OFF THE BEATEN PATH®
NORTHERN
CALIFORNIA →

Help Us Keep This Guide Up to Date

We would love to hear from you concerning your experiences with this guide and how you feel it could be improved and kept up to date. Please send your comments and suggestions to:

editorial@GlobePequot.com

Thanks for your input, and happy travels!

OFF THE BEATEN PATH® SERIES

EIGHTH EDITION

OFF THE BEATEN PATH® NORTHERN CALIFORNIA →

A GUIDE TO UNIQUE PLACES

Revised and updated by

Maxine Cass

gpp®
travel

Guilford, Connecticut

All the information in this guidebook is subject to change. We recommend that you call ahead to obtain current information before traveling.

Text design: Linda R. Loiewski
Maps: Equator Graphics © Morris Book Publishing, LLC

ISSN 1536-6286
ISBN 978-0-7627-5050-4

Printed in the United States of America
10 9 8 7 6 5 4 3 2 1

Contents

SHASTA
CASCADE

Eureka

Redding

NORTH
COAST

Sacramento

Auburn

THE
SIERRA
NEVADA

San Francisco

THE
BAY
AREA

San Jose

CENTRAL
VALLEY

Salinas

SOUTH
COAST

Introduction

California, more than any other part of the Union, is a country by itself, and San Francisco a capital.
—James Bryce, *The American Commonwealth,* 1901

How can anyone get "off the beaten path" in Northern California, you ask? This is the larger half of the country's most populous and most visited state, whose sights and attractions have become household names. Part of the answer lies in the sheer size of California and the astounding variety of natural and man-made wonders found here.

Another part derives from the nature of this book. It is not a guide to Fisherman's Wharf, Alcatraz, Yosemite, Lake Tahoe, Carmel, Sausalito, or any other well-trodden destination. We have deliberately chosen to ignore such people magnets as Napa Valley wineries, the Santa Cruz Boardwalk, Great America and other amusement parks, the state capitol, and a fistful of gold-country tourist traps. That's where most people go.

The nice flip side, however, is that with everyone visiting those places, the rest of Northern California is surprisingly crowd free most of the time. (Try to heed the experienced traveler's motto: "Never on Sunday.")

Nor is this book a guide to the rural "back roads" of Northern California, at least not by definition. You will indeed be sampling several country roads, but there are as many little-known, seldom-visited places in urban San Francisco as in the sticks.

With this guide you'll be able to explore the dank streets of Chinatown or sip espresso with an aging Beat poet in North Beach. You'll go to an island that was off-limits until recently or follow the bloodstained trail of Sam Spade and other characters from *The Maltese Falcon.*

San Francisco is only the beginning, just one of seven geographical areas covered by this book. More than one hundred different attractions are highlighted in detail, a kind of personal "best of" Northern California based on years of experience. Although this may seem a bit arbitrary, a selective guidebook allowed us to go beyond the once-over-lightly approach to an endless number of places. It was also a lot more fun to research and write.

This book will help you discover that California means Chinese Joss houses and a Russian fort as much as Spanish missions, and that Hollywood was really just an upstart when it came to making movies; the first film capital was right here at Niles. Everyone knows about the gold rush, but what about the great "California Coal Rush"? You can visit the mines of black gold and a cemetery with gravestones inscribed in Welsh. And if that doesn't excite you, choose instead to stroll around the ornate Sacramento mansion that the Reagans refused to live in.

You will visit museums on everything from Egyptian history to cartoon art, surfboards to pickup trucks. The book will show you a slew of superlatives: the world's smallest mountain range and tallest tree, matched by a pygmy forest of the shortest full-grown trees on earth, some less than a foot tall. You'll take a behind-the-scenes look at the world's only cable-car system and find out about beer and sake making. Enjoy a belt-stretching meal at the last lumberjack-style cookhouse in the West, and for visitors with adventuresome palates, we describe a restaurant that specializes in artichokes cooked two dozen different ways.

If you equate California with sandy beaches and warm Pacific waves, you may want to take a sharp left when you get to Fresno (if coming from the east, that is) and head for Southern California. The north, on the other hand, offers spectacular seacoast drives past Big Sur and Mendocino, the hissing volcanic terrain of Lassen and Lava Beds parks, wild river canyons, and a snow-shrouded peak with its own mystical powers. And if California means freeways to you, get ready for a visit to the state's Empty Quarter, where you will see more buzzards than cars.

Man-made marvels are also included in the bargain, from landmark lighthouses to ultramodern cathedrals and temples. And, yes, we take you along some of those scenic shortcuts and elusive back roads to places called Volcano and Fiddletown and to a region whose name speaks for itself: the Lost Coast.

For their generous assistance in the preparation of this book, we would like to offer our sincere appreciation to the following: San Francisco Convention & Visitors Bureau; Monterey Peninsula Chamber of Commerce; Redwood Empire Association; Mariposa Chamber of Commerce; Amador County Chamber of Commerce; Sacramento Convention and Visitors Bureau; Chico Visitor & Information Bureau; Shasta–Cascade Wonderland Association; Golden Gate National Recreation Area; Carmel Valley Chamber of Commerce; Pacific Grove Chamber of Commerce; California Artichoke Advisory Board; National Steinbeck Center, Salinas; San Juan Bautista Chamber of Commerce; Humboldt County Convention & Visitors Bureau; Lake County Marketing Program; Fort Bragg–Mendocino Coast Chamber of Commerce; and Mono Lake Tufa State Reserve.

California Welcome Centers (Northern Area)

Anderson, 1699 Highway 273, (530) 365-1180, (800) 4-SHASTA
Arcata, 1635 Heindon Road, (707) 822-3619

Auburn, 13411 Lincoln Way, (530) 887-2111
Merced, 710 West Sixteenth Street, Suite A, (209) 724-8104
San Francisco, Pier 39, Building P, 2nd Level, Suite 214-B, (415) 981-1280
Santa Rosa, 9 Fourth Street, (800) 404-7673

Helpful Phone Numbers and Web Sites

California Tourism: (800) 462-2543; www.visitcalifornia.com
California State Coastal Conservancy: www.scc.ca.gov
California Travel and Park Association: www.camp-california.com
Department of Transportation Road Conditions: (800) 427-ROAD
National Park Service: www.nps.gov
Sierra Club: www.sierraclub.org
Ski Reports: www.californiasnow.com
State Fish and Game: www.dfg.ca.gov
State Parks Camping Reservations: (800) 444-7275
State Parks Information: (800) 777-0369-; www.parks.ca.gov

Major Newspapers

Contra Costa Times
Fresno Bee
Marin Independent Journal
Monterey County Herald
Oakland Tribune
Redding Record Searchlight
Sacramento Bee
San Francisco Chronicle
San Jose Mercury News
Santa Rosa Press Democrat

Transportation

Air: Major airports with regularly scheduled out-of-state flights include San Francisco, Oakland, San Jose, Sacramento, Fresno, Monterey, Arcata, and Reno, Nevada (for Lake Tahoe area).
Train: Amtrak provides passenger travel between all major cities; the Coast Starlight runs from Los Angeles along the coast to the Bay Area (Emeryville), then inland and north to Redding, Mount Shasta, and Oregon. (800) USA–RAIL; www.amtrak.com; www.trainweb.com.
Bus: Greyhound is the major carrier with service to most towns; (800) 231-2222; www.greyhound.com.

Climate

Northern California's climate is characterized by general sun and warmth, with rain mainly in winter. It does vary greatly based on distance from the ocean and elevation, however. There are five main climatic zones in the area: coastal (mild temperatures and moderate rainfall); desert (great variations in temperature with very little rainfall); mountain (sunny summers and cold winters, heavy snowfall); valley (high temperature/low humidity in summer, low temperature/high humidity in winter); foothill (1,000 to 3,000 feet in elevation, similar to valley but with more rain and less fog).

Famous Northern California Natives

Ansel Adams (photographer); Lloyd Bridges, Clint Eastwood, and Tom Hanks (actors); Dave Brubeck (musician); Joe DiMaggio, Tom Seaver, and Billy Martin (baseball players); Peggy Fleming and Kristi Yamaguchi (figure skaters); Ernest and Julio Gallo (winemakers); Jack London, William Saroyan, and Irving Stone (writers); George Lucas (filmmaker); Mark Spitz (swimmer).

Recommended Reading

GUIDEBOOKS, TRAVEL, AND ECOLOGY

Bakker, Elna. *An Island Called California: An Ecological Introduction to Its Natural Communities*. University of California Press, 1985.

Braasch, Barbara. *California's Gold Rush Country*. Johnston Associates International, 1996.

Brower, David R. *Not Man Apart: Lines from Robinson Jeffers*. Photographs of the Big Sur Coast. Sierra Club Books, 1965.

California Coastal Access Guide. University of California Press, 2003.

Donley, Michael. *Atlas of California*. PacificBook Center, 1979.

Emory, Jerry. *The Monterey Bay Shoreline Guide*. University of California Press, 1999.

Hanson, Victor D. *Craft of Northern California*. Alcove Books, 2003.

Laws, David. *Steinbeck Country: Exploring the Settings for the Stories*. Windy Hill Press, 2002.

Lewkowicz, Bonnie. *A Wheelchair Rider's Guide: San Francisco Bay and Nearby Coast*. California Conservancy Association, 2006.

O'Brien, Robert. *This Is San Francisco: A Classic Portrait of the City*. Chronicle Books, 1994.

O'Reilly, James, Larry Habegger, and Sean O'Reilly, eds. *Travelers' Tales: San Francisco*. Travelers' Tales Inc., 2003.

Ostertag, Rhonda. *California State Parks: A Complete Recreation Guide*. Mountaineers Books, 2001.

HISTORY AND LITERATURE

Clemens, Samuel L. (Mark Twain). *The Celebrated Jumping Frog of Calaveras County* and *Roughing It*. Various editions.
Eisen, Jonathan, and David Fine. eds. *Unknown California*. Collier, 1985.
Fracchia, Charles A. *City by the Bay: A History of Modern San Francisco*. Heritage Media, 1997.
Haslam, Gerald W. *The Other California: The Great Central Valley in Life and Letters*. University of Nevada Press, 1993.
Kowalewski, Michael. *Goldrush: A Literary Exploration*. Heyday Books, 1997.
McPhee, John A. *Assembling California*. Noonday Press, 1994.
Muir, John. *The Nature Writings of John Muir*. Library of America, 1997.
Richards, Rand. *Historic San Francisco: A Concise History and Guide*. Heritage House, 2007.
Rohrbough, Malcolm J. *Days of Gold: The California Gold Rush and the American Nation*. University of California Press, 1998.
Rolle, Andrew F. *California: A History*. Harlan Davidson, 2003.
Starr, Kevin. *California: A History*. Modern Library, 2005.

Fast Facts

- Time: California is in the Pacific time zone and observes daylight saving time.
- Taxes: The state sales tax is 7.25 percent; local taxes may add as much as 2.5 percent.
- The region's most visited amusement/theme parks are: Santa Cruz Beach/ Boardwalk; California's Great America (Santa Clara); Monterey Bay Aquarium; Six Flags Discovery Kingdom (Vallejo).
- Northern California's professional sports teams include the Oakland A's and San Francisco Giants (baseball), Oakland Raiders and San Francisco 49ers (football), Golden State Warriors and Sacramento Kings (basketball), San Jose Sharks (hockey), and San Jose Earthquakes (soccer).
- Among U.S. states, California has the largest number of senior citizens living within its borders. More than five million residents are over sixty years of age.
- California produces more than $1.5 trillion worth of goods and services each year, which is about 13 percent of the U.S. gross national product. California has the world's seventh-largest economy.

- The Bear Flag Revolt in 1846 achieved California's independence from Mexico, and the banner used became the state's official flag.

SAN FRANCISCO

Walter Cronkite once said: "Leaving San Francisco is like say-ing good-bye to an old sweetheart. You want to linger as long as possible." As visitors know, there is something special about the place that sets it apart from other cities. How else could San Francisco be known as America's most European and its most Asian city? To most Northern Californians it's merely "the City," as if none other exists or matters.

Mention just about any place and a postcard vista snaps into view. Images carried like baggage by first-time visitors to San Francisco include all the famous sights (and sites) on everyone's must-see list: Coit Tower, Fisherman's Wharf, Chi-natown, Union Square, Golden Gate Bridge, Alcatraz, and, of course, the cable cars.

But beyond these the city packs a dazzling assortment of attractions into its compact site, just 47 square miles at the tip of a narrow peninsula between the Pacific and San Francisco Bay. Dig a little deeper and the landscape will yield still more nuggets, from a stupendous, soaring cathedral and the delight-fully cramped shops of North Beach to the haunts of fictional detective Sam Spade.

SAN FRANCISCO

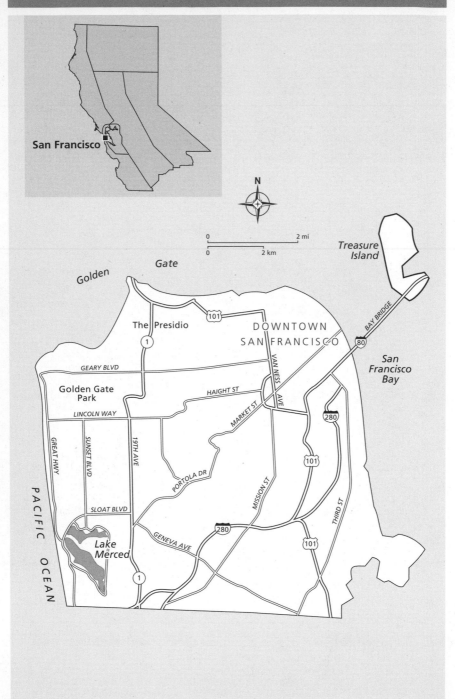

San Francisco

N

0   2 mi
0   2 km

Treasure
Island

Golden   Gate

The Presidio

DOWNTOWN
SAN FRANCISCO

BAY BRIDGE

San
Francisco
Bay

GEARY BLVD

Golden Gate
Park

HAIGHT ST

VAN NESS AVE

LINCOLN WAY

MARKET ST

280

PACIFIC OCEAN

GREAT HWY

SUNSET BLVD

19TH AVE

PORTOLA DR

MISSION ST

101

SLOAT BLVD

Lake
Merced

GENEVA AVE

280

THIRD ST

101

1

San Francisco is one of the world's most scenic cities, and it's also one of the easiest to explore. If you can't walk to your destination, you can reach it via an extensive public transportation system that includes the cable car—a national historic landmark in motion. So let us take you off the beaten path through a San Francisco most visitors never see.

Hidden Chinatown

During the gold rush many Chinese who didn't make it as far as the mines sought their fortunes on the streets of Gum San Dai Fow, "Big City on the Golden Hill." Their laundries and cafes formed the nucleus of Chinatown, presently the largest Chinese settlement outside Asia, comprising about 25 square blocks where thousands live and do business. Many live above the stores, their laundry drying on the balconies.

Chinatown is a top attraction, but it's also a real community, with its own schools, industries, banks, shops, social clubs (called family or benevolent associations), and chamber of commerce. Grant Avenue overflows with tourist shops and restaurants, although there are interesting shops like Chinatown Kite Shop (717 Grant), the Wok Shop across the street, and Ten Ren Tea (at 949), where dozens of exotic blends kept in hermetically sealed containers can be purchased by the ounce. But just 1 block over lies Stockton Street, where Chinatown's real business is carried on (especially between Jackson and Pacific Streets).

The street comes alive during the day with the vibrant pace of grocery shoppers busily sifting through mounds of exotic produce such as fuzzy melon and bok choy. Exotic food shops abound—oriental bakeries selling turnip cakes, Chinese donuts (not round and without holes), and sesame

AUTHOR'S TOP TEN FOR SAN FRANCISCO

Hidden Chinatown	The Presidio
Cable Car Barn	Victorian Homes Tour
Italian North Beach	Cathedral of St. Mary of the Assumption
The Embarcadero	Golden Gate Park
Treasure/Yerba Buena Islands	Mission District

San Francisco Don'ts

There's plenty to do, but here are a few tips for what not to do, with help from the San Francisco Convention & Visitors Bureau.

- Don't pack a tropical wardrobe for sunny California. It's often cool to downright cold, even in summer.

- Don't stand directly behind a cable-car gripman unless you want the wind knocked out of you when he brakes.

- Don't board a bus or cable car without coins; drivers don't make change.

- Don't park on a hill without curbing your wheels or you may end up chasing a runaway car.

- Don't wear shorts and T-shirts to the opera or symphony; these are formal affairs.

- Don't try swimming in San Francisco Bay without a wet suit, unless you're part polar bear.

- Don't expect Golden Gate Bridge to be golden; it's red-orange in color.

- Don't ask for Rice-A-Roni in any restaurant; it's virtually unknown despite decades of ads to the contrary.

- Above all, when visiting the city, please don't call it "Frisco," especially if you're from L.A.

balls; open-air stands overflowing with strange fruits and vegetables with delightful shapes and colors and unpronounceable names. In the fish markets old women in quilted jackets poke at gills of fat catfish and prod live crabs amid wicker baskets filled with pancake-flat pressed duck and gobs of bright red fish eggs.

Herbal shops offer a peek into another form of medicine, in which ailments are treated with roots, bark, and berries. Wan Cheong Ginseng Company (1043 Stockton) sells ginseng in its many forms, including candy and such medicinal oddities as dried sea horse and starfish. There are scores of similar shops offering an assortment of strange ointments and pills, including the Great China Herb Company at 857 Washington Street and Hue An Company at 776 Jackson.

Between Grant and Stockton a series of dank alleys and cramped streets seem to shelter the secret business of Chinatown. These narrow corridors at one time provided havens for prostitution, gambling, and opium dens, and many cellars still connect through a maze of tunnels, or so it's said.

In 1879 Waverly Place (between Sacramento and Washington Streets) witnessed the first Tong War, fought over the affections—and ownership—of a Chinese slave girl named Kum Ho. Now it's noted for ornate balconies, herbalists, and places of worship. The *Tin How Temple* at 125 Waverly Place honors the Taoist Queen of Heaven, the protectress of travelers, sailors, and ladies of the night. Open to respectful visitors (daily, 10:00 a.m. to 4:00 p.m.), Tin How occupies the top floor of a ramshackle building. You must climb four flights of wooden stairs and ring a buzzer to enter the sumptuous interior, done up in gold and lots of red, the color of good luck. Amid bowls of fruit, porcelain statues, and tasseled lamps, clouds of incense rise from a three-legged bronze pot as old women kneeling on cushions quietly fold offerings to be burned at the main shrine. Stay a while and soak up the mystical energy.

Spofford Lane (between Clay and Washington Streets) is a corridor of painted doorways and brick facades that hums with the strains of peculiarly Chinese melodies, like the click of mah jong tiles and animated talk behind the floral curtains. Crossing Washington, Spofford becomes Old Chinatown Lane, formerly famous for its brothels and gambling dens.

Fog

San Francisco's prize-winning columnist Herb Caen once wrote of the joy "after a hot spell, being awakened by the fugue of five foghorns, rattling the windows." Indeed, many San Franciscans love their special weather, where temperatures rarely rise above 75 degrees or sink below 40. Nature provides a kind of air conditioner, so that after three or four hot days a fog bank (now called a marine layer) is created offshore by a rare combination of ocean water, wind, and topography. This sits off the coast waiting to be pulled in by rising air currents when the land heats up. The fog is held back by coastal mountains, but it enters through passages such as the Golden Gate. But as the land cools, the vapor vanishes, so the city can be socked in at 8:00 a.m. but fog free by noon. Neighborhoods like the Sunset and Richmond can be cloaked in fog, while downtown might be sunny.

Fog can appear like mist or pea soup. When visibility drops to less than 5 miles at the mouth of the bay, foghorns begin to sound. There are thirty-two fog signals, not counting bells, only half audible within the city, and the loudest is the big diaphone on Golden Gate Bridge. These are joined by a cacophony of strange sounds across the bay, some activated manually but most set off by automated fog detectors. Due to the seasonal weather patterns, fog signals occur most frequently during summer months, and unwary visitors come to know the truth of Mark Twain's oft-quoted adage: "The coldest winter I ever spent was summer in San Francisco."

(If you want warmer weather, simply head inland. It can be several degrees warmer in the East Bay and Contra Costa County.)

TOP ANNUAL EVENTS IN SAN FRANCISCO

Chinese New Year Celebration, Chinatown (February)

St. Patrick's Day Parade, along Market Street to the Civic Center (March)

Cherry Blossom Festival, Japantown (April)

Bay to Breakers Footrace, the Embarcadero to the Great Highway (mid-May)

Carnaval, Mission District (May)

North Beach Festival, Washington Square, Grant Avenue, and Green Street (mid-June)

San Francisco LGBT (Gay) Pride Parade, Market Street (late June)

San Francisco Opera in the Park, Golden Gate Park (early September)

Italian Heritage Parade/Fleet Week, North Beach/Fisherman's Wharf (mid-October)

San Francisco Jazz Festival, various venues (late October—early November)

Among the hundreds of Chinatown restaurants, *Sam Wo's* (813 Washington Street) has become a landmark of sorts. To enter you pass right through a frenetic kitchen crammed with shouting cooks juggling exotic dishes between the hot iron stoves. Unflustered diners proceed upstairs via a rickety staircase to a cramped but colorful dining room. The restaurant is open for lunch and dinner until the wee hours.

Nearby Ross Alley claims the Golden Gate Fortune Cookie Factory at number 56; the owner often leaves the door open, and you can find out how they get those little messages inside. In the days when Ross boasted twenty-two fan-tan parlors, it earned the nickname "the street of gamblers." The dens were heavily fortified with doors of boilerplate iron to stave off police raids.

At 27 Ross Alley there's a factory filled with Chinese women sewing busily. There's also an old-fashioned barbershop whose proprietor plays the violin between customers, and one of Chinatown's original dry cleaners.

East of Grant (between Washington and Clay Streets) sits the cynosure of Old Chinatown. At Portsmouth Square clusters of wizened old men laugh and argue passionately while playing cards and board games, and here you fully realize that Chinatown is not so much a tourist destination as a real community. Some tourist-free streets nearby to explore include Wentworth and Beckett; you might end up trying an acupuncture session or a foot massage. At the corner of Jackson sits Red's Place, a genuine hole-in-the-wall hangout for locals. A couple of blocks away, at 916 Grant, the Li Po Bar looks and feels like an opium den, complete with cavelike design and basement funk music nights. The Buddha Bar across the street is another intriguing dive.

Before the earthquake and fire of 1906, Grant Avenue was called Dupont Street and was infamous as a red-light district in the heart of gang-controlled Chinatown. One island of faith in a sea of sin was *Old St. Mary's Church* (corner of Grant and California). California's first Roman Catholic Cathedral was built in 1853 with bricks shipped from Boston around Cape Horn, and it survived the '06 quake only to burn in the subsequent fire. The restored church, with its clock tower message "Son Observe the Time and Fly from Evil" that once warned patrons of nearby brothels and gambling halls, is open daily, with a classical music concert every Tuesday at 12:30 p.m.

History buffs should also visit the *Chinese Historical Society of America Museum,* which highlights Chinese contributions in areas such as agriculture, mining, and railroad construction during their 150-plus years in California. Among dozens of artifacts on display are a braided queue, opium pipes, a Buddhist altar, a three-pronged fishing spear, and a water cannon used during the gold rush. The museum's redbrick building at 965 Clay Street was designed by renowned architect Julia Morgan and is open Tuesday through Friday from noon to 5:00 p.m. Exhibits include the Ching Collection of negative stereotypes of Chinese found in advertising and news media. Call (415) 391-1188 for admission fees, or go to www.chsa.org.

Most visitors to San Francisco ride one of those little cable cars "that climb halfway to the stars." But does it really dawn on them that the cars have no motor and are actually towed along the tracks by a moving cable? That's why they are called cable cars, and it is like no other system in the world. Just 2 blocks up from Chinatown, the *Cable Car Barn* provides a fascinating behind-the-scenes look at this unique form of public transportation.

Built in 1907, this three-level brick building was enlarged and completely renovated with the rest of the 4.4-mile-long system during the eighties. Both the Powell–Mason and Powell–Hyde lines run past the barn, and you can watch the ten-ton cars coming and going. Inside, on the mezzanine level, you look down on twelve winding sheaves that look like giant wagon wheels. This is the guts of the system: machinery that winds four separate cables, each in a closed loop, for the four lines traversing 69 blocks at a steady 9.5 miles per hour. That's 57,300 feet, or 10.85 miles, of 1.25-inch-diameter steel cable moving up and down some of the city's steepest terrain.

Most of the system's forty cars were built between 1887 and 1914. A museum here features several of the oldest cars and scale models of others. According to legend, kindhearted Andrew S. Hallidie dreamt up the ingenious system after he watched a team of horses pulling a wagon falter and tumble backward down a steep hill.

Hallidie operated the very first cable car for a disbelieving crowd on August 2, 1873. Car no. 8 on display here was among the first cable cars in San Francisco.

trivia

In the 1890s cable cars left the Ferry Building as often as every fifteen seconds. Almost abandoned in 1947, the system was saved by private citizens. Twenty years later cable cars were declared a moving National Historic Landmark.

The Cable Car Barn is the powerhouse and repair shop that keeps the simple yet delicate system in working order. In addition to design flaws that crept in during renovation, there is the problem of the cable itself, which has a limited life. New wire must be spliced in when the old wears out, and there's a strand on display. As a finale, descend to the underground sheave-viewing room and watch the cable being neatly and methodically wound into figure-eight patterns 365 days a year.

The Cable Car Barn and Museum, 1201 Mason Street (at Washington), is open daily from 10:00 a.m. to 5:00 p.m. (to 6:00 p.m. April through September); no admission charged. For information call (415) 474-1887 or go to www .cablecarmuseum.org.

Italian North Beach

North Beach, a flat sliver of land between Telegraph Hill and Chinatown, means different things to different people. Many visitors see only the raucous street scene and lewd revues along Broadway. Others can recall the beatniks of the fifties, the poets and painters whose legacy still lives on at City Lights Bookstore and the Tosca Cafe. Yet long before, North Beach was called "Little Italy," and quite a few traces of the old Italian neighborhood still survive.

But where's the beach? The name goes back to the 1850s, when a narrow finger of the bay extended inland. As generations came and went, the bay was slowly filled in. Italian immigrants arrived in force, and they fished from what is now called Fisherman's Wharf and lived in North Beach. Their story, from Bank of America founder A. P. Giannini to poet Lawrence Ferlinghetti, is told at the **North Beach Museum** at 1435 Stockton Street. It is open Monday through Thursday from 9:00 a.m. to 4:00 p.m., and Friday from 9:00 a.m. to 6:00 p.m.; no admission charged. Call (415) 391-6210 for more information.

Although North Beach is slowly becoming an extension of Chinatown, you can still see a glimmer of the city's most European neighborhood. The heart of the Italian community is the fairy-tale ***Church of Saints Peter and Paul*** on Washington Square. Built in 1924, it is a dim and quiet retreat filled with incense and flickering candles. Stained-glass windows and bronze fixtures lead to an elaborate altar where daily Mass is offered. And Italian Americans from the city and beyond still come for baptisms, confirmations, weddings, and funerals.

Outside, Washington Square (with a statue of Benjamin Franklin, not Washington!) is a pleasant park lined with shops, restaurants, and stubborn holdouts such as the San Francisco Italian Athletic Club for members only (1630 Stockton). At Mario's Bohemian Cigar Store (566 Columbus), you can sip a cappuccino at a table overlooking the square. Nearby are a few cafes and bars where elderly Italians enjoy red wine and discuss the day's affairs. Gino and Carlo (548 Green Street), for example, has been a local hangout since 1948.

> ## trivia
>
> The Cliff House above the beach has welcomed presidents, tycoons, and ordinary visitors since 1863. Now in its third incarnation, the impressive structure welcomes 1.5 million visitors annually.

North Beach remains a self-contained enclave. The Italian imprint lingers in the old-style family businesses, although high rents are slowly driving them out. There are bakeries and pastry shops, delicatessens and butcher shops, sausage and pasta factories, and little neighborhood markets with fruits and vegetables so fresh they glow.

Pastry shops feature rum babas, marzipan, cannolis filled with sweetened ricotta cheese, and multi-tiered cakes. Each bakery boasts a specialty in addition to long loaves of sourdough bread and panettone, a round, sweet loaf filled with raisins and candied fruit. Specialty shops sell noodle machines and cheese graters, ravioli rolling sticks and baking irons for pizzelle, and you can find carpetto, prosciutto, and provolone at any corner deli.

Wander around and savor the sounds, smells, and tastes of old North Beach while you still can. Here are some traditional Italian businesses still going strong.

- Molinari Delicatessen (373 Columbus) offers a wide selection of Italian cheeses, sausages, olive oil, and red wine in outrageously twisted bottles.
- Victoria Pastry Co. (1362 Stockton; www.victoriapastry.com) offers zuccotto, a frozen dessert soaked in liqueur, and has specialized in towering wedding cakes since 1914.
- Liguria Bakery (1700 Stockton) makes only one thing, a thin bread called focaccia that is covered with different toppings and is said to be the forerunner of pizza.

- The Italian French Baking Company (1501 Grant) specializes in thick, handmade bread sticks (grissini), biscotti, and tubular cialdi cookies.
- Danilo Bakery (516 Green; www.danilobakery.com) specializes in wood oven-baked breads and pizzas at a small corner café.
- Caffè Trieste (601 Vallejo; www.caffetrieste.com) sells espresso machines and a variety of roasted coffees, including the "North Beach Blend," at the West Coast's first coffeehouse, started back in 1956.
- A. Cavalli & Co. (1441 Stockton), which has been around since 1880, features Italian books and magazines, records and tapes, as well as travel posters, opera prints, and other curiosities.
- Biordi Art Imports (412 Columbus; www.biordi.com) works directly with artists to bring high-quality, handcrafted ceramic pieces to San Francisco. The store is like a gallery, filled with exquisite *majolica* dishware, vases, and lamps.

Another North Beach institution is **City Lights Bookstore** at Broadway and Columbus (www.citylights.com), owned by poet Lawrence Ferlinghetti since 1953. It started as the nation's first bookstore featuring paperbacks only, then rocketed to literary fame for selling Allen Ginsberg's now-classic poem "Howl," once judged obscene, a decision reversed on the grounds that it held redeeming social importance. City Lights boasts unusual books, ignoring best sellers for mostly leftish political titles, Eastern religions, avant-garde fiction, and poetry. The regular clientele includes many writers, some from the Beat Generation, who drop in to pick up their mail. Ferlinghetti maintains an office on an open balcony overlooking the main floor.

Just across Jack Kerouac Alley at 255 Columbus, sits the classic North Beach bar and coffeehouse Vesuvio Cafe (www.vesuvio.com), which has been serving the community, literary and otherwise, since 1948. On a tiny alley across the street is Spec's Bar, a classic bohemian watering hole with sawdust on the floor and wall-to-wall posters.

Minimuseums

Museums come in all shapes and sizes, especially in a city as diverse as San Francisco. At some of the larger museums, you might have to purchase advance tickets for well-publicized shows. But at the lesser-known repositories, you may find yourself sharing the premises with the caretaker. Here are some of the city's best small museums.

It was in the heart of San Francisco at the Six Gallery on October 7, 1955, that Allen Ginsberg first read "Howl." From that moment on the Beats would become known as a significant cultural influence that would challenge and ultimately change American society. Jack Kerouac, Allen Ginsberg, William Burroughs, and Neal Cassady are just a few of the people who encompassed the spirit that became the Beat Generation.

Take a walk through the ***Beat Museum*** and step back in time to where it all began. Landmark events of the era include the arrest of Lawrence Ferlinghetti and subsequent "Howl" trial, the publication of *On the Road* by Kerouac, the influence of the cold war on society, the rise of Beat Generation women writers, and the advent of gay rights and environmentalism. Displays feature first editions, autographs, an original "Beat Pad," the sixties room, Ken Kesey and the Merry Pranksters, plus the theater room always showing a movie from the period.

The Beat Museum showcases the spirit of the Beats through writings, photos, and history. It provides a historical background of twentieth-century counterculture, with its themes of tolerance, inclusiveness, compassion, and having the courage to know, speak, and live your own individual truth. The rich influence of the Beat Generation lives on here with regular book signings, poetry readings, and other events highlighting the spirit and talent of today's artists as well as those from half a century ago.

The Beat Museum in the heart of North Beach (540 Broadway) is open Tuesday and Thursday noon to 10:00 p.m. and Wednesday and Friday through Sunday from 10:00 a.m. to 10:00 p.m. Museum admission is $5 for adults with discounts for students and seniors. For more information call (415) 399-9626 or go to www.thebeatmuseum.org.

The ***San Francisco Fire Department Museum*** holds an outstanding collection of historical photos, memorabilia, and fire-fighting equipment going back to the first volunteer brigade in 1849. It sits right next to a modern station, and you may have to ring the bell to gain entrance.

The very first engine—a hand-pulled, hand-pumped beauty—is there, piled high with trophies won by modern-day firefighters at various pumping competitions. The department's biggest challenge—the three-day blaze following the 1906 earthquake—is remembered in a wealth of photos and documents.

A glass-enclosed display tells the story of Lillie Hitchcock Coit, an eccentric millionaire who used to follow the brigade to fires and became an honorary member. To pay homage to the city's firemen, she financed the building of Coit Tower on Telegraph Hill, which bears an uncanny resemblance to the nozzle of a fire hose.

Several fire engines in mint condition show how far techniques have come since pioneer days, when the bucket brigade would put out blazes using water-filled buckets made from buffalo hide. Other curiosities include brass "speaker trumpets," a kind of early megaphone for issuing orders at the scene of a fire, and the city's first fire hydrant, formerly used by pioneer dogs.

The museum, at 655 Presidio Avenue, is open free of charge Thursday through Sunday from 1:00 to 4:00 p.m. For information call (415) 563-4630 or go to www.sffiremuseum.org.

The *Museum of Russian Culture* is a treasure chest devoted to Russia's troubled history before the fateful 1917 revolution. Now fifty-plus years old, the museum sits at the top of a dark staircase in the gracefully aging Russian Center. This monument to Old Russia displays an eclectic collection gathered mostly from the mementos brought here by refugees from the Communist regime. One of these old-timers is usually on hand to greet visitors and provide personal details that help bring the collection to life.

Among hundreds of items on display are fading photographs of Czar Nicholas II with his family, all of whom (including Anastasia, despite Hollywood mythology) were murdered by the Bolsheviks. Historical novelties include a captured German flag from World War I and a model of Fort Ross on the Northern California coast, a little-known Russian outpost nearly two centuries ago. There are even tributes to famous inventions by Russian Americans, such as the helicopter and cathode-ray tube (forerunner of television).

Russia's history stretches back many centuries, and the emphasis here is on this lengthy tradition. There's a suit of chain-mail armor made with thousands of individual rings, and the small collection of paintings contains a rendering of the Tartar invasion back in 1237. But the emphasis is on the Romanov dynasty that ruled Russia for three centuries: a silver tea service, military medals, imperial currency, as well as correspondence and photographs of the ill-fated royal family and other nobles. A picture of the teenage heir, Crown Prince Alexei, taken just months before his murder, is especially touching. The Museum of Russian Culture, located at 2450 Sutter Street, is open Wednesday and Saturday only from 10:30 a.m. to 2:30 p.m.; free admission. There's also a library with 14,000 books in Russian and hundreds of original manuscripts, not to mention a rare photograph of Leo Tolstoy. Call (415) 921-4082 or go to www.museumofrussianculturesf.org for further information.

Anyone interested in Russian culture should also visit one of San Francisco's eight Orthodox churches. The golden-domed *Holy Virgin Cathedral* in the Richmond district is the largest Russian Orthodox church in the West. Located at 6210 Geary Boulevard at 26th Avenue, it's open during services only: 8:00 to 9:00 a.m. and 5:30 to 6:30 p.m. weekdays and 8:00 a.m. to noon on Sunday. Another noteworthy church, Holy Trinity Cathedral, sits at the corner of Green and Van Ness Streets.

Everyone should see the spectacular **San Francisco Museum of Modern Art** (www.sfmoma.org) and adjacent Yerba Buena Gardens (especially during the Gardens Festival from May to October; go to www.ybgf.org). But just a block away is a lesser-known gem, the **Cartoon Art Museum,** with a collection of 6,000 items: from a 1760 engraving to Walt Disney's pre–Mickey Mouse sketches of Oswald the Rabbit to original pasteup boards of *Peanuts*.

Everyone has a favorite cartoon, and it's the first thing they reach for in the Sunday paper: *Nancy and Sluggo, Green Lantern, L'il Abner, The Wizard of Id, Superman, Dick Tracy,* or *Fritz the Cat.* Here, too, are western cartoons such as *Blueberry* in other languages, and you learn that although "Bam!" is universal, "Pow!" becomes "Paw!" when translated into French.

Cartoons are not always a laughing matter, and the museum does not ignore the darker side of the art form: old Marvel boards so realistic that the weapons seem to literally drip with blood, and underground and avant-garde drawings that are violent or obscene. And then there are the political cartoons and caricatures of celebrities.

The collection is rotated constantly, and there are frequent special exhibitions. Located at 655 Mission Street, the museum is open daily except Monday 11:00 a.m. to 5:00 p.m.; admission is charged. Call (415) 227-8666 or go to www.cartoonart.org for hours and information on current exhibitions.

Two excellent museums in the heart of the financial district focus on the history of California and the West. After the discovery of gold in 1848, banks played a lively role in that story, and Wells Fargo & Company got its start in 1852 by supplying banking and express delivery service.

Billions in Sierra Nevada gold and Comstock silver thundered into San Francisco on the two-man, six-horse Concord stagecoaches that formed the backbone of the company's transport network. A perfectly restored specimen of these coaches forms the centerpiece of the **Wells Fargo History Museum.** These 2,500-pound vehicles were as much a fixture in the Old West as the six-gun and tin star. Wells Fargo used them to transport passengers (up to nine

trivia

The Clarion Music Center (816 Sacramento Street, (415) 391-1317; www.clarionmusic.com) carries exotic instruments—Australian didgeridoos, African drums, Chinese gongs, and Tibetan singing bowls—and even offers workshops on how to play them.

fit snugly inside) and freight, especially gold. An upstairs exhibit details the skills involved in the forgotten craft of building these fine coaches. There's also a collection of framed letters using Wells Fargo's own stamps used before the U.S. Postal Service took over in 1865.

Charles E. Bolton, alias Black Bart, never cowered before a company shot-gun. From 1875 to 1883, Bart ambushed twenty-seven coaches, often leaving comical verses at the scene of the crime in which he claimed to be a Wild West version of Robin Hood. Bart, whose artifacts are preserved, was finally tripped up by Wells Fargo's top detective who traced the bandit through a laundry mark on his handkerchief.

Naturally, the gold rush receives most of the attention, with exhibits of strongboxes, photos from those raffish days, stock certificates, and, of course, the glistening gold itself. Only experts could tell real gold from fool's gold, there was such a wide variety of colors and textures, until it was refined and made into jewelry or shiny twenty-dollar gold pieces.

The Wells Fargo History Museum, at 420 Montgomery Street, is open free of charge Monday through Friday (except bank holidays) from 9:00 a.m. to 5:00 p.m. For information call (415) 396-2619 or visit www.wellsfargohistory .com/museums.

The *Bank of California Museum* is just a couple of blocks away in the basement of the Union Bank of California. The bank is the oldest on the West Coast, and its headquarters sits entrenched in a neoclassical 1906 building that looks more like a temple than a financial institution. Beckoning from behind glass museum cases are nuggets of gold and quartz, bullion, ingots, and shiny coins in flawless condition. Many coins on display were minted by various states, such as Utah (known as Deseret at the time) and Colorado but were phased out once the U.S. Mint was established in San Francisco. (Look for one privately minted coin with the imprint "In Gold We Trust.")

The Bank of California Museum, at 400 California Street, is open Monday through Friday 9:00 a.m. to 4:30 p.m.

Along the Bay

The City by the Bay does in fact sit perched on a narrow peninsula between San Francisco Bay and the Pacific Ocean. And, naturally enough, the north and east shore is fringed with quite a few docks and piers, known collectively as the *Embarcadero.* Here lies the city's attractive, usually sunny, waterfront boulevard and promenade.

From the gold rush through World War II, great ships came and went, bringing passengers and cargo from distant places. The cavernous pier sheds overflowed with the exotic and the mundane, from oriental spices to Kansas wheat. A plaque on the Embarcadero Promenade tells the story of longshore-men's leader Harry Bridges, who became a union hero during the Great Depression of the 1930s. He led a bitter strike for better conditions.

As times changed most waterborne trade moved across the bay to the more modern port at Oakland. What's left is the Embarcadero. The city demolished an ugly freeway here and replaced it with palm trees and other landscaping to create a showcase of urban renewal, including beautiful AT&T Park, home of the baseball Giants. In addition, the stretch south of Pier 35 is home to several smart cafes such as the Waterfront Restaurant and no-frills eateries like Red's Java House. Public transportation (Muni) runs from China Basin at the Embarcadero's south end to Market Street. From here the F line continues north as far as Fisherman's Wharf using historic trams and streetcars such as Presidential Conference Cars, nicknamed "green torpedoes."

Follow the Bird: The 49-Mile Scenic Drive

This is the city where the number 49 has been nearly sacred from gold rush days to its 49ers football team. So naturally the city provides a 49-mile auto (or even bicycle) route, and it's an easy way for visitors to glimpse the most important sights without a tour guide or bus. Allow about four to five hours for the drive, a loop that starts and ends at city hall, and simply follow the gull emblazoned on blue directional signs en route. Take pit stops as the spirit moves you; there's lots of room for spontaneity within the structured route (although admittedly parking in the city is a challenge).

From Civic Center you'll traverse Japantown, and then back downtown along Post Street to Union Square, up Nob Hill, along Grant through Chinatown and into North Beach, a popular place to stop for lunch. From here it's on to Fisherman's Wharf, though overcrowded still on everyone's must-see list, through the Marina District and along Marina Green, passing some sumptuous homes and the Palace of Fine Arts. You will enter the Presidio at the Lombard Street Gate and head toward Golden Gate Bridge, a nearly mandatory stop for everyone. Then travel south along Lincoln Boulevard and into Lincoln Park with its impressive Legion of Honor fine art museum.

Right at the ocean are Sutro Heights Park and the landmark Cliff House restaurant. Instead of going right into Golden Gate Park, the drive proceeds south along the Great Highway all the way to Lake Merced and the San Francisco Zoo, then back up Sunset Boulevard (northern edition, that is), and finally into the park. Warning: Here drivers often get lost because some markers are stolen or turned the wrong way by pranksters. So watch that bird!

Once out of the park, the route skirts the western border of former hippy enclave Haight-Ashbury and then up over Twin Peaks and into the gay Castro district and the Mission via palm-lined Dolores Street. The last leg takes you along the Embarcadero, past the Giants' AT&T Park and the Ferry Building, finally meandering through the Financial District, past SFMOMA and back up Howard Street to City Hall. Now it's time for a cup of espresso or a cool brew because you are officially a Forty-niner!

Fresh Veggies!

The twice-weekly Ferry Plaza Farmers Market draws thousands of shoppers looking for the best local produce, flowers, artisan-made products, and cooking demonstrations by local chefs. The large Saturday market surrounds the Ferry Building from 8:00 a.m. to 2:00 p.m. Tuesday's farmers market is on the Embarcadero sidewalk from 10:00 a.m. to 2:00 p.m.

The Embarcadero's centerpiece remains the *Ferry Building* at the foot of Market Street, at one time the tallest structure along the waterfront but now dwarfed by modern high-rises. From the Ferry Building radiate the city's old piers—odd numbered to the north, even numbered to the south. Before the two great bridges were built during the 1930s, this terminal was the hub of traffic to and from Marin County and the East Bay. During its peak period eight ferries made 170 trips daily, moving as many as 100,000 passengers at 10 cents a ride. Although this number has declined dramatically, ferries still commute several times a day to Larkspur and Sausalito in Marin County, Vallejo, and Oakland and Alameda in the East Bay.

Designed in the Beaux-Arts style by architect Arthur Paige Brown, the Ferry Building opened in 1898. Brown modeled its 245-foot tower on the Giralda Tower in Seville, Spain. At 5:12 a.m. on April 18, 1906, the hands on the tower's clock stopped; exactly a year later they were set in motion again. Yet the building survived undamaged by the great earthquake, and the beautiful clock still chimes the hour.

The Ferry Building underwent later restoration and reopened in 2003. Massive restoration uncovered the 660-foot-long grand nave and its stunning skylight, hidden for fifty years. On the floors of the building, 16,000 square feet of mosaics were replaced with about 140,000 individual tiles and columns and arches grace the interior. The street-level Ferry Building Marketplace (www .ferrybuildingmarketplace.com) blends upscale shops, local artisan food producers, restaurants, ice-cream and flower stands—even a couple of outdoor cafes, rare in chilly San Francisco.

Immediately behind the Ferry Building is the modern terminal and a wide plaza with an oddly out-of-place statue of Gandhi. Just beyond this area anglers can try their luck. Sinbads Restaurant (www.sinbadsrestaurant.com) nearby offers terrific views.

The city has created a delightful walk along the shoreline south of the Ferry Building called the *Embarcadero Waterfront Promenade.* It's an ideal spot for strollers, picnickers (there are benches), and anyone interested in stunning views of the bay and the Bay Bridge. A colossal metal sculpture called *Cupid's Span,* a bow and arrow impaling the Rincon Park lawn, was created by Claes Oldenburg and Coosje van Bruggen. Other points of interest along the promenade include the city's fireboat, berthed next to a historic firehouse at Pier 22½; the old redbrick Hills Brothers Coffee building at the foot of Harrison Street, and "tidal stairs" leading into the lapping waters of the bay.

For most commuters **Yerba Buena Island** is merely considered the principal anchor of the San Francisco–Oakland Bay Bridge. Yet this densely wooded isle and adjacent **Treasure Island,** formerly an important naval base, offer several points of interest and the best overall view of San Francisco's skyline.

Costanoan Indians used the island as a fishing station, and archaeologists have unearthed the remains of a village and cremation pits, along with contraband from smugglers and part of a shipwrecked galleon. Spanish explorers called the island Yerba Buena because of a fragrant herb that grew there in abundance.

Things remained quiet until builders used the island as the midpoint of the Bay Bridge, completed in 1936. Then ambitious promoters decided to create an artificial island on 400 acres of shoals offshore to serve as the site for a world's fair celebrating completion of the span, as well as the Golden Gate Bridge, finished about the same time. More than a year of dredging and a seawall built with 300,000 tons of rock went into the project, and in 1939 the Golden Gate International Exposition opened on the new Treasure Island.

That same year the famous China Clippers were launched as a trans-Pacific air service for mail and passengers. In 1941, after the bombing of Pearl Harbor, the U.S. Navy took over Treasure Island, and legions of sailors were trained here and shipped off to the Pacific. The military handed over the base to the City of San Francisco in 1997. Whimsical art deco architecture for the 1939 fair included the 400-foot-tall Tower of the Sun, with dozens of plazas, pyramids, fountains, and statues created for this "Pageant of the Pacific." One survivor is the semicircular building right inside the main gate, the base commander's one-time center of operations. Sharp-eyed movie buffs will recognize it as the setting for Captain Queeg's trial in *The Caine Mutiny* and the Berlin Airport in *Indiana Jones and the Last Crusade.*

Now people come for the spectacular views and the chance to glimpse a movie star when old hangars are used for film productions. A shuttle to the island from Transbay Terminal (SF Muni Line #108) operates hourly. If driving, take the Treasure Island exit from the Bay Bridge and continue north. The island is open to the public all day.

The best spot (with parking) for photographing the city skyline, especially in the early morning and at dusk, lies just outside the entrance gate. Here seabirds frolic and ships glide past as you take in an inspiring panorama of city and bay. Entering the old base, you follow a palm-lined avenue fronting the bay. A bit north is the Perimeter Walking Path, affording phenomenal views of Alcatraz, Angel Island, and the East Bay.

Yerba Buena Island itself is home to a sumptuous mansion formerly used by navy admirals as well as several U.S. Coast Guard facilities. West of the crowded Fisherman's Wharf area, San Francisco's northern waterfront opens out into the *Fort Mason* complex (now part of the Golden Gate National Recreation Area). The former military base serves as home to cultural activities (such as art fairs and blues festivals) as well as Greens, (415-771-6222; www.greensrestaurant.com), a renowned vegetarian restaurant in Building A. Next door in Building C sits the Museo Italo-Americano, (415-673-2200; www.museoitaloamericano.org), devoted to Italian art and culture. Farther on lies the fashionable Marina District, whose residents include a few older Italian families (Joe DiMaggio grew up here) and well-off urban professionals.

Tucked away on Baker Street, a block off the bayside promenade, sits the neoclassical *Palace of Fine Arts,* a true gem of a building built for a world's fair in 1915. It was designed by architect Bernard Maybeck to house a priceless art collection from around the world, and the remaining outer shell features a rotunda and sweeping colonnade. In front is a large pond where regal swans glide by. After serving two centuries as a military base under three flags, the *Presidio of San Francisco* is now a national park unlike any other, about 1,500 acres of historic sites, woods, and hiking and biking trails spread across the city's northwest corner.

A good place to enter the park is the Arguello Street gate at the southern boundary, first passing a golf course, then stopping at Inspiration Point, which looks out on the Palace of Fine Arts and Alcatraz and Angel Islands. The main entrance is actually at Lombard Street, not far from the Palace of Fine Arts.

The visitor center is found at the old Officers Club (building no. 50 on Moraga Avenue), its entrance flanked by two seventeenth-century cannons emblazoned with the royal Spanish crest. Spanish soldiers founded the Presidio (the word means "armed fortification") in 1776, years before the city itself. The club, built atop an adobe structure dating to around 1800, hosts rotating art exhibits. The visitor center, open daily from 9:00 a.m. to 5:00 p.m., is the information hub for maps and details about various walking tours. A free PresidiGo shuttle bus passes here on the half hour (every hour on weekends) and provides an overview of the Presidio complex.

Sights and activities, mostly reachable on foot, break down generally into historical and nature oriented. For example, near the visitor center are several refugee huts built by the army for homeless families after the great 1906 earthquake. At the post chapel nearby you can view a large mural depicting the Presidio's history up to the 1930s, painted with a federal grant during the Great Depression. Military remnants and relics are everywhere: artillery batteries, barracks, stables, and more than 200 historic buildings, though few are open. There are parade grounds and a World War II memorial to the west, just two places included on a 7-mile walking tour of the Presidio's illustrious history.

The most serene self-guided walk is within the National Military Cemetery, where many "Buffalo Soldiers" (as African Americans were dubbed by the Indians) are buried alongside hundreds of other fallen veterans from nearly all the nation's wars. Their graves are marked by plain white marble slabs with an occasional elaborate pillar or statue. Just down the hill is another poignant cemetery devoted to beloved military pets. Both areas are open daily from dawn until dusk.

Best of the nature walks is the Coastal Trail at the Pacific shoreline, a spectacular route along Baker Beach to the Golden Gate Bridge. The Ecology Trail runs south from behind the visitor center, loops through woods sheltering thirty kinds of trees, then links up with Lover's Lane (once used by strolling military couples the day before the soldier was shipped out to battle). All told the Presidio has 11 miles of hiking trails and 14 more for bicyclists.

Everyone's favorite walk is the *Golden Gate Promenade* along the bay from the Marina district to the bridge, much of it atop the old Crissy airfield, torn up and converted to wetlands, sand dunes, and beaches and restored with thousands of native plants. Nature festivals and environmental workshops take place at the community environmental center on Mason Street. This Crissy Field stretch at the Presidio's north end blends seamlessly into the surrounding urban landscape and is perhaps the nation's most beautiful walking/jogging route. The promenade ends nearly beneath the bridge, where there are more dazzling views with few tourists.

For further information about the Presidio, part of the Golden Gate National Recreation Area, call (415) 561-4323 or go to www.nps.gov/prsf. The Presidio Trust partially manages facilities and provides information at www.presidio.gov or call (415) 561-5418.

Fort Point, a mammoth brick Civil War era bastion in the Presidio hunkers down beneath the Golden Gate Bridge. The bridge's architects created a graceful arch over the fort to save it from demolition. The old stronghold served as the operations base during bridge construction. During World War II, about one hundred soldiers manned searchlights and guns to help protect a submarine net that stretched across the entrance to San Francisco Bay.

Catching a Play

Seeing live theater can be a costly affair, but here's a checklist for getting good seats without breaking the budget.

- **Get half-price tickets at Union Square.** The TIX Bay Area booth in a pavilion on Union Square sells tickets for the same day of performance and only selected shows and seats, but some bargains can be had, especially on orchestra seats. Open Tuesday through Thursday from 11:00 a.m. to 6:00 p.m., Friday through Saturday to 7:00 p.m. and Sunday from 11:00 a.m. to 3:00 p.m. Call (415) 433-7827 for information or check www.theatrebayarea.org/tix/tix_booth.jsp.

- **Take your chances at the theater.** Unused house seats and cancellations often turn up at bargain prices an hour or so before show time.

- **Go with friends.** Many theaters give discount ticket prices to groups.

- **Watch for special offers.** Sale prices are offered even on hit shows during slow times of the year—January and February—and during certain holiday weekends.

- **Catch a preview.** Preopening performances are normally cheaper (up to half off) and sometimes more exciting.

- **Choose a weeknight or matinee.** Many theaters discount tickets on certain days and times.

- **Sit in the balcony.** A good seat higher up is always cheaper than the orchestra and often better for seeing the show. The city's best balconies are at the Orpheum, A.C.T. (Geary Theater), and Club Fugazi ("Beach Blanket Babylon").

Millions of bricks shaped and supported Fort Point's 5- to 12-foot-thick walls. When complete in 1861, it was the largest brick structure west of the Mississippi. Fort Point protected the bay. No enemy ship ever entered, nor was a single shot fired in battle. Pass through a large wood-and-iron door and enter a chilly, dank courtyard. National Park Service guides recount the fort's quiet but colorful history. The site was originally a high promontory where, in 1776, Colonel Juan Bautista de Anza raised the Spanish flag. Spaniards erected the adobe Castillo de San Joaquin here, but in 1853, the U.S. Army blew up this fortress and the cliff on which it stood to make way for Fort Point.

The courtyard displays several types of cannons, including a stumpy mortar that could fire a 100-pound shell 1 mile, piles of black cannonballs, and a covered wagon. Fort Point housed 600 soldiers and could mount up to 126 cannons that were located in arched cubicles called casemate rooms.

Spiral staircases made with granite slabs lead to the upper levels. Wander through the tiers of casemates that acted as bombproof shelters for the big guns. At the top, stand directly under the concrete pillars and steel girders of the Golden Gate Bridge and hear the clank of cars passing above. Also topside are a lighthouse built in 1864 and emplacements for thirty-six pieces of artillery.

The museum contains a collection of old photos, a sampling of uniforms, and a special historical tribute to black soldiers. Fort Point National Historic Site is open Friday through Sunday only from 10:00 a.m. to 5:00 p.m.; call (415) 556-1693 for more information or go to www.nps.gov/fopo.

To reach the fort from inside the Presidio, take Long Road off Lincoln Boulevard, or walk down from the bridge observation area. San Francisco's waterfront begins here, and it's a fabulous spot to watch stormy Pacific waters surge through the Golden Gate and slam into the seawall. Fort Point is also the terminus of the Golden Gate Promenade and one of the best spots to watch windsurfers on the bay.

Above It All

Everyone goes to look at the Golden Gate Bridge, but there must be hundreds of great spots to catch an eyeful in San Francisco. It's a city of forty-two hills, and dozens of skyscrapers boast spectacular viewing rooms. Classic view points such as Twin Peaks and Coit Tower get very crowded at times. So here's an insider's selection (in no particular order) of great places to see San Francisco from on high.

Little-known *Tank Hill,* south of Golden Gate Park, provides a wrap-around view of the city and East Bay in a tourist-free environment. Go to the south end of Stanyan Street and turn left onto Belgrave Street; go to the end and take the footpath to the top.

Corona Heights offers superb views but also the chance to get a good workout. Located above a maze of winding streets not far from Market and Castro Streets, the outcropping of rock is reached via a precipitous trail. Take Roosevelt Way to Museum Way.

From the top of *Nob Hill,* look east down California (at the Powell inter-section) for a spectacular view of the bay. Office towers of the financial district and the tiled roofs of Chinatown bracket the Bay Bridge.

There's a public park, McKinley Square, on *Potrero Hill,* at the corner of Vermont and Twentieth Streets, with good views of the downtown skyline, Twin Peaks, and Mount Davidson. Then you can drive south down Vermont on a route that's just as crooked as the famous (and traffic-choked) stretch of Lombard Street.

In the little-visited ***Sunset District*** on the west side of town are two parks, Grand View and Golden Gate Heights, that provide stunning views all the way from Fort Funston and the zoo north along a 3-mile beach to the Golden Gate Bridge. On exceptionally clear days the panorama stretches to Point Reyes and the Farallon Islands. The parks sit atop two small peaks reached from 10th Avenue between Noriega and Pacheco Streets south of Golden Gate Park.

At the northwesternmost point of San Francisco lies Land's End. ***Ocean Lookout,*** at the end of El Camino Del Mar off Point Lobos Avenue, offers a superb vantage point for seeing the Pacific and Golden Gate.

On ***Russian Hill*** go to the intersection of Hyde and Greenwich Streets to gaze upon Telegraph Hill and Coit Tower, then to Hyde and Chestnut for a gripping view of the Hyde Street Pier and Alcatraz Island. If you want to enjoy coffee or a snack while you gape, try the cafeteria at the San Francisco Art Institute, 800 Chestnut Street. (There's also a huge Diego Rivera mural.)

Great views abound, but there are other reasons to visit Russian Hill. Novelist Herb Gold called it "a metropolitan village," an unpretentious blend of redwood shingle houses, cobbled lanes, and towering pine trees just a few blocks from downtown. Blessed with picturesque cul-de-sacs and stunning bay views, Russian Hill possesses "patrician elegance and Bohemian charm," as one writer put it.

The name remains something of a mystery—the area was never a Russian colony, nor were there many immigrants until much later. One legend has it that some Russian seal hunters are buried here; another, that a Russian sailor fell into a well and drowned after drinking too much.

The Powell–Hyde cable car line goes right over Russian Hill along Hyde Street, but only get off at Lombard to take a photo—that's "the crookedest street in the world" and also one of the most crowded. Little-known Filbert Street between Hyde and Leavenworth

trivia

The famous Filbert Steps on Telegraph Hill are among 350 stairways that lace together San Francisco's forty-two hills, the highest of which is Mount Davidson at 925 feet. If you like really steep hills, go to Twenty-second Street between Church and Vicksburg, with a 31.5 percent gradient.

trivia

Sutro Tower (for radio and television broadcasting) atop Mount Sutro is the city's tallest structure at 834 feet, while the famous Transamerica Pyramid (where King Kong used to appear in TV commercials) is the tallest building at 853 feet.

is the steepest in town, with a 31.5 percent vertical grade that provides a heart-rending descent (compared with Lombard Street's paltry 18 percent).

The hill's rustic informality has always appealed to writers, and the sounds of clicking typewriter keys (or is that a laser printer?) can still be heard, if you listen carefully, as you stroll along byways like Russian Hill Place. At its literary zenith in the late nineteenth century, queen of the hill was Ina Coolbrith, California's first poet laureate, who edited the *Overland Monthly* with colleagues Bret Harte and George Sterling. The latter described San Francisco as "the cool, gray city of love" long before the hippies arrived with flowers in their hair. Other writers who drifted through included Mark Twain, Joaquin Miller, Ambrose Bierce, Jack London, Frank Norris, Robinson Jeffers, and Helen Hunt Jackson.

Macondray Lane, where Coolbrith had a home, captures the village atmosphere that still defines Russian Hill, despite the intrusion of high-rises and traffic. The lane makes for a tranquil, reflective walk, passing shingled houses with bay windows, eucalyptus trees, and lush vegetation alive with the sound of songbirds. Armistead Maupin based his *Tales of the City* here on a fictional Barbary Lane. Even though residents must struggle with their groceries down this car-free passageway, they swear by life on the lane.

The heart of Russian Hill is bordered by Broadway and Hyde, Taylor, and Greenwich Streets. Worth exploring is the 1000 block of Green, so elegant it's called the "Paris Block." A delicate Italian-style house built in 1886 and later redesigned in Beaux Arts style by architect Julia Morgan, occupies 1055 Green Street, and there's the Feusier Octagon House at number 1067, reminder of an architectural fad that swept the city during the 1850s. The old firehouse at number 1088 once served the neighborhood as Engine House 31, and the Tudor-style building has been remodeled for use as a private residence; the original fire pole still stands in the doorway.

The far end of Vallejo Street has an aloof air about it. The brown shingle house with the double gable at number 1013–1019 was built by renowned architect Willis Polk for his own family, and number 1034 and number 1036 are two more homes from the original row. Branching off Vallejo are Russian Hill Place, a brick-paved lane lined with Mediterranean-style villas, and Florence

trivia

For thrilling views of the city try a round-trip tour on a hotel exterior view glass elevator. Among the more spectacular are at the JW Marriott San Francisco near Union Square, the Fairmont San Franciso on Nob Hill, and the Hyatt Regency San Francisco on the Embarcadero. Just push the top floor's button and blast off!

Street, which boasts the oldest cottage on Russian Hill (1857), a stark contrast to the ornate Victorians.

Architectural Delights

Pacific Heights is San Francisco's finest residential area, and the western section in particular contains several blocks of grand residences. Not that the wealthy enclaves of other cities can't match the mansions here, but the stunning setting makes them unforgettable. Pacific Heights is sandwiched between the Marina and Western Addition Districts, but with one important distinction—it's higher up. In San Francisco property, values and rent increase in direct proportion to altitude.

Begin the tour on Pacific Avenue along one stretch that's an architect's dream, the 3200 block between Presidio and Walnut. On this steep hill are several of the city's finest houses, including number 3233 by renowned architect Bernard Maybeck, which features a distinctive balustrade. The deep brown weathered shingles of several homes along the block create a wonderful architectural harmony.

The view from the corner of Pacific and Lyon Streets looks down over neighborhoods called Cow Hollow and the Marina. Farther east along Pacific Street are a sprawling mansion at the corner of Baker, the Egyptian consulate, and an impressive row of redbrick and white-trim Georgian homes in the 2800 block. The Drisco Hotel, at number 2901, was for many years the El Drisco, the only hotel in Pacific Heights.

Broadway is definitely one of the more schizophrenic streets in San Francisco. From an inauspicious start at the Embarcadero, it plummets straight into a sleazy strip of bawdy nightlife, skirts the edge of Chinatown, then disappears into the Broadway Tunnel. Emerging on the other side, the street traverses the lower part of Russian Hill and all of Pacific Heights before dead-ending outside the walls of the former Presidio. Here is a splendid view of the city and the Lyon Street Steps, a flight of stairs down to Vallejo Street and more mansions.

One block east (2898 Broadway), at the Baker Street stairs, sits a stately redbrick Georgian that epitomizes the best of Pacific Heights mansions—dignified, conservative, and self-assured. You can also see the former James Leary Flood mansion at 2222 Broadway, now a complex for the tony Sacred Heart Schools. Here are a few more gems to look for among the scores of lovely Pacific Heights homes:

- The grand Renaissance mansion at the intersection of Vallejo and Divisadero Streets has been used in several movies, including *Bullitt*.

- The Adolph Spreckels Mansion at 2080 Washington Street is a French baroque palace from 1913, now the residence of author Danielle Steel.
- A former firehouse (1893) at 3022 Washington has been converted into a private residence.

You could hardly call San Francisco a Victorian city, except when it comes to architecture. Some 14,000 "painted ladies" of seemingly endless size, shape, color, and ornamentation stand proudly throughout the town. About half of these have been restored or kept up over the years in a state befitting their stylish past.

The survival rate is astonishing when you consider that more than 500 blocks went up in smoke after the infamous 1906 earthquake. The fire raged through the town's northeast side, wiping out nearly everything between the bay and Van Ness Avenue. The most sumptuous homes lined this wide street but were dynamited by the army to form a firebreak that finally halted the blaze. Thus the richest depository of Victoriana lies west of Van Ness in the Pacific Heights and Western Addition sections of town. (Many Victorians also reside in the Mission District and the Haight-Ashbury.)

Why so many Victorians in San Francisco? The "City of Bay Windows" boomed during a few hectic decades of post–gold rush building. Victorian architecture was the rage, a style oozing with decorative details—fretwork, friezes, corbels, cartouches, plaster rosettes, fluted panels, carved medallions, and stained glass.

A driving tour of the city's finest *Victorian homes* starts with a cluster of lovely ladies at the intersection of California and Gough Streets. One highlight is the stately *Haas-Lilienthal House* at 2007 Franklin Street, built in 1886 for a wholesale grocer from Bavaria. During the great 1906 fire, the Haas family climbed to the roof of the three-story house and watched nervously as the flames moved toward them, only to be halted a block away at Van Ness. Their descendants occupied the home until 1972, when they donated it to an architectural foundation that offers guided tours on Wednesday, Saturday, and Sunday afternoons. Call (415) 441-3004 for tour times and entrance fees or check www.sfheritage.org.

The *Octagon House* (2645 Gough) is a perfectly preserved treasure from

trivia

The Columbarium (1 Lorraine Court) is a four-story architectural gem that serves as a burial vault for some of San Francisco's most influential former residents, including the Magnin and Folger families. Ornate decorations include a Tiffany stained-glass window, intricate carvings, and a copper dome. Open daily.

1861. Eight-sided homes enjoyed a vogue because some people believed they made for a healthier lifestyle. (Tours are given three days a month; call 415-441-7512 for information.)

The 700 block of Steiner Street at Alamo Square flaunts a row of Victorians with a famous backdrop of downtown seen on countless postcards. Another impressive lineup stands on McAllister near Scott in the same neighborhood. Bush Street, between Fillmore and Webster, has a row of houses moved from former sites during urban renewal, then spruced up and given front gardens.

Among unusual places to stay is the Queen Anne Hotel (1590 Sutter; (415) 441-2828; www.queenanne.com), with forty-nine rooms in a building designed for Miss Mary Lake's School for Girls. Walking tours of Victorian and other vintage residential neighborhoods are conducted by San Francisco City Guides (415-557-4266; www.sfcityguides.org), Heritage Walks (415-441-3004; www.sfheritage.org), and Victorian Home Walk Tour (415-252-9485; www.victorianwalk.com).

Another architectural thrill is the *Cathedral of St. Mary of the Assumption,* perched regally atop Cathedral Hill. In 1962 a major fire gutted the seventy-two-year-old redbrick church at Van Ness and Post, but before long, monolithic concrete pylons began to rise 2 blocks away. By the time the dust had settled, the city could boast a remarkable, marble-covered structure that has been likened to a schooner in full sail or a washing machine agitator, among other striking metaphors.

The ornate main entrance of St. Mary's Cathedral opens onto a white-marble baptismal font with seventy-eight diamond-faceted sides. Then, as in the great Gothic churches, eyes sweep upward to the stunning 190-foot-high dome and its faceted colored-glass windows that scale the walls like colored streamers to form a cross. The windows symbolize the classical elements: water, earth, fire, and air. The entire colossal structure rests on four giant pillars; between them are curved walls made from 1,680 prepoured concrete coffers that form a vast, columnless nave. Windows at the four corners open to views of San Francisco.

The radiant colors of the window rising behind the main altar reflect in the free-hanging baldachin, a kinetic sculpture by Richard Lippold, suspended above the sanctuary. Natural air currents keep this shimmering pendant in perpetual motion. An enormous Ruffatti organ with 4,842 pipes rests on a contoured concrete pedestal to take advantage of the cathedral's exceptionally good acoustics. Cathedral of St. Mary of the Assumption, at 1111 Gough Street (at Geary), is open daily from 9:00 a.m. to 4:30 p.m. For information about tours and free Sunday organ recitals, call (415) 567-2020.

Civic Center

A very different kind of pilgrimage is devoted to a book and its author. It told the story of "the stuff dreams are made of," the black bird whose enamel hid a king's ransom in precious gems. But when Dashiell Hammett created his superb detective novel *The Maltese Falcon,* he could not have imagined the cult that would grow up around it. Of course, John Huston's film of the same name ensured the immortality of Sam Spade, the Fat Man, and the rest of Hammett's carefully etched characters.

Falcon buffs can spend a day (preferably a foggy one) poking around the fading reminders of this exciting tale on a **Maltese Falcon tour.** All the action of *The Maltese Falcon* took place in a 10-block area between Union Square and Civic Center. Moreover, Hammett lived in San Francisco during his formative years, roughly from 1921 to 1929, and began his writing career here.

On Eddy Street off Larkin, for example, the Hammetts paid $45 a month for a furnished apartment. A nondescript building at 891 Post Street was the first place the writer lived after separating from his wife; it also served as the address of the hero, cynical gumshoe Sam Spade. It was here that Hammett wrote the first draft of his mystery masterpiece. He also lived for a time at 20 Monroe, a short street between Bush and Pine.

The old Hunter-Dulin Building at 111 Sutter Street housed the offices of Spade and his partner, Miles Archer, and it was here that they first laid eyes on the fickle Miss O'Shaughnessy. Later, on a little alley called Burritt Street (off Bush just above the Stockton Tunnel), she bumped off Archer. A bronze plaque reads: ON APPROXIMATELY THIS SPOT, MILES ARCHER, PARTNER OF SAM SPADE, WAS DONE IN BY BRIGID O'SHAUGHNESSY.

Quite a lot of "bumping off" took place in the story. On Geary near Leavenworth, Floyd Thursby was done in by "the kid," aka Wilmer Cook. Another identifiable locale is the Geary Theater (now American Conservatory Theater), site of a meeting between Spade and "the oily Joel Cairo."

To wind up the tour, head for 870 Market Street and the Flood Building, a gray edifice jutting out like the prow of a battleship. At this address Hammett worked briefly as a Pinkerton detective, or so the legend goes. Walking through the neoclassical lobby, you'll come out on Ellis Street, and at number 63 sits **John's Grill,** a classic establishment since 1908, and one of Hammett's hangouts in the twenties. It also served as the setting for one minor scene in *The Maltese Falcon.* Before setting out on a wild goose chase after Brigid, Sam stops by the grill for a quick dinner of "chops, baked potato, and sliced tomatoes."

Done up in dark wood, leather, and glass chandeliers, the restaurant looks pretty much as it must have in Hammett's day. And the management really "hamms" it up, too, serving "Sam Spade's Lamb Chops" and the "Bloody Brigid," a potent concoction of vodka, soda, pineapple juice, lime, and grenadine. An excellent replica of the black bird rules the roost upstairs, and there are copies of Hammett's works; a letter from his longtime friend, Lillian Hellman; and lots of good stills and posters from the classic film. Some say the writer's ghost appears as a misty white presence around noon, as if he's waiting to be seated for lunch. John's Grill (415-986-3274; www.johnsgrill.com) serves as headquarters for the Dashiell Hammett Society of San Francisco.

For many years a local character named Don Herron has given animated tours of Hammett's San Francisco, covering the 3 miles of key locations in the Tenderloin, Nob Hill, and downtown hotel district. The walks leave the main branch of the San Francisco Public Library in the Civic Center Saturdays at noon, May and June only. You shouldn't have any trouble spotting Herron; he'll be the one in a trench coat and fedora hat emerging from the fog. For further information visit www.donherron.com.

While at the Civic Center, stop by **San Francisco City Hall,** beautifully restored to all its former glory. Designed by Arthur Brown Jr. in the Beaux-Arts style, the soaring edifice boasts a 306-foot dome modeled on St. Peters in Rome. (In fact, city hall and the entire Civic Center area, including the opera house, public library, and other buildings, look like they belong in Vienna or Paris rather than California.) Like the rest of the building, the dome was completely renovated in the late 1990s and now features its original copper gold color. It's larger than the dome of the U.S. Capitol and the fifth tallest in the world. Inside city hall there is a sweeping marble staircase and two "light courts" bathed in natural sunlight pouring through the glass ceiling. San Francisco City Hall, with a city museum and gift shop, is open weekdays from 8:00 a.m. to 8:00 p.m. Guided tours are available. For information, call (415) 554-4933.

trivia

The San Francisco Convention & Visitors Bureau sponsors a 24-hour visitor hotline of current events in six languages. For English dial (415) 391-2001; for Spanish (415) 391-2122.

Another recommended stop at Civic Center is the **Heart of the City Farmers Market,** 2 blocks east of the city hall on United Nations Plaza. Colorful and cosmopolitan—with a distinct Asian influence in produce selection—it unfolds under blue awnings every Wednesday 7:00 a.m. to 5:30 p.m. and Sunday from 7:00 a.m. to 5:00 p.m. For more information call (415) 558-9455.

Here farmers can sell only what they raise or catch themselves. Dozens of stands overflow with eggs, almonds, live chickens, fish on ice, oysters, flowers, leeks, and mushrooms the size of dinner plates. Shoppers poke and prod and finally pick their own produce, whether mangoes or garlic or lush red cherries. Many sellers will let you sample the goodies before you buy, but don't misuse the custom to have a free lunch!

And speaking of lunch, nearby **Hayes Valley** is a great local neighborhood to stroll, window-shop at chichi boutiques, sip espresso, or sample from a wide array of trendy restaurants such as Absinthe Brasserie (398 Hayes Street, 415-551-1590; www.absinthe.com) and the legendary Hayes Street Grill (320 Hayes Street, 415-863-5545; www.hayesstreetgrill.com). Octavia Boulevard, complete with belle époque streetlamps, provides a stylish cynosure for the neighborhood with galleries and elegant shops.

The West Side

On a nice day you can always head for the city's most famous retreat. **Golden Gate Park,** one of the largest man-made parks in the world, had to be wrested inch by inch from the grip of sand dunes and economically worthless land. San Francisco was much smaller when the 1,017-acre site was selected in 1870 from what were known disparagingly as "the outside lands." Yet "the great sand bank" grew into a lush urban paradise largely through the efforts of engineer William Hammond Hall and John McLaren, two farsighted landscape architects.

Naturally, an idyllic retreat attracts loads of visitors, especially on sunny weekends. Even so, the park is so vast that you can easily find solitude in a misty forest or by a tranquil pond. (Remember, after the 1906 earthquake some 40,000 refugees managed to camp here!) Generally, the park's eastern half is busier, especially around the complex of excellent museums.

Nearby, ride a painted pony—and a dog, frog, or reindeer—on the vintage **carousel** in the Koret Children's Quarter. Built in 1912 and fully restored, this rare, wood-carved Herschell-Spillman merry-go-round is housed inside a pillared rotunda. It features a pipe organ, gleaming brass poles, dazzling mirrors and glass jewelry, and pictorial panels painted with idyllic scenes of bygone times. And, of course, the delightfully carved animals, lined up in four bobbing rows, including giraffes, ostriches, camels, cats, roosters, and horses with roses in their manes and cherubs on their saddles. Even if you don't hop on for a ride, it's worth a trip just to see the superb craftsmanship and attention to detail, such as real horsehair in the tails of those wonderful painted ponies.

Located off Bowling Green Drive at the park's eastern edge, the Golden Gate Park Carrousel is open daily from 9:00 a.m. to 4:00 p.m.

If ruins are your thing, head over to tiny Lloyd Lake, just west of Cross Over Drive, to see the strangely evocative **Portals of the Past.** This curious landmark consists of six white marble pillars that at one time formed the entrance to the grandiose A. N. Towne residence atop Nob Hill. But they were all that remained after the 1906 disaster.

Next take a trip to the **Buffalo Paddock** in the park's wide-open western spaces. The fences here are so carefully concealed by artful landscaping that the bison seem to be roaming free. Across from the Buffalo Paddock sits another unique attraction, the **Flycasting Pools.**

There are no fish here, but fishermen find the next best thing: an enormous cement-lined pool with almost two acres of water for practicing distance casting, accuracy, and the difficult technique of fly casting. The Golden Gate Angling & Casting Club makes its headquarters in the Angler's Lodge. Inside, paneled knotty pine walls are hung with classic rods, mounted trout, and displays of hand-tied flies. For information check www.ggacc.org.

Next head west to the final stop of a crowd-free trip to the park. At the far end of John F. Kennedy Drive, just before it reaches the Great Highway, is the **Dutch Windmill,** another lesser-known jewel. Built in 1902, the mill was designed to pump water to the reservoir atop Strawberry Hill. It has been restored with a new copper dome and scalelike shingles, and it turns happily in the breeze. The Queen Wilhelmina Tulip Gardens erupt in a symphony of color early each spring.

For further information about Golden Gate Park, visit www.parks.sfgov.org.

A great way to get a different perspective on San Francisco's seemingly endless diversity is to visit one of the outlying neighborhoods seldom frequented by tourists. Among the more intriguing count Potrero Hill, Haight-Ashbury, the Sunset, the Richmond, and, perhaps most diverse of all, the **Mission District** in the south central area of town.

The Mission District was San Francisco's first neighborhood, and today it's largely ignored by visitors but loved by locals. It's an exciting, albeit sometimes bewildering, cultural and ethnic mix; once Italian and Irish, now chiefly Hispanic, but with many African Americans, Filipinos, and Samoans. This diversity brings with it a delightful blend of food choices, with an emphasis on Latin but not necessarily Mexican dishes. You can find cornmeal pancakes called arepas and sea bass seviche (raw with seasoning) from South America; Salvadoran *pupusas* (stuffed with pork and cheese); and Guatemalan specialties like tamales steamed in banana leaves. Burritos are served so widely in the Mission that some speak of a burrito cult or subculture. Especially popular at all hours are the "little burros" made at El Farolito at 2779 Mission Street (415-826-4870). But if Latin food doesn't appeal, try organic meat loaf, homemade gnocchi, Chinese yin yang prawns, and even great schnitzel and potato dumplings. The nearby gay mecca of Castro Street helped bring the neighborhood great food and chic boutiques, avant-garde theaters, and torrid nightlife, whether it be jazz, stand-up comedy, Chinese opera, flamenco, salsa, or drag shows.

But before the sun sets, be sure to take in the Mission's cultural attractions. These include old **Mission Dolores,** whose correct name is Mission de San Francisco de Asis, at Dolores and Sixteenth Streets; it was founded five days before the Declaration of Independence was signed in 1776. View the beautiful Mission Dolores Basilica dome and an interior window depicting St. Francis of Assisi. Mission Dolores is open daily from 9:00 a.m. to 4:00 p.m.

The Mission District's colorful and flamboyant murals—about 200 in all—are a local art form with national recognition. Found throughout the area but concentrated on a few key streets are walls of every description, from the sides of three-story buildings to garage doors, transformed into outdoor canvases by a wide range of artistic talent. Often they speak to Hispanic heritage and human rights; in fact, the mural tradition got its first big push back in 1971 when more than thirty works were created to call for peace in Central America. The murals that line an entire block of Balmy Street between Twenty-fourth and Twenty-fifth Streets are an eclectic mixture of Hindu goddesses, portraits of peasants with clenched fists, whimsical childlike fantasies, and dark religious themes. Many more wall paintings are found on bustling Twenty-fourth Street, and at number 2981 is the Precita Eyes Mural Arts and Visitors Center, which conducts guided tours every Saturday of eight important blocks featuring more than sixty murals. Call (415) 285-2287 for tour details.

Twenty-fourth Street is really the heart of the district and a welcome respite from the hectic pace of Mission Street itself. The flavor is definitely Hispanic, with *Mexicatessens, panaderias* (for bread), and even *esoterica gitana* (a gypsy fortune-reading parlor). Places of note include the popular Roosevelt Tamale Parlor at 2817 Twenty-fourth Street and Galería de la Raza (at 2857; 415-826-8009; www.galeriadelaraza.org) featuring primarily politically oriented Latino art.

If Twenty-fourth Street is the heart of the Mission, then Valencia Street is its soul, and San Franciscans flock here for neighborhood bookstores (specializing in sci-fi, Eastern religions, and leftish

trivia

According to statistics, hard-driving S.F. cab drivers burn out their brakes every 2,000 miles.

politics), trendy shopping (from designer clothes, vintage furniture, candles and incense, to a vintage record store), and even a mind-boggling array of adult toys at the famous Good Vibrations store (603 Valencia Street). The best strolling section of Valencia Street lies between Twenty-second and Seventeenth Streets.

Valencia Street really comes alive on weekend nights, with scores of interesting dining choices: Ethiopian cuisine or Spanish tapas; smart bistros like Garcon! (1101 Valencia; 415-401-8959; www.garconsf.com) and Mexican restaurants. Nightlife begins with happy hour at the Phoenix Bar (at 811), an Irish pub where they pour Guinness correctly, a procedure taking almost ten minutes, time to peruse pithy quotes from Oscar Wilde, travel posters, and memorabilia from Ireland. More exotic imbibers crave an almond mocha chocolate martini at Blondie's (540 Valencia; 415-864-2419; http://blondiesbar .com). Once you've supped and sipped you might try the gay-oriented Theatre Rhinoceros at 2926 Sixteenth Street (415-861-5079; www.therhino.org) or the Marsh (1062 Valencia; 415-826-5750; www.themarsh.org), with live theater and stand-up comedy on weekends. One final tip: When heading back from the Mission at night, it's best to take a taxi.

The Final Stop

Finally, you can go south of Market Street to find out what happens when the scion of one of America's wealthiest industrial families decides to become a brewmaster. Young Fritz Maytag of the famous washing-machine empire heard that the maker of his favorite beer, Anchor Steam, was tottering on the edge of bankruptcy. So, back in 1965, he decided to step in and save the ***Anchor Brewing Company.*** One delightful result of Maytag's personal passion is a great forty-five-minute tour. It begins by meeting the guide and fellow beer-lovers in the tasting room, done up nicely with antique brewing paraphernalia and serving trays from around the world. A wall of windows looks out on gleaming copper kettles used in the beer-making process.

First, the guide describes the origin of steam brewing, a unique process developed in the nineteenth century to get around the need for ice, then scarce in San Francisco. Without ice, the unfermented beer is transferred to large, shallow pans instead of to deep vats so that the larger surface area can dissipate the heat faster. Although the origin of the term *steam beer* remains obscure, one version says that the final product emerged so heavily charged with natural carbonation that it appeared to let off steam when kegs were tapped.

First the barley is malted and crushed for mashing, then blended with warm water and gradually heated in huge copper kettles. The filtration process yields wort, an unfermented liquid that will eventually become beer. The wort is boiled and combined with whole hops that lend beer its aroma and slight bitterness. For fermentation, yeast is introduced into the wort, which has meanwhile been transferred to shallow pans for cooling. Three days later, it's beer!

The tour group—by now having worked up a tremendous thirst—marches off to the tasting room to sample steam beer, three kinds of ale, a dark porter, and a wheat beer. On a tour between Thanksgiving and the end of January? Expect an extra treat: a spicy Christmas ale brewed to the carefully prepared specifications of master brewer Fritz Maytag.

The Anchor Brewing Company, at 1705 Mariposa Street, conducts free tours and tastings by reservation only on weekdays at 1:00 p.m.; call (415) 863-8350 for information or go to www.anchorbrewing.com.

Places to Stay in San Francisco

UNION SQUARE/ NOB HILL

Adagio Hotel,
550 Geary Street;
(800) 228-8830

Andrews Hotel
624 Post Street
(800) 926-3739

Beresford Hotel
635 Sutter Street
(415) 673-9900

Cartwright Hotel
524 Sutter Street
(800) 227-3844

Chancellor Hotel
433 Powell Street
(800) 428-4748

Cornell Hotel de France
715 Bush Street
(800) 232-9698

Handlery Union Square Hotel
351 Geary Street
(415) 781-7800

Hotel Abri
127 Ellis Street
(866) 823-4669

Hotel Triton
342 Grant Avenue
(800) 433-6611

Orchard Garden Hotel
466 Bush Street
(888) 717-2881

WORTH SEEING/DOING IN SAN FRANCISCO

Alcatraz Island Tour

Asian Art Museum, Civic Center

Bay Cruise

Cable Car Ride

California Academy of Sciences, Golden Gate Park

Coit Tower, North Beach

De Young Art Museum, Golden Gate Park

Golden Gate Bridge

Japantown

Legion of Honor (fine art museum), Lincoln Park

San Francisco Museum of Modern Art/Yerba Buena Gardens

York Hotel
940 Sutter Street
(800) 808-9675

**EMBARCADERO/
FISHERMAN'S WHARF**

Best Western Tuscan Inn
425 North Point Street
(800) 648-4626

Harbor Court Hotel
165 Steuart Street
(866) 792-6283

**Hyatt Regency San
Francisco**
5 Embarcadero Center
(415) 788-1234

Wharf Inn
2601 Mason Street
(800) 548-9918

VAN NESS/LOMBARD

Broadway Manor Inn
2201 Van Ness Avenue
(800) 727-6239

Castle Inn Motel
1565 Broadway
(800) 822-7853

Comfort Inn by the Bay
2775 Van Ness Avenue
(800) 228-5150

Pacific Heights Inn
1555 Union Street
(800) 523-1801

Ramada Limited
1940 Lombard Street
(800) 272-6232

Travelodge by the Bay
1450 Lombard Street
(800) 578-7878

Places to Eat in San Francisco

(All area codes are 415)

**UNION SQUARE/
DOWNTOWN**

Akiko's Sushi (Japanese)
542 Mason Street
989-8218

**Annabelle's Bar and
Bistro (American/
Californian)**
68 Fourth Street
777-1200

Cafe Claude (French)
7 Claude Lane
392-3505

**Cafe de la Presse
(Continental)**
352 Grant Avenue
398-2680

Café Tiramisu (Italian)
28 Belden Place
421-7044

David's (Jewish)
474 Geary Street
276-5950

Grand Cafe (Continental)
501 Geary Street
292-0101

Jeanne d'Arc (French)
715 Bush Street
421-3154

**Johnny Foley's Irish
House (pub food)**
243 O'Farrell Street
954-0777

Le Central (French)
453 Bush Street
391-2233

**Le Colonial
(Vietnamese/French)**
20 Cosmo Place
931-3600

**Marrakech Moroccan
Restaurant
(North African)**
419 O'Farrell Street
776-6717

**Sam's Grill & Seafood
Restaurant**
374 Bush Street;
421-0594

**Sushi Boat Restaurant
(Japanese)**
389 Geary Street
781-5111

**NORTH BEACH/
CHINATOWN**

Caffe Sport (Italian)
574 Green Street
981-1251

Calzone's (Italian)
430 Columbus Avenue
397-3600

**Chinatown Restaurant
(Chinese)**
744 Washington Street
392-7958

**Great Eastern Restaurant
(Chinese)**
649 Jackson Street
986-2500

**House of Nan King
(Chinese)**
919 Kearny Street
421-1429

**North Beach Restaurant
(Italian)**
1512 Stockton Street
392-1700

The Pot Sticker (Chinese)
150 Waverly Place
397-9985

Rose Pistola (Italian)
532 Columbus Avenue
399-0499

**The Stinking Rose
(Italian/Garlic)**
325 Columbus
781-7673

**Tomasso's Restaurant
(Italian)**
1042 Kearny Street
398-9696

Yank Sing (Chinese)
101 Spear Street
957-9300

EMBARCADERO/WHARF

**Buena Vista Cafe
(American/Californian)**
2765 Hyde Street
474-5044

**Castagnola's Restaurant
(seafood)**
286 Jefferson Street
776-5015

**Fog City Diner
(American/Californian)**
1300 Battery Street
982-2000

Gary Danko (French)
800 North Point
749-2060

Globe (American)
290 Pacific Avenue
391-4132

**Slanted Door
(Vietnamese)**
1 Ferry Building
The Embarcadero
861-8032

Tadich Grill (seafood)
240 California Street
391-1849

**Waterfront Restaurant
(American/Californian)**
Pier 7
The Embarcadero
391-2696

**VAN NESS/CIVIC
CENTER/MISSION**

Dosa (Indian)
995 Valencia Street
642-3672

**Greens Restaurant
(vegetarian)**
Fort Mason Building A
771-6222

**Harris' Restaurant
(American/Californian)**
2100 Van Ness Avenue
673-1888

**Hayes Street Grill
(seafood)**
320 Hayes Street
863-5545

Matterhorn (Swiss)
2323 Van Ness Avenue
885-6116

**Max's Opera Cafe
(American/Californian)**
601 Van Ness Avenue
771-7300

Suppenkuche (German)
601 Hayes Street
252-9289

Zarzuela (Spanish)
2000 Hyde Street
346-0800

HELPFUL WEB SITES FOR SAN FRANCISCO

City Search:
http://sanfrancisco.citysearch.com

Golden Gate Park:
www.parks.sfgov.org

San Francisco *7x7* Magazine:
www.7x7.com

San Francisco Arts: www.sfarts.org

San Francisco Chronicle:
www.sfgate.com

**San Francisco Convention & Visitors
Bureau:** www.onlyinsanfrancisco.com

San Francisco Guide:
www.sfguide.com

San Francisco Magazine: http://media
.modernluxury.com/digital.php?e=SANF

TIX outlet: www.theatrebayarea.org

THE BAY AREA

Most visitors are amazed to discover that San Francisco has only about 825,000 residents, hardly big enough, it would seem, for its big-city reputation. But taken as a whole, the San Francisco Bay Area (including Marin, Alameda, Contra Costa, Solano, San Mateo, and Santa Clara Counties) is home to more than seven million people, making it one of the nation's largest metropolitan areas. Many people commute daily to San Francisco, while others rarely visit, preferring to live quietly in their own self-contained communities.

Geologists conclude that the famous bay was formed many thousands of years ago, when rising water levels caused the Pacific to punch through the Golden Gate and fill a valley that had been carved by river runoff from the interior. The bay still receives drainage from the San Joaquin and Sacramento Rivers, as well as a number of smaller streams, and has been a major shipping avenue since the California Gold Rush of 1849.

Although many visitors find it hard to pull themselves away from San Francisco, it's definitely worth the effort. The Bay Area is among the country's most diverse places in terms of natural beauty and visitor attractions. Using San Francisco as

THE BAY AREA

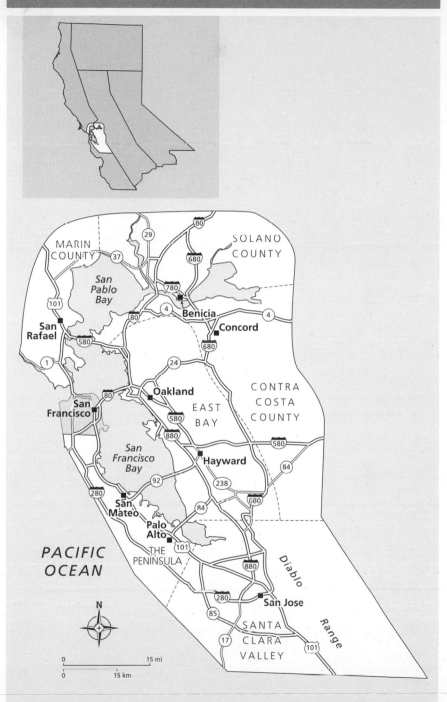

MARIN COUNTY

SOLANO COUNTY

San Pablo Bay

San Rafael

Benicia

Concord

CONTRA COSTA COUNTY

Oakland

EAST BAY

San Francisco

San Francisco Bay

Hayward

San Mateo

Palo Alto

THE PENINSULA

PACIFIC OCEAN

Diablo Range

San Jose

SANTA CLARA VALLEY

N

0   15 mi
0   15 km

a base, most of the area's scenic and cultural delights are within reach by car or public transportation in little more than an hour.

Marin County

Jutting down from the north toward San Francisco, Marin County is accessible via the Golden Gate Bridge or by ferry across the bay. The coastal mountains neatly divide Marin—one side fronts the bay and the other, the ocean. The east is known for its fashionably cute seaside towns like Sausalito and Tiburon, getaways to shop, stroll, and watch sailboats skim the surface of the bay. A windy, often fog-draped landscape of mountains and craggy shoreline awaits to the west. San Francisco seems close enough to reach out and grab, yet nature remains remarkably unspoiled by modern incursions.

trivia

San Francisco Bay is the largest natural harbor and estuary on the West Coast.

Just a mile of bridge separates hectic San Francisco from the grassy slopes and windswept ridges of the *Marin Headlands,* which stretch from the bridge to Muir Beach. The area encompasses jagged coastline, tranquil valleys, and isolated beaches; grassy bluffs high above the surf provide spectacular views of San Francisco and the bay. Although close to the city in distance and time, the headlands seem far removed from urban life.

The area has remained so relatively unspoiled because from the 1870s to 1972 much of it belonged to the U.S. Army and thus escaped commercial development. (The rest of the land belonged to dairy farmers and a hunting group.) You can still sense the military's legacy everywhere, especially in three forts and numerous concrete artillery batteries that protect the entrance to the bay.

AUTHOR'S TOP TEN IN THE BAY AREA

Marin Headlands	Alameda Island
Tiburon	Stanford University
Angel Island	Skyline Boulevard
Benicia	Rosicrucian Egyptian Museum
Oakland Temple	Mount Hamilton

For a good overview of the Marin Headlands, take the loop drive on Conzelman and Bunker Roads. Along the way you'll spot several turnouts offering magnificent views, and at Kirby Cove you can take a 1-mile hike down to the beach to see the Golden Gate Bridge from below (a *must* for photographers). The visitor center sits at the junction of Bunker and Field Roads. (It's open daily from 9:30 a.m. to 4:30 p.m.; 415-331-1540.) Around you are the white frame structures of Fort Barry, a turn-of-the-twentieth-century seacoast artillery post. Just uphill from the visitor center is the historic Nike Missile Site, an outdoor museum of cold war–era defenses. Now fully restored, the site is open Wednesday, Thursday, Friday, and the first Saturday of each month from 12:30 to 3:30 p.m.

At the far western end of this driving route lies the unique ***Marine Mammal Center,*** run by a private organization dedicated to rescuing and rehabilitating injured and ailing ocean animals—seals, sea lions, and the occasional whale or dolphin—then releasing them. The group patrols the coast from San Luis Obispo to the Oregon border and treats marine mammals brought in for anything from skin diseases to injuries from boats. A new facility and visitor center is open daily; for information call (415) 289-7355 or check www.marine mammalcenter.org.

Another popular place is ***Point Bonita Lighthouse,*** perched like a sentinel at the peninsula's southern tip. Drive part way out, then follow a trail along a wind-pummeled ridge, through a tunnel, and across a 120-foot-high bridge before reaching the light. Here, see the Golden Gate as if approaching from the ocean. The station still uses the original hand-ground French lens, installed after the first system (an army sergeant firing a cannon every half hour during foggy spells) failed. The lighthouse and trail are open Saturday, Sunday, and Monday from 12:30 to 3:30 p.m. but are subject to closure due to high wind. Check at the visitor center for information about guided tours and consult www.nps.gov/goga/pobo.htm.

The Marin Headlands are a favorite with hikers. The Coastal Trail scrambles over spectacular shoreline and can be reached at the trailhead just west of Rodeo Lagoon. The 1.7-mile Tennessee

trivia

It's said that Marin County has the world's highest concentration of hot tubs and BMWs.

Valley Trail goes to Tennessee Beach. The ***Tennessee Valley*** was named for a shipwreck lying just offshore, a steamer called the *Tennessee,* which went down in 1853. The beach is quiet, and the warm, sheltered valley is great for walking. Nothing bigger than a bush is indigenous to the headlands, and any trees you see were planted by the military, mostly as camouflage for

The Wonderful Bay

I'm sitting here beside the little ferry dock at Tiburon in Marin County, marveling at my good fortune. It's December 31, and the weather is sunny and warm, almost balmy. Sailboats glide across the water, and seagulls flutter overhead. Except for a few cottony clouds, the sky is clear and the views superb: south across the bay to San Francisco, its larger avenues visible as they climb the city's hills. I scan the skyline 10 miles distant, spotting familiar landmarks like Coit Tower and the Transamerica Pyramid.

Glistening in the morning sun, the bay is sprinkled with sailboats and catamarans, rubber dinghies, and much larger vessels. I can see Alcatraz clearly off to the left, and Angel Island sits directly across narrow Raccoon Strait like a pocket-size Isle of Capri. (It's accessible by ferry on weekends from this same dock.) The ferry from San Francisco pulls in several times a day after a stop at Sausalito, and the ride back to the city takes just fifteen minutes.

The cute, upscale village of Tiburon (which means "shark" in Spanish) sits on a 4-mile-long peninsula crowded with expensive homes and clapboard-sheathed condominiums clinging to the hills. Tiburon faces south, which means great views and lots of sunshine, and I stop to partake of both blessings and a cappuccino at Sweden House Bakery on Main Street, one of several cafes with outdoor terraces. (Other popular spots are Sam's Anchor Cafe and Guaymas Restaurant.) I'm looking out on a small marina flush with craft belonging to the exclusive Corinthian Yacht Club.

Afterward I stroll along Main Street, which old-timers say hasn't changed much in decades, though most stores are now gift shops and galleries, and there's even a wine-tasting room for visitors. From here a pleasant promenade skirting the shore is alive with people walking dogs, in-line skating, or just lounging on benches and enjoying the views. But it's not crowded even on this holiday weekend.

At the far end of the promenade, I decide to stop for lunch at Caprice Restaurant overlooking the bay, and my jaw drops when I see the menu—and the prices. It's expensive, but I don't worry about such things today. After all, how many people are lucky enough to visit a place like this?

artillery. But wildlife abounds, including the highest concentration of hawks on the Pacific coast. From September through November bird-watchers flock to Hawk Hill west of Kirby Cove as thousands of birds from various species of raptors (hawks and kestrels) stop here before hopping across the bay on thermals.

To reach the Marin Headlands, northbound drivers must take the Alexander Avenue exit from U.S. Highway 101; southbound drivers should get off at the second Sausalito exit (the last exit before the bridge). Follow the signs to

Conzelman Road or Fort Cronkhite to join the loop. For more information go to www.nps.gov/goga/mahe.

Among Marin's many popular sights are Muir Woods and Mount Tamalpais, and they are often jammed with camera-clicking visitors. Yet the north side of the mountain, the rainiest spot in the Bay Area, offers several small lakes little known even to residents.

Part of the twenty-acre **Mount Tamalpais Watershed,** these lakes (Bon Tempe, Lagunitas, Alpine, and Phoenix) are actually man-made reservoirs built between 1873 and 1954 in the shadow of the mountain. The water is clear and clean, and there is some trout fishing but no swimming or boating. There are many easy trails around the lakes (get a map at the entrance) that wind through woods of oak, madrone, Douglas fir, and redwood. One steep trail at Alpine Lake leads to beautiful Cataract Falls, and many animals thrive in the area: deer, jackrabbits, squirrels, raccoons, bobcats, and birds such as red-tailed hawks.

To reach the Mount Tamalpais Watershed, drive north on US 101 to Sir Francis Drake Boulevard, then west to Fairfax. Take Bolinas–Fairfax Road south and turn left at Sky Oaks Road, leading to the entrance. Open sunrise to sunset daily; $7 per vehicle. Call (415) 945-1181 for information.

trivia

Arguably the best view in the Bay Area is from the top of East Peak Lookout (2,571 feet) in Mount Tamalpais State Park.

Another pleasant side trip from the affluent town of Fairfax (go west 4 miles on Nicasio Valley Road) leads to the tiny village of **Nicasio.** Lying at the geographical center of Marin, early settlers tried to make it the county seat. But San Rafael prevailed, and Nicasio remains rustic and unspoiled. grazing sheep and dairy farms, golf courses, and big, beautiful homes (George Lucas's Skywalker Ranch is nearby).

The village itself, once the home of Grateful Dead guitarist Jerry Garcia, is like something from a pleasant daydream, with a little red schoolhouse, the white-steepled St Mary's Church, and a Little League baseball diamond in the old town square. Across the street Rancho Nicasio Restaurant (415-662-2219; www.ranchonicasio.com) has a big western-style bar, music events, and outdoor tables for a lazy lunch.

Most visitors see a very different side of Marin County's split personality: yacht harbors, trendy restaurants, smart boutiques, and a profusion of BMWs. Sun-splashed Sausalito is quintessentially quaint, and most visitors are happy to stroll, shop, and eyeball the high-living locals. But Sausalito boasts a most unusual attraction: the **San Francisco Bay and Delta Model.**

TOP ANNUAL EVENTS IN THE BAY AREA

San Mateo International Sportsmans Expo, San Mateo (mid-January)

Tet Festival (Vietnamese Lunar New Year), San Jose (mid-January)

Golden Gate Kennel Club Dog Show, Daly City (late January)

Sonoma-Marin Fair, Petaluma (late June)

Los Altos Arts and Wine Festival (mid-July)

Roaring Camp Mountain Man Rendezvous, Felton (August)

Chinatown Street Fest, Oakland (late August)

Sausalito Art Festival, Sausalito (Labor Day Weekend, early September)

San Jose Mariachi Festival, San Jose (September)

Half Moon Bay Art & Pumpkin Festival (mid-October)

Day of the Dead *(Dia de los Muertos)*, Oakland (Sunday nearest November 1)

Lighted Yacht Parade, Oakland (early December)

Las Posadas, Mission San Jose, Fremont (early December)

Built by the U.S. Army Corps of Engineers to simulate bay conditions, this mass of concrete, water, wires, and gauges sprawls over a 1.5-acre site inside an old World War II warehouse. Grasp how big the model is by walking around it and seeing things from a simulated height of 12,000 feet. Entering the building, head up a ramp to journey through the San Francisco watershed via the *From the Mountains to the Sea* exhibit. A twelve-minute video describes the San Francisco Bay's complex watershed from the Sierra Nevada to the Pacific and the role of the bay model. The sprawling model, the size of two football fields, re-creates 343 square miles of the bay on concrete slabs ingeniously formed to mimic the real landscape.. It was designed almost half a century ago to find answers to complex hydrodynamic problems by monitoring the effects of tides, currents, geology, pollution, and other natural and human factors, including studying the delicate dynamics of water mixing in the narrow Carquinez Strait.

The 360-foot-deep Golden Gate Channel is 3.5 feet deep in the scale model. San Francisco Bay, San Pablo Bay, the Carquinez Strait, and the Sacramento/San Joaquin Delta are modeled. That's a lot of ground—and water—to cover. The Delta alone has 700 miles of waterways, sloughs, and bays, and San Francisco Bay is already one-third filled in. To re-create actual conditions, 185,000 gallons of water were mixed with seventeen tons of salt and pumped into the model at a precise rate, pouring through the Golden Gate, swirling around Alcatraz and into the bay. In seven-and-a-half minutes the simulated tide rises and falls, compared with six hours in real life, and a day passes in about fifteen minutes. A year lasts just three-and-a-half days; that's one hundred times faster than in nature.

The Bay Model has provided valuable data coordinated in computer simulations that have been used to evaluate oil and chemical spills, dredging, and the impact of landfill, and to study the mixing of fresh with salt water.

Visitors "Take the Water Challenge" by trying to allocate California's precious water supply to competing interests—agriculture, wildlife, industry, and cities—as politicians have to do. An excellent one-hour self-guided audio tour is available.

The San Francisco and Delta Bay Model, at 2100 Bridgeway (accessed via Marinship Way), is open Tuesday through Saturday from 9:00 a.m. to 4:00 p.m. Call (415) 332-3871 for further information, or visit www.spn.usace.army .mil/bmvc.

Best Factory Tours

Hundreds of thousands of people visit Bay Area factories each year, sampling everything from beer to banana splits and seeing how things get made, not to mention learning secrets like how they get those little messages into fortune cookies. Here's a list of the best tours around:

- **Fortune Cookie Factory,** 261 Twelfth Street, Oakland; (510) 832-5552, Monday through Friday from 10:00 a.m. to 3:00 p.m.; $1 per person to see how a fortune cookie is made.

- **Intel Museum,** 2200 Mission College Boulevard, Santa Clara; (408) 765-0503; www.intel.com/museum. Open weekdays from 9:00 a.m. to 6:00 p.m.; Saturday from 10:00 a.m. to 5:00 p.m. Free. Self-guided exhibits in the heart of Silicon Valley show the chip-manufacturing process and the history of the microprocessor.

- **Marin French Cheese Factory,** 7500 Red Hill Road, Petaluma; (800) 292-6001; www.marinfrenchcheese.com. Tours daily at 10:00, 11:00 a.m., noon, and 3:00 p.m. Free. See cheese-making and packing rooms with free tastes of Brie, Camembert, and other soft cheeses.

- **Mrs. Grossman's Paper Co.,** 3810 Cypress Drive, Petaluma; (800) 429-4549; www.mrsgrossmans.com. Open weekdays, tour times vary; $3 admission charged; reservations needed. See how stickers are made; free stickers are handed out.

Falling Waters

Perhaps the Bay Area's greatest secret is its hidden waterfalls, often seen along the trails of some great hikes. There's nothing like the sound of rushing water to drown out the cacophony of modern life, but in this area the falls come and go like wildflowers. Try to visit in winter or spring after any significant rainfall. Here are some favorites.

Berry Creek Falls, Big Basin State Park, Boulder Creek. Reached by a 4.7-mile hike (allow about six hours round-trip), this 70-foot cascade is enclosed in a redwood canyon and lush grotto of ferns and sorrel.

Cataract Falls, Mount Tamalpais Watershed. Hike from the Laura Dell Trailhead about 2 miles to the falls, a long and dramatic series of cascades.

Brooks Falls, San Pedro Valley Park, Pacifica. A stunning 175-foot silver strand in three tiers tumbles down into a canyon. Take the Montara Mountain Trail.

Silver Falls, Big Basin State Park, Boulder Creek. A pristine cascade that fronts a hollowed-out cavern, just upstream from Berry Creek Falls.

Castle Rock Falls, Castle Rock State Park, Los Gatos. This 50-foot cataract is a powerful surge of white, pounding water. The trail to the viewing platform is about a mile long.

Carson Falls, Marin Water District, Fairfax. A series of pools and falls rushing over giant boulders and leading to a 40-foot silvery chute. The round-trip is 3 miles over easy terrain.

Diablo Falls, Mount Diablo State Park, Danville. Hidden on the mountain's north flank are two falls forming a combined 85-foot drop. Reached by a steep and difficult hike, 9 miles round-trip.

Triple Falls, Uvas County Park, Coyote (Santa Clara County). A series of three cascades, about 40 feet in all, hidden in the foothills. Reached by a 2.5-mile hike from the trailhead.

Cascade Falls, Elliot Nature Preserve, Fairfax. Though not high, these falls are set in near-perfect surroundings of moss-lined rocks; also easy to reach, only 2 miles round-trip.

Murrieta Falls, Sunol Regional Wilderness, Livermore. At 100 feet this is the Bay Area's highest waterfall, but reaching it requires a long and strenuous hike (11 miles round-trip) from the trailhead at Del Valle Regional Park.

Angel Island sits a mile offshore from the affluent Marin town of Tiburon. Though it is the bay's largest island (about 740 acres), it is often ignored by visitors eager to see that neighboring isle of ill repute—Alcatraz. Yet Angel Island is easily reached by ferryboat from Marin County or San Francisco.

Except for staff vehicles, cars are not allowed on the island—but there will be cyclists with their bikes, hikers with backpacks, boys with fishing rods, and families lugging picnic baskets (sorry, no dogs). After a short trip, the ferry arrives at Ayala Cove, named for Spanish explorer Juan Manuel de Ayala, whose ship, the *San Carlos,* first anchored here in August 1775. Ayala used the island as a base for mapping the bay and named it Isla de Los Angeles.

Ayala Cove faces Tiburon, a mile across Raccoon Strait. When the same spot served as a quarantine station for ships with infected crews, it was nick-named Hospital Cove. Now a ranger's kiosk at the dock provides information and maps.

You can visit **Camp Reynolds,** a military garrison built during the Civil War to guard against the unlikely prospect of Confederate ships slipping into the bay. The remaining seventeen structures are the nation's largest collection of Civil War–era army buildings. Much later, Angel Island felt the shadow of its notorious neighbor. At "Alcatraz Gardens" prisoners ferried over from the "Rock" raised vegetables to supplement their meager diet.

One trail leads to North Garrison, the "Ellis Island of the West," an Immigration Station for the waves of Europeans anticipated when the Panama Canal opened. But they never arrived; instead, tens of thousands of Asians (mostly Chinese) were held and interrogated before being admitted. The station operated until 1940, then was used to process enemy prison-ers during the World War II. One of the old barracks serves as a museum preserving the cramped, dingy quarters where new arrivals were held for questioning. Look for Chinese writing scratched on the walls, bitter poems composed by disillusioned immigrants. (Translations are on display in the visitor center.)

But Angel Island has more than an historic past. Thin strips of sand are perfect for beachcombing and sunbathing (but not for swimming in the ice-cold bay). With 13 miles of trails and fire roads threading across the land-scape, hiking is excellent. The trek up the North Ridge Trail weaves through cool groves and across meadows to the top of 781-foot Mount Livermore, where a grandstand view awaits. Stand at the heart of the Bay Area and feel its pulse. Along the way, spot some of the 200 or so resident deer. Although there are many good trails, the island's main street is a 4.8-mile-long perim-eter road that is very popular with bicyclists. (Bicycles can be rented on Angel Island or brought over by ferry.) Campsites are often booked weeks in advance.

Ferry schedules vary depending on the season. For more information call (415) 435-1915 or visit www.angelisland.org.

Straits and Bays

If you like islands—and have a taste for the unusual and exclusive—don't miss tiny **East Brother Island,** home to a bed-and-breakfast inn built right inside a working lighthouse. Four rocky islands occupy San Pablo Strait where San Francisco and San Pablo Bays meet: the Sisters, near the Marin coast; and the Brothers, just west of Point San Pablo. They can be seen from the Richmond–San Rafael Bridge (Interstate 580), which links Marin County and the East Bay.

West Brother Island is uninhabited except for a few seabirds and water-fowl. The old U.S Lighthouse Service built a station on East Brother back in 1873, and it was deemed the "Riviera Station" by keepers because of its favor-able location—sheltered from winds, storms, and fog. After automation the old building was nearly razed, until a conservation group stepped in and offered to transform it into a profit-making venture. Today, the West Coast's bed-and-breakfast lighthouse has five rooms to let.

You don't have to stay at the inn to visit the island, however. Lighthouse buffs can grab a picnic lunch and take the day excursion (11:15 a.m. to 3:30 p.m.) from Point San Pablo Yacht Harbor May through September, Saturday only, $20 round-trip per person. After a ten-minute ride, the carpenter's Gothic-style cottage comes into view—with its fish-scale shingles, gingerbread trim, and picket fence—perched on a lump of land less than an acre in size.

Inside, the rooms are furnished with antiques and provided with those extra touches not found elsewhere, such as a set of earplugs at bedside in case the foghorn is in use. The inn is open Thursday through Sunday; over-night rates are on the expensive side but include transportation, historical tour, and gourmet meals. For further information call (510) 233-2385 or visit http://ebls.org.

The Carquinez Strait is a deep channel between San Pablo Bay and Suisun Bay that, in turn, leads to the Sacramento–San Joaquin River Delta. A vital ship-ping lane since the days when paddle wheelers plied these waters, the strait retains some of that bucolic atmosphere. Get there by heading east toward Sac-ramento on Interstate 80 and cross the Carquinez Bridge into Solano County.

Continue east on Interstate 780 to the town of **Benicia.** Entering this quiet community, it's hard to believe that it served for a year (1853–1854) as Califor-nia's state capital and stood ready to challenge San Francisco as the Bay Area's chief port. Founded in 1847, the town was more accessible to the interior and also boasted a better harbor and climate.

The heart of Benicia is First Street, lined with antique and craft shops, restaurants, and boutiques. Centerpiece of forty historic sites is the **Old State**

Capitol on West G Street. This redbrick, Georgian-style building had its brief moment of glory back in 1853, when Benicians convinced California's new legislature to locate here. Legend has it that the politicians' wives demanded the move to Sacramento thirteen months later because of Benicia's licentious reputation A peek inside reveals original whale-oil lamps, quill pens, and brass cuspidors. It's open Wednesday through Sunday from 10:00 a.m. to 5:00 p.m. A small admission is charged for self-guided tours of Benicia Capitol State Historic Park; (707) 774-3385.

The first Masonic Temple in California (1850) at 110 West J Street, was constructed with lumber shipped around Cape Horn. There are dozens of restored Victorians, with a superb collection on East D Street.

First Street begins (at Military Road) with a lovely little park and a white gazebo, then slopes gently toward the strait. Benicia is a great town for walking, with first Street the focus for browsing in shops and short detours to the historical sights, such as the state's first Protestant church on West K Street.

Captain Blyther's Restaurant (123 First Street; 707-745-4082; www.captain-blythers.com) occupies an old clapboard house that at one time served as a brothel. It stands near the restored train depot. From here it's a short walk to a pier poking out into Carquinez Strait, almost within handshaking distance of passing vessels. Benicia once was a key railroad crossing for the two largest train ferries ever built. Each carried thirty-six cars and two locomotives and crossed the strait to Port Costa from 1879 to 1930.

Benicia also attracts visitors with its Waterfront Trail (at the foot of Twelfth Street) along Southhampton Bay. Farther along is a thriving port, and a large oil refinery. In 1851, the U.S. Army built an arsenal that stored weapons and ammunition for troops that fought in conflicts from the Indian campaigns through the Korean War. The former arsenal includes the clock tower, commander's home, guardhouse, cemetery, and *Camel Barns.* These date from the army's ill-fated camel corps, seventy-seven beasts of burden brought from the Middle East in 1855 for use in the arid Southwest. One camel barn houses the Benicia Historical Museum, open Wednesday through Sunday from 1:00 to 4:00 p.m. For information about tours call (707) 745-5435 or go to www.beneciahistoricalmuseum.org.

Benicia is renowned for its large artists' colony, dedicated to crafts such as glassblowing as well as to the fine arts. Many artists have studios in former arsenal warehouses and hold an open house in May. Antique stores sponsor an annual fair in August. For further information contact the Benicia Chamber of Commerce at (707) 745-2120, consult www.beniciachamber.com, or stop by the office at 601 First Street, Suite 100.

Contra Costa County

Cross the Carquinez Strait again on the Benicia–Martinez Bridge (Interstate 680) and enter Contra Costa County. Towns such as Concord, Walnut Creek, and Danville are known as long on subdivisions and shopping malls and short on visitor attractions. Yet there are several excellent regional and state parks that locals enjoy.

The great 1849 California Gold Rush was a crazy stampede for riches that hurled a sleepy territory onto a dazzling path of fame and fortune. But what about the great coal rush of the 1860s, which led to decades of mining "black diamonds"?

A few years after the glittering golden stuff turned up in the Sierra foothills, California's largest known coal deposit opened for mining on the northern slope of Mount Diablo. From these foothills, a cluster of mines disgorged $20 million worth of coal, about four million tons in all.

Square-jawed miners from around the world joined Americans in a life of hard work and long hours, occasionally relieved by a holiday or social event. Next to the mines small, dust-choked settlements—like Nortonville and Somersville—sprouted, thrived, then wilted when mining ceased after the turn of the twentieth century. There was a comeback of sorts during the 1920s and 1930s with the mining of silica sand.

This mining legacy lives on at **Black Diamond Mines Regional Preserve** south of Antioch, where about 6,300 acres have been carved out of the grassland and smoothly contoured foothills. Although most mines were abandoned long ago and sealed over, there is still plenty of evidence of the backbreaking life.

trivia

Two national historic sites in Contra Costa County feature the homes of naturalist John Muir (Martinez, www.nps.gov/jomu) and playwright Eugene O'Neill (Danville; www.nps.gov/euon).

Black Diamond offers the chance to explore 40 miles of trails. Rose Hill Cemetery's chipped and broken gravestones tell sad tales (some in Welsh) of the harsh lives of miners and their families, who died from epidemics, childbirth, mining accidents, or, if they were fortunate, from natural causes.

Miles of trails crisscrossing the preserve go past a number of abandoned mines, one of which has been converted into an underground museum. Open weekends, March through November from 10:00 a.m. to 4:30 p.m., the Greathouse Visitor Center displays photographs and artifacts from the period. Hundreds of feet of old mining tunnels are open for exploration, but bring a flashlight! The star attraction is the Hazel-Atlas Mine, where a guide walks groups through a 400-foot underground chamber.

Black Diamond Mines Regional Preserve (925-757-2620; www.ebparks .org/parks/black_diamond) is open daily, from 8:00 a.m. to dusk; call for admission prices. To reach it, take Highway 4 to Antioch and exit at Somersville Road; then go 3 miles south.

Contra Costa is also home to the Bay Area's most majestic lookout point. A trip to the summit of 3,849-foot **Mount Diablo** takes in 20,000 square miles spread over parts of more than thirty California counties. Because few other mountains lie nearby, Diablo stands like a lofty island amid the surrounding flatland. But one word of warning: Wait for a windy day or a day right after a storm to avoid peering down into thick layers of haze.

Local Indians considered Diablo a place of power, the only point not submerged by a primordial flood in tribal legend. The mountain was the center of the universe, home of the gods and a magical place both respected and feared. The only thing to fear today is the spine-jangling drive up a tortuous road.

A wide range of vegetation is caused by sharp differences in temperature, rainfall, and wind exposure. Mountain landscapes vary from shady cottonwood canyons, open woodlands, and erosion-carved gullies to wind-sharpened crags.

Mount Diablo State Park covers an 18,000-acre chunk of the mountain accessed via Walnut Creek or Danville by one of two separate entrances. Where these roads join at about 2,200 feet, sits a ranger station. Stop for a detailed map of the hiking trails. After the 4.5-mile final ascent to the summit, an observation tower looks out on the Delta and Wine Country, the bay and San Francisco, Mount Tamalpais in Marin, and, on an exceptionally clear day, to Lassen Peak in the Cascade Range.

The trails beckon. An hour's walk traverses grassland to bay laurel-scented canyons strewn with wildflowers like the endemic globe lily. High above soar golden eagles, red-tailed hawks, and horned larks.

Mount Diablo State Park is open daily from 8:00 a.m. to sunset year-round; for more information and directions, call (925) 837-2525. There is a $6 day-use fee charged per vehicle. Camping is available. More information is found at www.mdia.org.

The East Bay

What has come to be known as the East Bay lies directly across the water from San Francisco and is normally reached via the Bay Bridge or BART (Bay Area Rapid Transit). Along a narrow strip of land between the hills and the bay lie a string of communities with widely differing appeal. Most travelers concentrate on two: Oakland, with one of the world's largest ports; and Berkeley, the perennial home of excellence and eccentricity.

Takara Sake Brewery in Berkeley is the place to taste the famous Japanese drink—"Happiness you can pour," is the company motto. Takara has been making sake—rice wine—in Kyoto for more than eighty-five years, and the Berkeley brewery produces the Sho Chiku Bai brand.

The serene, wood-paneled tasting room is bathed in subtle light. Japanese poems and woodblock prints decorate the walls, shoji screens cover the windows, and bright lanterns hang from the ceiling. Taste several varieties of sake, filtered or with rice residue, and sweet plum wine.

Two millennia ago in Japan, sake fermentation was induced by villagers chewing rice and spitting the resulting wad into a wooden tub. Sake, with a 16 percent alcohol content was reserved for only the most sacred events, and the *toji* (sake master) was revered as an artist.

All Takara Sake rice is grown in California's Central Valley, then milled and polished, soaked, and steamed. Next the rice is seeded with a special culture that is combined with more rice, yeast, and water and allowed to ferment for about twenty-five days. After several filterings, the raw sake is pasteurized and aged for six months.

The Takara Sake USA Brewery, at 708 Addison Street in Berkeley (just off University Street near I-80), is open daily (except November through February when it's closed on Sunday) from noon to 6:00 p.m. Call (510) 540-8250 for information about group visits.

Visiting the University of California and its famous museums and libraries takes days. One lesser-known Berkeley sight lies south of the campus: the *Judah L. Magnes Museum.* Named for an Oakland rabbi who helped found the Hebrew University in Israel, this was the first Jewish museum in the western United States and is now the nation's third largest of its kind.

The permanent 8,000-artifact collection will move in 2010 from a three-story villa in a neighborhood to 2222 Harold Way in downtown Berkeley. Special exhibitions change every three months, and the facility houses an historical archive and research library, and a rare book and manuscript collection. The theme is the universality of Jewish culture from biblical times to the present. An embroidered velvet wedding dress from Turkey, a Persian illuminated manuscript, or an amber necklace from Yemen may be some items on view. The gilded wood carving used by the Jews of Cochin, India, served as an ark for the sacred Torah, the basic canon of the Jewish Scripture.

The permanent collection concentrates on textiles and ceremonial objects such as Hanukkah lamps made from pewter, bronze, silver, and stone; a large

There's a *There* There

Writer Gertrude Stein supposedly remarked after visiting Oakland: "There was no there there." The city unquestionably lives in the shadow of its illustrious neighbor, yet Oakland can make a multitude of fascinating claims.

- Lake Merritt downtown is the largest saltwater body within a U.S. city. It encompasses the country's first official wildlife refuge.

- Writer Jack London ran for mayor of Oakland on the Socialist ticket.

- Oakland International Airport is closer to San Francisco than S.F. International, and was the starting point of Amelia Earhart's final flight, the first trans-Pacific flight, and the first global circumnavigation by air.

- Oakland may be America's most racially diverse city, where everyone is a minority. Blacks, Asians, and Hispanics comprise two-thirds of the population, and at least one hundred languages and dialects are spoken.

- The Port of Oakland is the West Coast's leading container port and the fourth busiest in the United States.

- The Oakland Asian Cultural Center is one of the largest of its kind in the United States, with classes in martial arts, yoga, and music, and art exhibits and cultural programs.

- Oakland was the birthplace of the Black Panthers and the notorious Raiders pro football team.

collection of Torah binders; framed ketubbahs—decorative calligraphic wedding contracts; and objects used at circumcisions. The rare book and manuscript library houses works by Jewish typographers and book designers. The 5,000-item manuscript collection includes Albert Einstein's personal papers. The Judah L. Magnes Museum, at 2911 Russell Street in Berkeley until 2010, is open by appointment from 2:00 to 4:00 p.m. Sunday, Tuesday, and Thursday with a $6 admission charge. For information about current exhibits, call (510) 549-6950 or go to www.magnes.org.

Straddling the border between Berkeley and Oakland, high in the hills, the *Claremont Resort* has been a Bay Area landmark since its completion in 1915. It's a big, white wedding cake of a place, with soaring towers, a steeply sloped roof, and dozens of gables, set amid twenty acres of palm trees, roses, swimming pools, and tennis courts. Lots of mystique surrounds the old girl, such as the story of how Frank Havens won the estate in a checkers game from millionaire miner Borax Smith at Oakland's Athenian Club. The old Claremont reached a zenith of popularity in the 1930s and 1940s with radio broadcasts from "High Atop the Hill" and big band dances in the Garden Room. (Lawrence Welk made his West Coast debut here.)

Each room is unique because of the building's curved shape: Some rooms have three walls, others five, and one suite boasts its own private sauna. Stroll around the gardens or partake of the stirring views from the cocktail lounge.

The Claremont Resort & Spa is located at Ashby and Domingo Avenues in Oakland; for information call (510) 843-3000 or consult www.claremontresort.com.

Another East Bay landmark clutching the hills is the **Oakland Temple,** one of just fifteen such sanctuaries worldwide run by the Church of Jesus Christ of Latter-day Saints, better known as the Mormons. This majestic structure stands out like a beacon, especially when illuminated by floodlights at night.

The design, contemporary with a slight oriental motif, features an exterior faced with Sierra white granite and topped with several pinnacle-like towers decorated with gold and blue mosaics. Two large sculptured exterior panels depict Christ in Palestine and Jesus with the Indians of America shortly after his resurrection, an event accepted as fact by Mormons.

After noting the temple's design and enjoying outdoor fountains, pools, and palm-lined gardens, the visitor center provides background on the building and the church. Using a series of panels, a guide narrates the story of how the angel Moroni visited Joseph Smith and delivered the Book of Mormon. Only church members can enter the temple, but visitors see a film showing the interior. After the presentation the guide escorts visitors to the impeccable terraced gardens, a spectacular spot overlooking most of the Bay Area.

The visitor center at the Oakland Temple, 4677 Lincoln Avenue, is open without charge daily from 9:00 a.m. to 9:00 p.m. There is also a genealogical library open Tuesday through Friday to the general public; for information call (510) 531-1475 or go to www.lds.org/placestovisit.

Another local landmark is the **Paramount Theatre of the Arts,** a former movie palace of the grand old style whose glamour refuses to fade. Built in 1931, it is an outstanding example of art deco architecture and decor, including carved walls of faux gold and softly lit ceilings. The theater has been called "the most exquisite restoration of a movie palace in the entire world."

Guided tours (first and third Saturday of each month at 10:00 a.m.) provide a complete view of the 3,000-seat

trivia

A dozen popular restaurants sitting along Berkeley's Shattuck Avenue (between Vine and Hearst) have been dubbed the "Gourmet Ghetto." Among them are the famous Chez Panisse of master chef Alice Waters and the Virginia Bakery, a local landmark since 1934.

theater, which hosts a full schedule of musical and theatrical events, from Willie Nelson to Vladimir Horowitz. The Paramount Theatre is located in downtown Oakland at 2025 Broadway; for current program information call (510) 893-2300 or visit www.paramounttheatre.com.

Oakland has an intriguing trio of major attractions: the Oakland Museum, Jack London Square, and Lake Merritt. Water is in Oakland's heart and history. Franklin Delano Roosevelt's presidential yacht *Potomac* is docked in Oakland. The thirty-second president used his boat to escape hot summer confinement in the White House and planned military strategy on the vessel during World War II. Guided dockside tours with a video introduction are given on Wednesday and Friday from 10:30 a.m. to 2:30 p.m. and Sunday from noon to 3:00 p.m. A visitor center is open weekdays from 9:00 a.m. to 4:00 p.m. Several times a month, the *Potomac* cruises San Francisco Bay from its dock at 540 Water Street. For information on tours and cruises call (510) 627-1667 or consult www.usspotomac.org for current hours and admission.

Alameda Island was created in 1902 when engineers dug a tidal canal between the Alameda Peninsula and Oakland's shore. The town had its resort era when San Franciscans built weekend homes here, and there was a huge amusement park called Neptune Beach. The military era began with the outbreak of World War II, when Alameda served as a naval air station for training aviators and maritime officers. Forty-seven graduates of the school lost their lives in the Pacific conflict with the Japanese.

Part of this story is told at the Crab Cove Visitor Center (1252 McKay Avenue; 510-521-6887; www.ebparks.org/parks/vc/crab_cove), an educational center with interesting displays about San Francisco Bay. One shows how alien marine species of crabs and snails have invaded the bay to the detriment of the ecosystem; in another, a crab can be constructed from the inside out. The center, with its 800-gallon aquarium, is open from Wednesday through Sunday from 10:00 a.m. to 5:00 p.m. It sits at Crab Cove at the north end of Crown Memorial State Beach, a long swath of park fronting the bay on Alameda's west shore; it's right off Central Avenue on the way out to the island's top attraction, the famed aircraft carrier ***USS* Hornet.**

This proud vessel served with distinction from World War II through Vietnam and welcomed back the first moon-walking astronauts from NASA mission Apollo 11. After entering the ship on the hangar deck, there's a display of the *Hornet*'s role in destroying enemy ships and planes, including a record 62 Japanese aircraft in one day and 255 in one month. Well-informed docents (many of them navy vets) lead several different tours of the enormous vessel, all the way from the once sweltering engine room (where conditions were nearly unbearable), through the general mess (where most of the 3,500 crew ate Spam and other delicacies) and sick bay, up to the navigation bridge, where the captain's plush chair is irresistible if the docent is looking the other way. In the primary flight control room, five levels above the flight deck, the air boss controlled all aircraft traffic, including the slingshot-style takeoffs and often perilous landings. Visitors emerge with a real feeling of the confined and dangerous experience the many sailors and airmen lived through.

The USS *Hornet* is open daily from 10:00 a.m. to 5:00 p.m. Admission charged; for more information call (510) 521-8448 or visit www.uss-hornet.org.

The heart of Alameda's business district resides along Park Street and Central Avenue. Nearby Park Avenue, with a gazebo and arboreal strip of mature trees running down the middle, contains dozens of stylish old Victorian homes built for bankers, judges, and an admiral or two.

trivia

Miniature trains wind through the woods at Tilden Regional Park in Berkeley, gem of the East Bay public greenbelt. At this 2,077-acre refuge you can also swim, play golf, ride the animals on a 1911 carousel, or feed real barnyard animals at Little Farm. The ten-acre botanical garden boasts the most complete collection of native California plants anywhere.

Before there was a Hollywood, there was *Niles,* the short-lived movie-making capital of California. On the side of a hill overlooking the town, large white letters spell out NILES, just like in Hollywood. This evocative town at the mouth of Alameda Creek, actually a district of Fremont in south Alameda County, got started as a flour mill in 1842. The community was known as Vallejo Mills for more than twenty years, until the influential Western Pacific railroad renamed it after a company bigwig. Niles was an important link in the rail network between the Bay Area and Sacramento, and from there to the rest of the nation.

Essanay Film Studios started in 1912 and ran the show from offices at First and G Streets, producing one- and two-reelers starring Wallace Beery and Ben Turpin. Old frontier houses and the Niles Canyon's creek and forests were an ideal location for filming westerns. More than 450 movies were filmed here, including *The Tramp* with Charlie Chaplin, before the film industry shifted south to a quiet district of Los Angeles. Niles still has a Wild West feeling today, with false-front buildings lining the main street on one side. Antiques shops abound, as do bare-knuckle bars like Joe's Corner (37713 Niles Boulevard, Fremont; 510-648-2681), allegedly once owned by a local character named Bronco Billy. Shops sell everything from Indian art to incense, a nod to Fremont's populations with roots in India and Afghanistan. There's an interesting walking tour of the old town; for details go to www.niles.org.

Alameda Creek slices through the hills behind Niles and forms 6-mile-long Niles Canyon, blessed with some of the area's most rugged and beautiful scenery. Along Niles Canyon Road are rolling hills, grazing cattle, steep slopes, and idyllic places to stop for a picnic or to fish. The town of Sunol lies at the canyon's far end.

Nearby at 505 Paloma Way is the ***Sunol Water Temple.*** This neoclassical monument features fluted columns, a dome painted with exotic figures, and noble inscriptions chiseled in stone. Designed by famed architect Willis Polk, it pays tribute to a system that brings water from the Sierra Nevada. To reach the temple, follow Niles Canyon Road to the sign for I-680, then take an immediate right through the gates. It's open weekdays only from 10:00 a.m. to 3:00 p.m.

The Peninsula

The San Francisco Peninsula is an arm of land south of the city, split by the coastal mountains into two distinct regions. The bay side has the airport, light industry, and a string of small towns that have melded into an uninterrupted suburban sprawl. Peninsula life is comfortably well-off (very comfortably in posh Hillsborough and Atherton), without the trendiness of Marin County. West of the mountains, the peninsula's ocean side (discussed in the South Coast chapter) marches to the beat of a different drummer—a world of farms and fishing far removed from the Bay Area's hectic pace. The peninsula

Last of the Yana Indians

Ishi, the last known Stone Age survivor in North America and the last wild American Indian, was formerly entombed in Olivet Memorial Park in Colma, just south of San Francisco. His story is told in a famous book, *Ishi in Two Worlds,* by Theodora Kroeber.

Ishi was first glimpsed in 1911 hiding near Oroville and was taken into custody. Anthropologists soon learned of his existence, and he was taken from the most primitive of existences to live in a San Francisco anthropology museum run by the University of California, a place of clocks and calendars, money and newspapers. But Ishi chose to stay on as janitor rather than go to a reservation, and he lived in the museum until his death in 1916. He was cremated along with bow and arrows, a basket of acorn meal, and other personal items, and the ashes were placed in a black clay urn inscribed "Ishi, the last Yana Indian, 1916." In 2000, related tribal leaders reunited Ishi's brain, which had been kept by the Smithsonian Institution, with his ashes and reburied the remains somewhere secret in Northern California's Ishi Wilderness.

extends south as far as Palo Alto, and beyond lies the Santa Clara Valley, better known as Silicon Valley.

Jets soar overhead, and all around humans have taken over the once pristine bay. Yet the ***Coyote Point Museum for Environmental Education*** tries to make people aware of the complex ecosystem disrupted in the process. The museum inhabits a spectacular site along the shore just south of San Francisco International Airport in San Mateo.

Outside are various man-made wildlife habitats, a kind of minizoo for animals formerly abundant in the area: bobcats and raccoons, scaly snakes and playful river otters that are fed at 12:30 p.m., badgers and tree frogs. A walk-through aviary, with a huge tentlike net to keep the birds from escaping, is home to long-billed herons, owls, scavengers like turkey vultures, and a watchful golden eagle peering down on visitors from its perch.

Inside, the museum boasts an impressive architectural design of ascending ramps, lofty beamed ceilings, and redwood paneling. Exhibits stress man's intrusive role in the environment, which is based on a delicate balance between the many species sharing our planet, with a message: There are too many people. An eye-catching pyramid of ersatz dead animals (e.g., stuffed snakes, rats) demonstrates how just one hawk will eat about 1,200 other creatures in a year, consumption not even the most voracious human can manage.

There is a giant sperm whale cranium and a hive cutaway to show thousands of bees at work producing honey (the queen is marked by a green dot). Listen to the hum of their wings in the original key of E when the bees are tired and in the key of A when they speed up!

The Coyote Point Museum, 1651 Coyote Point Drive, San Mateo, is open Tuesday through Saturday from 10:00 a.m. to 5:00 p.m. and from noon to 5:00 p.m. on Sunday; admission charged. For information call (650) 342-7755 or visit www.coyoteptmuseum.org.

Burial Grounds

Because land was so expensive in the city, Colma on the borderline of San Mateo County became the burial place for most San Franciscans. At present there are seventeen cemeteries here with the grave sites of historical personages such as Wyatt Earp (Hills of Eternity) and a lineup of millionaire tycoons: Crocker, Flood, Spreckels, and Hearst (all at Cypress Lawn Memorial Park). To learn more about visiting famous grave sites, contact the Colma Historical Association at (650) 757-1676, or www .colmahistory.org, or stop at the museum at 1500 Hillside Boulevard, Colma, which is open Tuesday through Sunday from 10:00 a.m. to 3:00 p.m.

The *Hiller Aviation Museum* in San Carlos is dedicated to humanity's dream of flight as well as to one man's stunning achievements in the field. Stanley Hiller Jr. was only eighteen when he built his first successful helicopter, the XH-44 (on display), and he went on to found Hiller Aircraft Corporation in the Bay Area. Over the years he became involved in all sorts of interesting projects, like a one-man flying platform (used in a James Bond film) and the 290-pound collapsible Rotorcycle. Small enough when folded to carry in a pod under an aircraft's wing, it could become a full-sized helicopter in a matter of minutes. (The museum hosts the country's largest helicopter show each June.)

Hiller was also the driving force behind this fine museum, which is like a mini-Smithsonian in layout and quality of exhibits. Check out the whalelike *Avitor,* which made its first flight in 1869—at which time only one Wright brother had been born—up the peninsula near San Francisco. This was the very first motor-powered, unmanned plane in the world, designed and built by an Englishman. The Hiller collection, mostly original restored aircraft, contains many other aviation landmarks: first controlled glider, first experimental wind tunnel, first plane to fly from the Pacific to the Atlantic (across the Isthmus of Panama in 1913), and first takeoff and landing from a ship (the Curtiss Pusher in 1911). The Condor robotic spy plane, fully automated and capable of flying at 67,000 feet, cost $300 million to create and made a grand total of eight flights before being abandoned by the government. The only surviving example of the massive plane, with a wingspan of 201 feet, lords over the entire collection. One of the collection's rarest pieces is the Gonzales plane, designed by two fif-

> ## trivia
>
> The unusually sleepy town of Colma, with its constant fog and abundant cemeteries, inspired an award-winning 2006 film entitled *Colma: The Musical,* which has given new life to the town of about 1,200 living residents.

teen-year-old brothers in San Francisco. The Hiller Aviation Museum is located next to San Carlos Airport at 601 Skyway Road (take the Redwood Shores Parkway exit off US 101). Open daily from 10:00 a.m. to 5:00 p.m.; admission charged. For information call (650) 654-0200 or visit www.hiller.org.

While on the San Francisco Peninsula, take a trip south to Palo Alto to visit "the Farm." At one time a trotting-horse ranch in the middle of nowhere, *Stanford University* has a beautiful, sun-drenched campus filled with palm trees and Romanesque-style buildings of sandstone and red tile roofs. Getting there involves taking Highway 101 south to the University Avenue exit and heading west until it becomes Palm Drive. Or preview the campus at www.stanford.edu.

Quarks and Charms

A century ago scientists believed that the eternal and indestructible atom was the smallest thing in nature. Then the nucleus was discovered: ten thousand times smaller than an atom and composed of neutrons and protons surrounded by whizzing electrons. Surely that was the ultimate building block, it was thought. Not for particle physicists. At the Stanford Linear Accelerator Center near the famous university, top scientists (with 150 Ph.D.s among them) struggle to unlock the ultimate secrets of the universe.

The linear accelerator here is like a giant electron microscope in allowing physicists to see particles smaller than light waves—except that this "microscope" is a 2-mile-long copper tube buried 30 feet underground in a tunnel. Inside this tube tiny particles are hurtled toward one another at nearly the speed of light, the collisions producing energy and even smaller particles. Electrons and positrons "surf" along waves of electromagnetic radiation created by giant microwave power generators 600 times more powerful than the average oven. The accelerator can emit electron beams with energy up to fifty billion volts, which makes for one heck of a power bill!

Extremely dense subatomic particles called quarks and leptons, each with its own name and "flavor" (mass and electrical charge) are now considered the smallest things in nature. Physicists here have discovered the psi (a quark called a "charm") and the tau (an exotic lepton). But all this is no laughing matter. The discoverers of these particles were rewarded with the Nobel Prize in physics. Meanwhile, with high energy physics giving way to photon science, the search for even smaller particles goes on.

The Visitor Center of the Stanford Linear Accelerator (SLAC) intends to resume temporarily suspended free tours; check www.slac.stanford.edu. SLAC's Virtual Visitor Center is online at www2.slac.stanford.edu/vvc.

A visitor information center in the Memorial Auditorium lobby is open Monday through Friday from 8:00 a.m. to 5:00 p.m. and from 9:00 a.m. to 5:00 p.m. on weekends. Call (650) 723-2560 for tour schedules. An outstanding overview is available daily from the fourteenth-story observation platform of nearby 285-foot Hoover Tower; open from 9:00 a.m. to 5:00 p.m., with a small admission fee; call (650) 723-2053.

One highlight is **Memorial Church,** which dominates a central courtyard called the Inner Quad. Luminous stained-glass windows and a mosaic reproduction of Cosimo Rosselli's *Last Supper* fresco behind the altar are renowned. Master stonecutters carved transept inscriptions using ancient religious symbols. The church is open weekdays from 8:00 a.m. to 5:00 p.m. weekdays and during services on weekends, with free tours Friday at 2:00 p.m.

The university's sterling visitor attraction may be the ***Cantor Arts Center Rodin Sculpture Garden.*** Twenty works by Auguste Rodin reside in a formal outdoor setting. Counting some 160 pieces housed inside the adjacent museum (the Iris & B. Gerald Cantor Center for the Visual Arts; 650-723-4177; museum. stanford.edu), Stanford now has the world's second-largest collection of Rodin sculpture, surpassed only by the Musée Rodin in Paris, although most works here were cast after the artist's death.

Crowning the outdoor display is The Gates of Hell—whimsical 21-foot-tall bronze doors considered the sculptor's greatest public work. Rodin toiled for two decades on this creation of 180 writhing figures, which represents a hell of unfulfilled dreams and passions. Another major work is titled *The Burghers of Calais*.

The sculpture garden is open continuously, with tours offered on Wednesday at 2:00 p.m., Saturday at 11:30 a.m., and Sunday at 3:00 p.m. Call (650) 723-4177 for details.

Driving US 101 gives the impression that the San Francisco Peninsula is not much more than an endless sprawl of suburbia, but taking Interstate 280 to the west presents a much different picture— wooded hills, lakes, and splendid vistas. An even more scenic route follows **Skyline Boulevard** (Highway 35), a two-lane road about 2,200 feet above

trivia

The Pulgas Water Temple in Woodside, modeled after temples of ancient Greece, celebrates the arrival of San Francisco's drinking water from the Sierra Nevada.

sea level hugging the spiny backbone of the Santa Cruz Mountains. Along the route is pleasant, wooded countryside and more great views, this time of both the Bay Area and the Pacific Ocean.

Reach Skyline Boulevard via Highway 92 from San Mateo, passing Crystal Springs Reservoir, which contains San Francisco's main water supply and is built atop the San Andreas Fault. This 23-mile scenic route, despite being named a boulevard, is really a well-maintained country road. The sights are pleasant if not spectacular: Christmas tree farms, nurseries growing rhododendrons, a few private homes, parks, and open-space preserves laced with hiking trails and picnic areas.

Purisima Creek Redwoods Open Space Preserve (4.5 miles south of the Highway 92 junction; check www.openspace.org/preserves/pr_purisima.asp) takes in 3,360 acres of the big trees and surrounding watershed. Views of the coast are exceptional, and there are some great footpaths, such as Soda Gulch Trail.

Two excellent county parks are Huddart, just below Skyline Boulevard at King's Mountain Road, with nature trails and facilities, and even less-known Wunderlich, near the junction of Woodside Road, which is popular with equestrians. The two are linked by the Bay Ridge Trail. Portola Redwoods State Park off Alpine Road offers camping and impressive stands of coast redwoods, and Windy Hill Open Space Preserve (www.openspace.org/preserves/pr_windy_hill.asp) has good trails, allows dogs, and is a mecca for kite-flying, hang-gliding, and paragliding.

The most unusual of the parks is **Los Trancos Open Space Preserve,** located about 1.5 miles off Skyline Boulevard along Page Mill Road. Follow the self-guided 1.5-mile San Andreas Fault Trail to study the seismic history of the past two million years. Halt at fourteen marked stops along the 1/3-mile-wide fault, to inspect earthquake evidence such as sag ponds, benches, and scarps, as well as a spot where a fence jumped 6 feet during the 1906 temblor. (The Pacific Plate normally moves about 1 inch per year.) Boulders en route at one time lay 23 miles to the southeast, according to geologists. The most striking view is from a high point near the parking lot, from which the fault is obvious, all the way to San Francisco. Los Trancos is open daily from dawn to dusk; see www.openspace.org/preserves/pr_los_trancos.asp.

Farther along Skyline Boulevard lies Long Ridge Open Space Preserve (www.openspace.org/preserves/pr_long_ridge.asp), featuring a beautiful little pond hidden in a stream-cut canyon. The park covers almost 1,000 acres, with trails in a variety of arboreal settings and views of Big Basin, Butano Ridge, and Devils Canyon.

Santa Clara Valley

Skyline Boulevard intersects Highway 9 at the Saratoga Gap, marking the end of the scenic driving route. Turn right and proceed to Santa Cruz, passing Big Basin State Park and the old railroad town of Felton. Stay on Highway 35 and continue 11 winding miles to Interstate 880 and the more direct route to Santa Cruz and San Jose. Or turn left on Highway 9 and drive to the town of Saratoga in the Santa Clara Valley, home to a main street of quaint shops and quality restaurants, plus little-known **Hakone Gardens** (7 miles from Highway 35).

This lushly planted slice of the Orient, spread over eighteen acres of gentle hills, is considered the most authentic example of Japanese gardens in America. Four different gardens display the art form—harmonious placement of plants, rocks, and water—and there are several discreet structures built without nails, including a cultural center modeled on a tea merchant's house.

Open daily to the public, Hakone Gardens (21000 Big Basin Way) also provides docent tours and tea service for groups. It's open from 10:00 a.m. to 5:00 p.m. and from 11:00 a.m. to 5:00 p.m. on weekends. Call (408) 741-4994 for parking fees and admission fee information or visit www.hakone.com.

The Santa Clara Valley is justly famous for its high-tech industry and also boasts a few well-publicized attractions, such as the Tech Museum of Innovation, California's Great America amusement park, and the Winchester Mystery House. Although receiving its fair share of visitors, San Jose's excellent ***Rosicrucian Egyptian Museum*** deserves more attention. Dedicated to the allure and romance of ancient Egypt, the museum is just one building in a complex that forms the American Grand Lodge of the Rosicrucian Order. This nonsectarian, fraternal group explores subjects such as occult knowledge from antiquity and expanding human potential.

Covering an entire square block, the grounds are an oasis of fountains, palm trees, a garden growing papyrus, hieroglyphics-covered shrines, stone sphinxes, and a carved obelisk. Buildings seem to have been transported from the banks of the Nile. The sand-colored administration building is a copy of the great temple of Medinet Habu in upper Egypt, and the planetarium was built to resemble a Moorish castle in North Africa. The shrine to Pharoah Akhnaton is a replica of the original in Luxor, and the temple of Amon at Karnak was inspiration for the museum itself.

A double line of kneeling rams flanks the entry walkway. Between them stands an 8-foot stone statue of Taurt, a hippopotamus symbolizing fertility. Enter through enormous bronze doors into evocative galleries, where the distant past seems alive. The museum conveys an almost childlike enthusiasm for the exotic and strange with its extensive collection of mummies—not just humans but also fish, falcons, cats, snakes, and a crocodile.

There's also a rare mummy of a baboon from Sakkara, where sacred temple animals were entombed, a set of X-rays of a mummy inside its sarcophagus, and canopic jars, in which the

trivia

The Museum of American Heritage at 351 Homer Avenue, Palo Alto preserves nineteenth-century inventions and a former lab with medical and pharmaceutical artifacts. Call (650) 321-1004 or visit www.moah.org.

deceased's vital organs were placed for the trip to the next world. (The brain was discarded.) The most remarkable mummy is Usermontu, a priest whose body lies stretched out with folded arms, eerily preserved right down to the teeth and fingernails. His metal leg pin is believed to be one of the first known examples of knee surgery.

A skillfully re-created rock tomb with inscriptions and false doorways were copied exactly from the famous tombs of Beni Hasan. Small carved figures called Ushabti acted as servants of the departed and there are personal collections of toys, jewelry, papyrus scrolls, and musical instruments. One of the most prized pieces is a black granite statue of Cleopatra.

The Rosicrucian Egyptian Museum, at 1664 Park Avenue at Naglee Avenue in San Jose, is open Monday through Friday from 9:00 a.m. to 5:00 p.m. and Saturday and Sunday from 11:00 a.m. to 6:00 p.m.; admission charged. For information call (408) 947-3636 or go to www.egyptianmuseum.org.

A block away lies the **San Jose Municipal Rose Garden,** five acres featuring 4,000 rose shrubs from nearly 200 varieties. A new flush of roses blooms every six to eight weeks from April through November. Located at Naglee and Dana Avenues, the garden is open daily from 8:00 a.m. to one-half hour after sunset; no admission charged.

trivia

Santana Row in San Jose is the "chic-est" spot in Silicon Valley. This 42-acre shopping center and residential zone features upscale stores like St. John, Ann Taylor, and Gucci plus some of the priciest restaurants in town.

At 4,200 feet, Mount Hamilton dominates the Santa Clara Valley. It can be reached via Highway 130 off Alum Rock Road. After 19 miles and a couple of hundred curves past hills covered with oak and chaparral, there's **James Lick Observatory.**

Named for the gold rush–era land entrepreneur whose $700,000 donation made it all possible, the observatory was finished in 1888. Early visitors had to take a horse-drawn stagecoach to see the famous 36-inch refractor telescope. Weighing fourteen tons, it's still the world's second largest of its kind. Visitors see this early telescope up close and watch the rotating dome's hydraulic floor rise 17 feet to accommodate star-gazing from different angles. James Lick himself is entombed under the oak floorboards.

Another dome houses a newer, 120-inch reflector telescope that weighs an awesome 275 tons and is used for important research by University of California astronomers. But don't expect to see them on duty—they all sleep by day and work by night, when the stars are out.

The Lick Observatory Visitors Center and the Shane Dome 120-inch telescope gallery are open from 10:00 a.m. to 5:00 p.m. on weekends, and Monday through Friday from 12:30 p.m. to 5:00 p.m. Daily tours available; call (408) 274-5061 for information or check http://mthamilton.ucolick.org.

Places to Stay in the Bay Area

MARIN COUNTY

Best Western Corte Madera Inn
56 Madera Boulevard
Corte Madera
(800) 777-9670

Casa Madrona Hotel
801 Bridgeway
Sausalito
(800) 288-0502

Gerstle Park Inn
34 Grove Street
San Rafael
(800) 726-7611

Hotel Sausalito
16 El Portal
Sausalito
(888) 442-0700

The Inn Above Tide
30 El Portal
Sausalito
(800) 893-8433

The Lodge at Tiburon
1651 Tiburon Boulevard
Tiburon
(415) 435-3133

Mill Valley Inn
165 Throckmorton Avenue
Mill Valley
(800) 595-2100

Mountain Home Inn
810 Panoramic Highway
Mill Valley
(415) 381-9000

EAST BAY

Hotel Durant
2600 Durant Avenue
Berkleley
(510) 845-8981

Inn at Benicia Bay
145 East D Street
Benicia
(707) 746-1055

Inn at Jack London Square
233 Broadway
Oakland
(800) 633-5973

Jack London Inn
444 Embarcadero West
Oakland
(510) 444-2032

Marina Village Inn
1151 Pacific Marina
Alameda
(510) 523-9450

Washington Inn
495 Tenth Street
Oakland
(510) 452-1776

PENINSULA/SOUTH BAY

Campbell Inn
675 East Campbell Avenue
Campbell
(800) 582-4449

Coxhead House Bed & Breakfast
37 East Santa Inez Avenue
San Mateo
(650) 685-1600

Embassy Suites
150 Anza Boulevard
Burlingame
(650) 342-4600

Granada Inn Silicon Valley
2515 El Camino Real
Santa Clara
(408) 241-2841

Homestead Studio Suites
1830 Gateway Drive
San Mateo
(650) 574-1744

WORTH SEEING/DOING IN THE BAY AREA

Filoli Mansion, Woodside

Jack London Square, Oakland

Lake Merritt, Oakland

Six Flags Discovery Kingdom, Vallejo

Muir Woods/Mount Tamalpais, Marin

Oakland Museum of California

California's Great America, Santa Clara

Tech Museum of Innovation, San Jose

University of California at Berkeley

HELPFUL WEB SITES IN THE BAY AREA

Berkeley Convention & Visitors Bureau: www.visitberkeley.com

City of Benicia: www.ci.benicia.ca.us

East Bay Regional Park District: www.ebparks.org

Marin County Visitors Bureau: www.visitmarin.org

Oakland Convention and Visitors Bureau: www.oaklandcvb.com

San Jose Convention & Visitors Bureau: www.sanjose.org

San Mateo County Convention & Visitors Bureau: www.sanmateocountycvb.com

Santa Clara Convention & Visitors Bureau: www.santaclara.org

Tiburon Peninsula Chamber of Commerce: www.tiburonchamber.org

---

Madison Street Inn
1390 Madison Street
Santa Clara
(408) 249-5541

Millwood Inn & Suites
1375 El Camino Real
Millbrae
(800) 516-6738

The Sainte Claire
302 South Market Street
San Jose
(408) 295-2000

Places to Eat in the Bay Area

MARIN COUNTY

Dipsea Cafe (American)
200 Shoreline Highway
Mill Valley
(415) 381-0298

Guaymas (Mexican)
5 Main Street
Tiburon
(415) 435-6300

Lark Creek Inn (American)
234 Magnolia Avenue
Larkspur
(415) 924-7766

Marin Joe's Restaurant (American)
1585 Casa Buena Drive
Corte Madera
(415) 924-2081

Panama Hotel & Restaurant (Californian)
4 Bayview Street
San Rafael
(415) 457-3993

Scoma's (seafood/Italian)
588 Bridgeway
Sausalito
(415) 332-9551

EAST BAY

Blackhawk Grille (American)
3540 Blackhawk Plaza Circle
Danville
(925) 736-4295

Cafe Rouge (Continental)
1782 Fourth Street
Berkeley
(510) 525-1440

Chez Panisse (Californian)
1517 Shattuck Avenue
Berkeley
(510) 548-5525

The Fat Lady (steakhouse)
201 Washington Street
Jack London Square
Oakland
(510) 465-4996

The New Zealander Restaurant and Pub (Kiwi cuisine)
1400 Webster Street
Alameda
(510) 769-8555

Soizic (French)
300 Broadway Avenue
Oakland
(510) 251-8100

Yoshi's (Japanese)
510 Embarcadero West
Jack London Square
Oakland
(510) 238-9200

Zachary's Chicago Pizza (pizza)
5801 College Avenue
Oakland
(510) 655-6385

PENINSULA/SOUTH BAY

Bella Mia Restaurant (Italian)
58 South First Street
San Jose
(408) 280-1993

Bella Vista Restaurant (Mediterranean)
13451 Skyline Boulevard
Woodside
(650) 851-1229

Blake's Steakhouse (American)
17 North San Pedro
Square
San Jose
(408) 298-9221

Cafe La Scala (Italian)
1219 Burlingame Avenue
Burlingame
(650) 347-3035

California Cafe (Californian)
50 University Avenue
Los Gatos
(408) 354-8118

Eulipia (cosmopolitan)
374 South First Street
San Jose
(408) 280-6161

Evvia (Greek)
420 Emerson Street
Palo Alto
(650) 326-0983

Hong Kong Flower Lounge Restaurant (Chinese)
51 Millbrae Avenue
Millbrae
(650) 692-6666

La Fondue (French)
14550 Big Basin Way
Saratoga
(408) 867-3332

Taxi's Hamburgers (American)
2700 South El Camino Real
San Mateo
(650) 377-1947

Vivace Ristorante (Italian)
1910 Ralston Avenue
Belmont
(650) 637-0611

SOUTH COAST

The South Coast of Northern California (and its interior valleys) is a world apart from San Francisco and the Bay Area and evokes wonderful travel images—barking sea lions and fresh fish dinners, primeval wildlife refuges and sunbaked adobes, ghostly cypress trees and coastal fog stretching to the horizon like strips of gauze.

The South Coast encompasses all or part of Monterey, San Benito, Santa Cruz, and San Mateo Counties and is reached and explored via Highway 1 or U.S. Highway 101. Although several small towns dot the area, it is overwhelmingly devoted to such nonurban pursuits as fishing and agriculture. The atmosphere is infectious, and you just might find yourself leaving with a string of garlic or a box of artichokes crammed into your trunk. You may even glimpse a bit of Old California (the Spanish period) as it was before American settlers changed life forever.

San Mateo/Santa Cruz Coast

Your magic carpet to the South Coast is Highway 1, whose various incarnations along the Pacific provide some of Northern

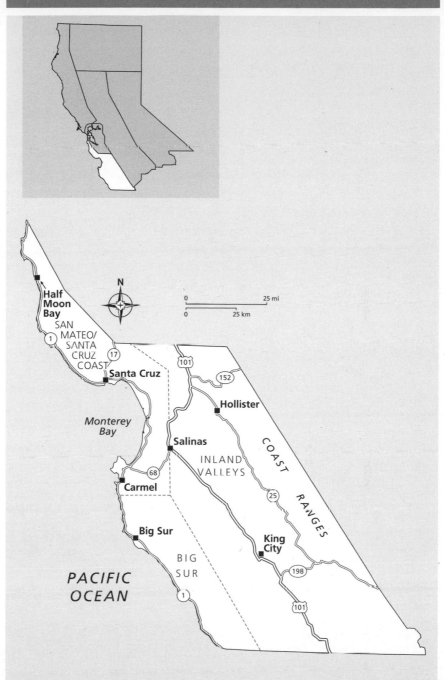

N

0   25 mi
0   25 km

Half Moon Bay

SAN MATEO/ SANTA CRUZ COAST

①

⑰

Santa Cruz

101

152

Hollister

Monterey Bay

Salinas

INLAND VALLEYS

COAST RANGES

⑥⑧

Carmel

25

Big Sur

BIG SUR

King City

198

101

PACIFIC OCEAN

①

California's most memorable sightseeing. The stretch between San Francisco and Santa Cruz, although busy at times, is relatively unheralded when compared with Highway 1 through Big Sur or north along the Mendocino coast. Yet on a clear day (fog is a frequent visitor), the scenery is a stunning marriage of land and sea.

Reach the coast of San Mateo and Santa Cruz Counties from San Francisco by heading south on Interstate 280, then taking the Highway 1 exit to Pacifica, a fog-shrouded bedroom community. South of town, the road narrows and snakes along rugged terrain. (The road is subject to closure at Devil's Slide.) Pass gnarled cypress trees, the golden sands and sheer cliffs of Montara State Beach, and the old Point Montara Lighthouse (1875), now doubling as a youth hostel (650-728-7177; www.norcalhostels.org/montara).

First stop is the *Fitzgerald Marine Reserve,* about 20 miles south of San Francisco in Moss Beach, which has one of the best tide pool reefs on the Pacific Coast, a thirty-acre tidal basin filled with 350 species of plants and tiny marine organisms. These include hermit crabs, giant green anemones, starfish, turban snails, and purple sea urchins, best seen when the ocean rolls back during minus low tides, especially from November through January. Open dawn till dusk; no admission charged. For tide schedules and other information, call (650) 728-3584 or consult www.fitzgeraldreserve.org.

Next stop is little *Princeton-by-the-Sea* and Pillar Point Harbor, the only port between the Golden Gate and Santa Cruz. According to local lore the village was named by an early developer for his dog, Prince. The harbor, on the north side of Half Moon Bay, was the site of shore-based whaling and sardine fishing that peaked during the 1940s. But just as in Monterey, the industry went belly up when the sardines mysteriously vanished. Ignored for years, Princeton finds itself riding the crest of a comeback.

AUTHOR'S TOP TEN ON THE SOUTH COAST

Pescadero

Pigeon Point Lighthouse

Pacific Grove

Carmel Valley

Big Sur

San Juan Bautista

National Steinbeck Center Museum and Archive

Salinas Valley wineries

Pinnacles National Monument

Mission San Antonio de Padua

The turnoff from Highway 1 is Capistrano Road, a semicircular route gliding past Princeton Inn (1906) and the harbor. ***Pillar Point*** has a breakwater, a marina with berths for hundreds of commercial and pleasure craft, and lots of opportunities for fishing. Walk to the end of Johnson Pier and watch fishmongers selling their catch. You can surf cast from the beach (license required), drop a line from the pier, or fish for lingcod or rockfish offshore. Several excursion outfits that operate daily, weather permitting, include Half Moon Bay Sportfishing (650-726-2913) and Huck Finn Sportfishing (650-726-7133).

If you're fortunate and here at the right time, you can spot gray whales migrating south from Alaska (November to January) or returning from Baja California with newborn offspring (March and April). Whale-watching cruises along the coast also leave from Pillar Point Harbor.

The Half Moon Bay Brewing Company (390 Capistrano Road; 650-728-2739; www.hmbbrewingco.com) is tucked in a New England–style cottage overlooking the harbor and features a separate oyster bar. Just across the road is Barbara's FishTrap (281 Capistrano Road; 650-728-7049), a cheap, cash only, friendly place to eat. On Johnson Pier, Princeton Seafood Company (650-726-7251; www.princetonseafood.com) serves chowder in a sourdough bread bowl. For ambitious hikers a wonderful trail leads around the tip of Pillar Point (beyond the radar tower) to a primeval world of sea lions, cormorants, pelicans, tide pools, and clusters of offshore rocks. Surfers flock here to a spot called Maverick's to take on some of California's most challenging waves, reaching heights up to 30 feet during winter storms. Each year dozens of the world's best surfers arrive for the Maverick's Men Who Ride Mountains surfing competition, although the dates are never certain due to changing surf conditions. For bulletins go to www.maverickssurf.com.

The coast's character begins to change noticeably after the growing community of ***Half Moon Bay,*** famous for its Art and Pumpkin Festival every October. (It's also the terminus of Highway 92 from San Mateo, an alternate route to the coast.) The small town is known for an eclectic blend of shops and cafes along Main Street, as well as the Coastal Flower Market on the third Saturday of every month except October. South of town lies the ultra-plush Ritz-Carlton Half Moon Bay (650-712-7000; www.ritzcarlton.com), a world-class resort perched between two challenging golf courses and a bit out of place in an area where bed-and-breakfasts predominate. The coastal strip south becomes thinly populated and heavily planted, the rocky shoreline giving way to long stretches of sandy beach, excellent for day use. At San Gregorio State Beach you can drive inland 1 mile on Highway 84 to see the hamlet of San Gregorio, with its historic Spanish-style San Gregorio General Store (650-726-0565; www.sangregoriostore.com) and post office on Stage Road.

Back on the coast, **Pescadero State Beach** has sand dunes, tide pools, and a creek where steelhead run. Right across the road is Pescadero Marsh Natural Preserve, habitat for 180 species of resident and migratory birds, including blue heron with 6-foot wingspans. Two trails loop through the marsh along nearly level ground (dogs not allowed). For information about guided walks, call (650) 879-2170.

An authentic slice of rural small-town California awaits 2 miles inland at the hamlet of **Pescadero,** set amid verdant vegetable fields with the hazy coastal range as a backdrop. It's a place of country stores and wood-frame houses, white-steepled churches and front-porch rockers. Founded by Portuguese whalers in about 1850, the town prospered and once boasted two first-class hotels.

Although the name *Pescadero* means "fisherman," most residents are farmers, and the town seems to float amid fields of artichokes, brussels sprouts, beans, and lettuce. Stage Road is the closest thing to a main street, and Duarte's Tavern at number 202 has a reputation for the best food, fresh pies, and drink in these parts. For several decades this raucous, down-to-earth establishment has served up Portuguese linguica sausage, fried artichoke hearts, crab cioppino, oysters, abalone, cream of artichoke soup, and other delights. For reservations call (650) 879-0464. Also on Stage Road you'll find the old Arcangeli Grocery (1929), now called Norm's, and the First Congregational Church (1867). You can enjoy edible flower gardens and 500 goats on a reservation-only tour of Harley Farms Goat Dairy on North Street or stop to taste at the cheese shop (650-879-0480; www.harley farms.com).

Several area farms offer "pick your own" opportunities for fruits and vegetables. If possible, come to Pescadero in May, when residents of the port community take to the streets en masse for the Chamarita Festival of the Holy Ghost.

More beach parks line the shore south of Pescadero, but for a change of pace try **Butano State Park,** 3,500 acres of dense redwoods and Douglas fir a few miles inland that conservationists barely managed to save. *Butano* is an Indian word meaning "a gathering place for friendly visits," and this little-known park features forty campsites, including one for backpackers atop a 1,600-foot grade, a creek, a small fern canyon, and several crowd-free trails. To get there take Pescadero Road to Cloverdale Road, or enter on Gazos Creek Road off Highway 1 about 10 miles south of the Pescadero turnoff. For further information call (650) 879-2040.

A few miles south of Pescadero State Beach stands **Pigeon Point Light-house,** the second tallest in the United States and the quintessential coastal beacon. This 115-foot, white-brick sentinel thrusting up from a dramatic promontory has guided ships away from a shallow reef since 1872. Ironically, the point was named for a clipper ship called *Carrier Pigeon,* which sank here twenty years earlier. Later it became a favorite unloading spot for bootleggers.

The double-walled brick lighthouse, part of a state historic park, has survived several major earthquakes, still has its original Fresnel lens in the glass-enclosed lantern room at the top, but is closed indefinitely for restoration. From 10:30 a.m. to 4:00 p.m., Friday through Sunday, volunteers describe the light station's history and the 144-step ascent for what is a gum-swallowing view of the coast. For real lighthouse buffs, three former Coast Guard bungalows now serve as a youth hostel open year-round; for reservations call (650) 879-0633 or book online at http://norcalhostels.org/pigeon/reservations. For those pea-soup days when the light can't be seen, there's also a fog signal that can be heard up to 5 miles away.

Continuing south along the coastal highway, you reach Santa Cruz County, where the scenery changes abruptly. The cliffs drop sheer to a road that hugs a narrow ledge overlooking the ocean. Look for the sign marking Waddell Creek Beach (a famous windsurfing spot) and pull over. On the other side of the road is *Rancho del Oso*—like Waddell Creek, part of Big Basin Redwoods State Park—where there's a trailhead for a wonderful though virtually unknown hike. About half a mile up a paved road sits a ranger station (open weekends only from noon to 4:00 p.m.) where further information and trail maps are available. Call the visitor center and nature center for more information; (831) 427-2288. For information about backcountry activities and camping, call (831) 338-8861.

For anyone in a hurry, the short marsh trail offers glimpses of the usual coastal fauna and flora, but the real attraction here is the Skyline to the Sea Trail. This scenic route along Waddell Creek is actually two trails—one for walkers and another for horses and bicycles—and it winds all the way to Big Basin State Park in the hills, about 5 miles away. The trail is like an old ranch road with few difficult stretches, so it's perfect for Sunday hikers. Along the way you may see California quail and other birds, deer, and even an occasional mountain lion (rangers recommend making noise as you walk to frighten them).

Waddell Creek is a pleasant stream that attracts steelhead in winter, and about 6 miles from the trailhead you reach beautiful Berry Creek Falls amid a redwood forest (see the "Falling Waters" sidebar in the Bay Area chapter). There are several campsites along the trail, but reservations are strongly recommended; call Rancho del Oso at (831) 338-8861 for information.

Just north of the town of Santa Cruz, at the water's edge and flanked by fields of brussels sprouts, lies the **Long Marine Laboratory.** Spread over forty acres of wetlands and seashore, this is primarily a research center for the University of California at Santa Cruz. But visitors are welcome, and unlike the famous Monterey Bay Aquarium on the other side of the bay, it's rarely crowded and it's cheaper.

At Long Marine Laboratory's Seymour Marine Discovery Center, two aquaria have excellent exhibits of local shells and fish, hermit crabs, starfish, monkeyface eels, and other marine life from Monterey Bay, including pint-size sharks. A touching tank for the youngsters swarms with creepy creatures from below.

trivia

The Mystery Spot near Santa Cruz has baffled visitors since its discovery in 1940. Even scientists can't explain why gravity and perspective behave so strangely in this one location.

In the afternoon docents lead brief tours to the outdoor tanks where sea lions, dolphins, and other marine mammals are studied and trained. Not only will you be entertained by the frisky critters, you'll learn such obscure details as how to tell a seal from a sea lion (check the ears) and the eating habits of a dolphin. And speaking of eating, there's an 87-foot skeleton of a blue whale that weighed about 130 tons when alive. As with others of the species, it ate four tons of krill shrimp a day just to survive!

To reach the Long Marine Laboratory, take Swift Avenue off Highway 1, turn right at Delaware Street, and continue to the end. It's open Tuesday through Saturday from 10:00 a.m. to 5:00 p.m. and opens at noon on Sunday; admission charged. Call (831) 459-3800 for information, or check http://seymourcenter.ucsc .edu for details.

Two miles east of Swift Street at 701 West Cliff Drive, at the north tip of Monterey Bay, is a small, brick lighthouse containing the **Santa Cruz Surfing Museum.** Started by a few barnacled old surf veterans, the museum traces sixty years of the sport through breathtaking photos and an exciting video, rubber fins, and an array of surfboards.

You can trace surfing's evolution from redwood boards weighing a hundred pounds to the shorter, lighter present-day variety, made from foam and fiberglass. There's even an exhibit on sharks and the mangled wet suit of a surfer attacked by a great white.

The Santa Cruz Surfing Museum is open Thursday through Monday from noon to 4:00 p.m., and longer hours in summer, with no admission charged. Call (831) 420-6289 and consult www.santacruzsurfingmuseum.org

TOP ANNUAL EVENTS ON THE SOUTH COAST

Artichoke Festival, Castroville
(mid-May)

Watsonville "Fly-In" & Air Show
(Memorial Day weekend)

**San Juan Bautista State Historic Park
Early Days** (mid-June)

California Rodeo, Salinas (mid-July)

Gilroy Garlic Festival (mid-July)

Carmel Bach Festival, Carmel-by-the-
Sea (mid-July to early August)

Steinbeck Festival, Salinas
(early August)

Capitola Begonia Festival
(Labor Day weekend)

Monterey Jazz Festival
(late September)

Pacific Coast Fog Fest, Pacifica
(late September)

Butterfly Parade, Pacific Grove
(early October)

Monterey Wine Festival (mid-October)

Art & Pumpkin Festival, Half Moon Bay
(mid-October)

Christmas in the Adobes, Monterey
(mid-December)

for information. Conclude a visit with a short walk to Steamer Lane, a popular beach for local surfers and their admirers.

Monterey Bay

Leaving the Santa Cruz area on Highway 1, enter Monterey County, renowned for its outstanding visitor attractions. First there's an unscheduled stop at a most unlikely place. As you approach the weather-beaten fishing village of **Moss Landing,** the first thing you'll notice are the two hideous smokestacks of a huge power plant. The temptation is to push the accelerator to the floor, but that would be a mistake.

Moss Landing is the one town on Monterey Bay that still looks like a rough-and-tumble fishing port. There are tuna and shellfish canneries, hundreds of chipped and rusting vessels, boats up on blocks, vacant lots filled with weeds—the kind of thing John Steinbeck saw when he wrote about Monterey decades ago.

This seaside settlement claims a curious history. A Frenchman named Paul Lezare founded "the city of St. Paul" in the 1850s. Two decades later Captain Charles Moss built some docks,

trivia

The Monterey Jazz Festival in September is the oldest of its kind in the world.

and Moss Landing boomed with grain shipments, sardine canneries, whaling, and boat building—before the inevitable decline. Now it's a center for oceanographic research as well as a threadbare working port. Restaurants and antiques shops have also cropped up along the main drag.

Elkhorn Slough, nearby, shelters a world of salt marshes and tidal flats inhabited by hundreds of species of birds and waterfowl, invertebrates and fish, not to mention sea otters, seals, and salamanders. This 2,500-acre estuary (where freshwater and saltwater meet) is one of the nation's most biologically productive habitats. Nearly 90 percent of California's wetlands have been destroyed by "progress," and Elkhorn is second in size only to the shores of San Francisco Bay. The slough straddles a 7-mile-long river channel winding through marshland blanketed with mustard plant, filaree, and lupine.

Elkhorn Slough National Estuarine Research Reserve forms about half of the entire slough and is open regular hours for visitors. The main channel outside the reserve is open continuously for fishing, kayaking, and the like.

Begin at the visitor center, which is well stocked with maps and interpretive displays; admission is free. Five miles of wide trails are accessible after paying a small fee; crisscross the sloping terrain leading down to the slough. Along the way you may spot a golden eagle or a peregrine falcon hunting for lunch among the impressive stands of eucalyptus or live oak. Patches of mugwort, lavender-colored wild radish, and hundreds of other botanical delights crowd the estuary banks and provide sustenance for the countless migratory and resident birds. (Late fall, winter, and early spring are the best times for birding.)

The stillness at Elkhorn is overwhelming, just as it must have been when the planet's first life oozed forth from a place like this. At present highly developed species such as the snowy egret share the marsh with one-celled life forms, spanning eons of evolutionary history. If you're lucky you may find as many as fifty seals lounging on the mud banks or spot the pattern of a leopard-shark's fin as it cuts the surface of the water.

Elkhorn Slough Reserve is open year-round Wednesday through Sunday from 9:00 a.m. to 5:00 p.m., with guided

The Truth about Artichokes

One of the oldest foods known, artichokes were cultivated in the Mediterranean region thousands of years ago. Catherine of Medici introduced them into France in the mid-1500s. In present-day France *les artichauts* are prepared in dozens of ways, including baked hearts au gratin.

Italian immigrants first brought artichokes to California in the 1920s, and today the state accounts for 99.9 percent of all American production, more than four million cartons annually valued at more than $50 million. About three-fourths of this crop is grown in Monterey County, where the climate and soil are considered ideal.

Artichokes belong to the thistle group of the sunflower family, and the "vegetable" we eat is really a flower bud. If allowed to bloom, the violet-blue blossom would measure 7 inches in diameter.

The artichoke is a thistlelike spheroid sheathed in tough, pointed leaves, what one food critic described as "an organic hand grenade." Yet within the tough exterior is palatable flesh with a subtle taste. It's said that eating artichokes makes other food taste sweeter and helps cheap wine resemble the vintage stuff.

Artichokes are high in folic acid, vitamin C, and fiber; low in calories and sodium; and contain no fat or cholesterol. They are also high in snob appeal and reputed to be an aphrodisiac.

Somewhat challenging to consume, artichokes are one of the last holdouts in an age of fast food. But aficionados swear all the effort is worth it. They can be steamed, boiled, baked, french-fried, marinated, and stir-fried with seafood, pasta, and so on. For some classic recipes send an SASE to the California Artichoke Advisory Board, P.O. Box 747, Castroville, CA 95012; call (831) 633-4411; or check out www.artichokes.org.

tours on weekends at 10:00 a.m. and 1:00 p.m. You can reach the reserve via Dolan Road (next to the power plant), heading east about 3 miles to Elkhorn Road, then another 2 miles north to the visitor center. For information call (831) 728-2822 or go to www.elkhornslough.org.

A company called Elkhorn Slough Safari out of Moss Landing offers nature tours aboard a 27-foot pontoon boat. The two-hour excursion is led by jocular Captain Yohn Gideon and a naturalist, who share an uncanny ability to spot the abundant wildlife as it appears. They also provide loads of information and anecdotes about the animals. This is one of the nation's top places for bird-watching: More than 340 species have been spotted here, many using the slough as a stopover on their migrant flyways. Cruising along the inland waterway, visitors help count the playful otters, constantly grooming themselves, and large numbers of harbor seals For details on the pontoon-boat excursion, call (831) 633-5555. Don't forget the camera and binoculars! For an upscale

B&B experience, the same folks run the Captain's Inn; call (831) 633-5550 or go online at www.captainsinn.com.

"Celebrate the thistle" a few miles away in **Castroville,** a town owing its entire identity to one thing—artichokes. The area's soil and mild climate create a kind of artichoke heaven, and Castroville claims about 90 percent of the total U.S. production. It's a one-vegetable town and isn't shy about proclaiming itself the artichoke center of the world in a sign fixed above Main Street. This town of about 6,800 lies at the western edge of the famous Salinas Valley, home to some of the nation's most fertile farmland.

Founded back in 1863 by Juan Bautista Castro, the town witnessed some bad times. Then, about 1920, Italian immigrants appeared with a curious Mediterranean plant and the crazy idea of cultivating it. The rest belongs to artichoke history.

Castroville boasts a 20-foot-tall, 16-foot-wide artichoke made of reinforced concrete that has become an icon of American roadside kitsch. This local treasure marks the location of the Giant Artichoke Restaurant (11261 Merritt Street; 831-633-3501). Here you can discover a multitude of tasty ways to prepare the thistle—boiled, marinated, sautéed, in soup, bread, cake, salad, omelets, quiches, pasta, and the restaurant's specialty—french-fried artichoke hearts.

When Castroville hosts its annual **Artichoke Festival** in May, visitors can discover even more ways to eat the beloved thistle as well as take part in a full-blown celebration that includes a parade, 10K run, and artichoke cooking and eating competitions. And there's one interesting footnote to it all: Back in 1947, none other than a budding starlet named Norma Jean Baker, who was later better known as Marilyn Monroe, reigned as Castroville's first "Artichoke" Queen. Today, Franco's Norma Jean, a Hispanic gay nightclub on Merritt Street, honors the star with her real name.

trivia

Mazda Raceway Laguna Seca in Salinas is home to numerous world-class racing events and historic automobile shows.

Castroville lies at the junction of Highways 156 and 183, about 7 miles from Salinas and 16 miles from the Monterey Peninsula.

Monterey and its well-known neighbors hardly require an introduction. Renowned indeed are the world-class golf, outstanding aquarium, Cannery Row, Fisherman's Wharf, and Carmel's quaint shops and restaurants. One lesser-known attraction, **Monterey's Path of History,** begins just a few steps from the wharf, yet few visitors find it.

Monterey is one of California's most historic places, with its best collection of Spanish colonial–period architecture. After early explorers made claims for

It's a Dog's World

My bouncy Samoyed and I often have trouble finding places—parks, trails, beaches, and motels—that let us enjoy the facilities together. Not so in Carmel-by-the-Sea, which welcomes dogs and "their people" with open paws.

Start with the city beach, a gorgeous swath of white sand bordered by cypress trees and a nice walking trail, located at the end of Ocean Avenue. Here my dog can join dozens of other pooches frolicking leashless with the full protection of the local law. This innocent play often turns into an authentic canine circus with all the normal instinctual behavior, so watch where you step. It's the only beach for many miles that allows such freedom (leashed pets are permitted at Carmel River State Beach south of town).

When we walk around Carmel, I can go into any shop without worry; there are special doggie hitching posts outside for pets to relax in the shade while waiting for their masters. (Many shops will allow them to enter.) The Fountain of Woof in Carmel Plaza Shopping Center is the town's only official dog drinking fountain. A woman named Gale Wrausmann runs Carmel Walks, a foot-and-paw tour of the quaint little town that not only allows dogs (on leash) but encourages them to come along. There's a special segment of the tour called "the canine culture of Carmel, past and present." Call (831) 642-2700 for information.

Finally, we know there will always be some place to sleep and eat while in Carmel. The Cypress Inn is an elegant Mediterranean-style hostelry replete with antiques and feather beds. It's part-owned by famous dog-lover Doris Day, which means your pooch will get the V.I.D. treatment, including his or her pet bed and an invitation to "Yappy Hour" each afternoon. But the Cypress Inn is very popular, and reservations are essential; call (800) 443-7443. Pets are also welcome at the Happy Landing Inn.

After a day of romping, my dog often likes to turn in early, but when we go out there's the chic Porta Bella Restaurant, where we can sit outside in a candlelit courtyard with other dogs and owners. For reservations call (831) 624-4395. If it's booked, we can dine at Forge in the Forest Restaurant, which has a "Dog Pound Menu" featuring canine treats like the "Quarter Hounder" served beside the firepit in the patio. Now that's something to bark about!

the crown of Spain (Vizcaino named the area for the count of Monte Rey), the peninsula was finally settled in the 1770s. Monterey became Alta California's liveliest town, not to mention a provincial capital under both Spanish and Mexican flags.

About forty buildings remain from before 1850, when the gold rush and San Francisco stole most of Monterey's thunder, and about a dozen are open along the Path of History. Ironically, they were less a product of any Spanish or Mexican influence than of Yankee settlers such as Thomas Larkin, who tried to build a New England–style house using local materials and created the "Monterey-style": two-story adobes with balconies, overhanging roofs, beamed ceilings, and plank floors.

The *Custom House,* at 1 Custom House Plaza, is the oldest surviving government building on the Pacific Coast (1827). Cargo was inspected and taxed here before it could be sold. Researchers have used an old ship's manifest to cleverly re-create a feeling for the times, with kegs of whisky, tallow candles, sacks of flour, and piles of "California banknotes," the cowhides used for bartering at the time. All this loot is lorded over by a gabby parrot. One historical note: At the Custom House the U.S. flag was officially raised for the first time in California—on July 7, 1846, during the Mexican-American War.

The *Pacific House,* 8 Custom House Plaza, was used for military storage and later as a tavern. Now it's a museum covering the Costanoan Indians through the early American period. The *Casa del Oro,* at the corner of Scott and Olivier Streets, contains a general store featuring novelty items and gifts that might have been sold in the 1850s and Russian-made goods and toys. You can see the old safe where gold was stored (*oro* means "gold" in Spanish) and an herb garden outside.

Just off the Path of History at 5 Custom House Plaza, in a modern building marked by the glow from a 580-prism Point Sur Lightstation Fresnel lens, is the *Maritime Museum of Monterey* (831-375-2553; www.montereyhistory .org). The free museum, open Tuesday through Sunday from 10:00 a.m. to 5:00 p.m., houses more than 6,000 artifacts, from sextants and maps to mementos from the USS *Macon* and Monterey's sardine fishery days. The reference library contains hundreds of books and 50,000 photographs.

Colton Hall, 522 Pacific, was built by a navy chaplain who became the town's first American mayor. The neoclassical building in Friendly Plaza became the site of California's constitutional convention in 1849. You can see the tables where delegates sat, as well as their notes, inkwells, and wire-rimmed spectacles. The realistic cells at Old Monterey Jail next door look ready for the next prisoner to arrive (it was used until 1956).

trivia

The Dennis the Menace Playground in Monterey was designed by Hank Ketcham, creator of the famous comic strip.

The *Larkin House,* 510 Calle Principal, remains the best example of the Monterey style. It was built in 1835 by the future U.S. consul to Mexico, Thomas Larkin. The *Cooper-Molera Adobe,* corner of Polk and Munras Streets, has been beautifully restored, right down to matching the original wallpaper, and it houses an interpretive center. Its three-acre walled garden is a flower-filled oasis. At the ***Stevenson House,*** 530 Houston Street, author Robert Louis Stevenson paid 25 cents per week in rent while visiting his wife-to-be, Fanny Osborne. Poor, unknown, and in frail health, he wrote articles for local newspapers and a book entitled *The Old Pacific Capital,* an account of Monterey in the 1870s.

These and some other buildings on the Path of History are part of the Monterey State Historic Park, open at various times throughout the week. Pick up a map at the Custom House or El Estero Visitors Center, Franklin at Camino El Estero, open daily from 9:00 a.m. to 5:00 p.m., or reserve a spot on a free guided walking tour. For more information call (831) 649-7118 or visit www.parks.ca.gov.

Old Monterey's downtown area, centered on Alvarado Street, is a seamless blend of historical and new attractions, with a fish restaurant housed in an old adobe, funky art galleries, and a classic film palace—now a movie and live performance venue—designed like a Moorish castle called the Golden State Theatre. The Old Monterey Inn is an imposing Tudor-style home built by a former mayor transformed into a quality bed-and-breakfast inn. Each of ten rooms features a different motif, and all are incredibly cozy; call (831) 375-8284 or check www.oldmontereyinn.com for reservations.

trivia

17-Mile Drive through Pebble Beach is a private toll road for cars and free for bicycles and pedestrians, though motorcycles are forbidden.

The tiny community of ***Pacific Grove*** may be the best-kept secret on the Monterey Peninsula. Clutching a finger of land immediately west of Cannery Row, it embraces a 4-mile stretch of spectacular coastline dotted with rocky beaches, tide pools, and seaside parks ablaze with the pink iceplant blossoms. A cool blanket of fog often hangs over its quiet streets that are lined with small cottages and inns replete with bay windows, gables, and stained-glass windows.

In 1875, 450 Methodists arrived here by horse and wagon to camp out and "sing praises to God in open air." Every summer the Methodist Seaside Retreat became a tent city, but before long visitors became residents and built modest homes in this nature-blessed spot. The retreat was something of a curiosity to its ripsnorting neighbors along the Cannery Row. For nearly a century in Pacific Grove liquor was outlawed and required a prescription, and not until 1969 did California's last dry town fall off the wagon. Laws also banned gambling, dancing, swimming without a proper costume (i.e., doubled crotched), fishing on Sunday, and fast buggy driving.

As far as anyone can tell, the mysterious monarch butterflies started arriving in Pacific Grove about the same time as the Methodists. Each fall tens of thousands of these orange and black creatures wing it from as far away as Alaska and the Canadian Rockies for a winter sojourn in Butterfly Town USA. From early October (when there's a festive Butterfly Parade) through early March, you can see butterflies hanging in clusters on the branches of cypress and eucalyptus trees. One spot in particular is a butterfly haven: the **Monarch Butterfly Sanctuary** just off Lighthouse Avenue. You can look, but don't touch; there's a thousand-dollar fine for anyone caught "molesting butterflies."

A special exhibit explains the monarch phenomenon at the **Pacific Grove Museum of Natural History.** Excellent displays showcase the peninsula's animal and plant life, from univalves and giant oysters to wild boars, playful sea otters, and the endangered California condor. The museum, at 165 Forest Avenue, is open Tuesday through Saturday from 10:00 a.m. to 5:00 p.m. No admission charged. For information call (831) 648-5716 or visit www.pgmuseum .org.

trivia

Early last century the Monterey Peninsula became home to a new school of landscape art called California impressionism, which sought to capture the fleeting effects of light in nature. This style survives today with the contemporary plein air artists found in many local galleries and art shows.

At the Pacific Grove Chamber of Commerce across the street, pick up a walking tour map of eighteen historical sites that includes old St. Mary's by-the-Sea Episcopal Church and the **Point Pinos Lighthouse.** This coastal beacon is the oldest in continuous operation on the West Coast, marking the entrance to Monterey Harbor since 1855, when it used a lard-oil lantern. A historical museum inside is open Thursday through Monday from 1:00 to 4:00 p.m. Call (831) 648-5716, ext. 13.

At the **Great Tide Pool of Point Pinos,** you can spy sea otters frolicking offshore in the kelp beds and hear the sharp crack of a clamshell being opened for lunch by one of these delightful creatures. Once thought extinct, otters have staged a remarkable comeback. You can watch them year-round from numerous points along Ocean View Boulevard, especially between the Hopkins Marine Station and the lighthouse.

Pacific Grove is also famous for its bed-and-breakfast inns, housed in creaky, charming Victorians amid storybook settings. Among the best are the Gosby House Inn (800-527-8828; www.gosbyhouseinn.com), Green Gables Inn (831-375-2095; www.greengablesinnpg.com), Seven Gables Inn (831-372-4341;

www.pginns.com), and the ultimate Victorian, The Centrella Inn (800-233-3372; www.centrellainn.com). For further information about touring the old Victorians, call the Pacific Grove Chamber of Commerce at (800) 656-6650.

The village of **Carmel,** next to Pacific Grove, is cute indeed. But the cuteness of no street addresses and no street lights pales when tourist crowds swarm into town. When that happens, it's time to head for the valley.

About 15 miles long from the mouth of the Carmel River to its headwaters in the Santa Lucia Mountains, the Carmel Valley is a sun-splashed retreat from the bustle of the peninsula. Coastal fog rarely comes this far, and 300 sunny days a year make it easy to enjoy swimming, golf, tennis, and hiking amid idyllic rural scenery.

trivia

Neon signs, billboards, and hot dog stands are prohibited in the quaint village of Carmel, and a permit is required to wear high-heeled shoes.

Just south of Carmel, Carmel Valley Road heads inland from Highway 1 and follows the river toward the hills. Along the way are fields of strawberries, fruit orchards, and grazing horses. The entire Monterey Peninsula is a golfer's paradise, and the valley claims some of the finest courses. At the Rancho Cañada Golf Club (800-536-9459; www.ranchocanada.com), a thirty-six-hole public facility about a mile inland, one of two scenic courses leaps the river five times. The Quail Lodge Golf Club (888-828-8787; www.quaillodge.com/golf.cfm) hosts resort guests and members of reciprocating private clubs. Quail Lodge Resort & Golf Club occupies a pastoral setting on 245 acres of lakes, woods, and meadows stretching more than 4,000 acres. Another private course at the Carmel Valley Ranch (866-282-4745; www.carmelvalleyranch.com) features nine holes along the river and the back nine climbing the hills, in addition to twelve tennis courts.

Although money definitely talks in the valley, fun is not the exclusive domain of high rollers. **Garland Ranch Regional Park** (www.mprpd .org/parks/garland.htm) provides picnic sites and more than 7 miles of trails

trivia

San Francisco artists and writers flocked to Carmel after the 1906 earthquake left them homeless — and a tradition was born.

through alluring hills and meadows stretching more than 4,500 acres. The park is especially beautiful in April and May with a fantastic array of wildflowers.

Right in the neighborhood is **Château Julien Winery,** housed in a beautiful replica of a French castle, with an elegant tasting room where six varieties of wine are sampled. The place is small enough that the winemaker himself sometimes assists with the tour. Château Julien is open from 8:30 a.m. to 5:00 p.m. weekdays and from 11:00 a.m. to 5:00 p.m. weekends. For information about tours call (831) 624-2600.

Other wineries with tasting rooms in the Carmel Valley village are Bernardus, 5 West Carmel Valley Road (800) 223-2533; Chateau Sinnet, 13746 Center Street, (831) 659-2244; Heller Estate, 69 West Carmel Valley Road, (831) 659-6220; Joullian, 2 Village Drive, (831) 659-8100; and Robert Talbot, 53 West Carmel Valley Road, (831) 659-3500.

Seclusion can be found at the ***Tassajara Zen Mountain Center.*** Operated by the San Francisco Zen Center as a monastic community, Tassajara is open to the public part of the year for overnight stays or pre-booked day visits. Seventeen hot mineral springs have been attracting bathers here since Indian days, and the spot was a fashionable resort in the early 1900s. Tassajara is open during summer but closed in winter for student training. Be forewarned: This is really off the beaten path. Call (831) 659-2229 for information or go to www.sfzc.org.

There are numerous shopping spots, accommodations, and dining possibilities throughout the area, especially at Carmel Valley Village. For information contact the chamber of commerce, P.O. Box 288, 13 West Carmel Valley Road, Carmel Valley, CA 93924; (831) 659-4000.

The busy four-lane section of ***Carmel Valley Road*** between Highway 1 and Laureles Grande gives way to a twisty two-lane blacktop that winds through vineyards and oak groves, narrow canyons, and green pastures. Allow about two hours for the one-way journey from Carmel Valley Village to the town of Greenfield on US 101.

For information about the entire county, contact the Monterey County Convention & Visitors Bureau at (877) 666-8373 or visit its Web site at www .montereyinfo.org.

Big Sur

Highway 1 south of Carmel, also known as the Cabrillo Highway, ranks as one of the America's great scenic roads—the greatest, say some. It winds for about 90 miles along the high cliffs of Big Sur toward San Simeon and San Luis Obispo County. Along the way are jagged mountains rising from the Pacific, grassy promontories sprinkled with wildflowers, rushing streams, and dense pockets of redwoods. Yet few people realize how wild Big Sur and the coastal mountains remain, despite their immense popularity with visitors. Forests and brush burned 200,000 acres to the edges of cliffs in mid-2008 when much of the Big Sur coast was threatened by a lightening-ignited wildfire.

For the Birds

The rare and regal California condor has lived in the Santa Lucia Mountains for at least ten millennia and once roamed as far north as British Columbia. It is North America's largest land bird, with a 10-foot wingspan and a range of 150 miles per day.

However, by the late 1980s these magnificent creatures were close to extinction due to hunting and egg collecting, and urgent action was required. The last known wild condor was taken into captivity to join twenty-six others. Working together, the U.S. government and Ventana Wildlife Society began a careful breeding program followed by reintroduction into the wilderness. Reintroduction continues, and has been extended to the Pinnacles area, Southern California, Arizona, and Baja California (Mexico). So far the program seems to be working, despite the threats from power line electrocution and lead poisoning.

The Ventana Wildlife Society has a research and education center beside the entrance to Andrew Molera State Park. Contact administrative offices at 19045 Portola Drive, Suite F-1, Salinas, CA 93908; call (831) 455-9514 or go to www.ventana ws.org for more information.

The Esselen Indians once inhabited this land, but whites did not settle here until after 1850, and the highway was not completed until 1937. During the 1950s, novelist Henry Miller became the focus of an artists colony, and a decade later, hippies arrived in droves, spurred on by tales of good vibes and beautiful scenery. But the hippies went again, and even now only about 1,500 permanent residents call Big Sur home. Amenities are few, just a smattering of resorts and campgrounds, and the sense of escape is compelling. To capture this feeling of quiet intimacy, try staying at *Deetjen's Big Sur Inn,* a collection of simple cabins built by Norwegian immigrants in the 1920s. Call (831) 667-2377 for information or check www.deetjens.com.

The dramatic 30-mile drive from Carmel to Big Sur takes about an hour along a road that clings desperately to the seaward face of the Santa Lucia Mountains. Along the way (about 15 miles south), you will pass the massive, 714 foot long Bixby Bridge, with a grace and grandeur almost equal to the natural wonders of Big Sur. It was built during the 1930s by prisoners eager to work time off their sentences. A bit south, the historic *Point Sur Lighthouse* sits perched 361 feet above the boiling surf. For information on guided tours, call (831) 625-4419 or look at www.pointsur.org. Farther along (30 miles south of Carmel) are the world-famous *Nepenthe restaurant* (once owned by Orson Welles, call 831-667-2345; www.nepenthebigsur.com) and the *Henry Miller Library,* with documents and artifacts on the life of the feisty

Esalen on the Edge

More than four decades ago, two unusual and highly motivated young men, Michael Murphy and Dick Price, put their heads together. They shared a mutual interest in meditation, spirituality, and psychology, and Murphy's grandmother just happened to own twenty-seven acres of land at the southern edge of Big Sur. And so the Esalen Institute was born.

This unique educational retreat enjoys a spectacular setting on a terraced hillside at the edge of the continent, with views of crashing waves, sea otters, whales, gulls, and mind-blowing sunsets when fog is not present, which is often the case at Big Sur. Gardens and flowers, some of them edible, abound.

A number of faults and fissures in the area allow underground water to break through the surface and create therapeutic springs, and Native Americans used them heal and purify. In fact, Esalen derives its name from the Esselen tribe, and the retreat sits on former ceremonial grounds once used to conduct peace gatherings. The Indians spoke of an energy vortex here, and something about the land still feels sacred.

Since the late 1960s that energy has drawn notable teachers such as Alan Watts, Aldous Huxley, Joseph Campbell, and Buckminster Fuller, and the illustrious guest rolls have included George Harrison, Bob Dylan, Andrew Weil, and even former Russian leader Boris Yeltsin. In fact, during the 1980s hundreds of top Soviet scientists, intellectuals, and diplomats came here to engage with their American peers in "hot tub diplomacy" and got a taste of new ideas and the good life. Some claim this eventually led to glasnost.

That life includes organic meals at the lodge (about 600 served daily), the renowned Esalen massage therapy—which can be almost a religious experience, some say—and above all the massive stone tubs filled with 119-degree Fahrenheit geothermal water, rich in sulfur and known to heal both body and spirit. The hot tubs sit in a templelike sanctuary on a rocky cliff high above the shoreline. Nearby the water-bearing creek forms a waterfall and joins the Pacific, and many feel this spot is especially powerful, a portal for inner pilgrimage.

The spirit of Big Sur and Esalen is purging, renewal, and preservation. The institute was at the forefront of the human potential movement of the 1970s with a unique blend of Eastern and Western philosophy whose central thread was the mind-body connection. Today Esalen draws about 10,000 guests a year from around the world for a wide array of workshops, from atomic physics to alternative sexuality and from the environment and alternative energy to the role of psychedelics in society. One recent topic was achieving cultural diversity in visual arts, music, and dance; another, the disturbing rise of fundamentalism in the world's leading religions. Workshops may seem trendy, but Esalen takes pride in being on the cutting edge. Top-level intellectuals explore themes that may never reach the mass culture except by a kind of trickle-down theory of ideas that can sometimes create change.

For further information about staying at Esalen, go to www.esalen.org. The hot tubs are open to the general public by reservation from 1:00 to 3:00 a.m. each morning; call (831) 667-3047 for details.

writer and painter. It's open Wednesday through Monday from 11:00 a.m. to 6:00 p.m. For information call (831) 667-2574 or visit www.henrymiller.org.

trivia

You can tour a chocoholic's paradise at Monterey Bay Chocolates' factory in Seaside, near Monterey.

One truly beautiful sight is the waterfall at *Julia Pfeiffer Burns State Park,* sitting right off Highway 1 a short walk from the parking area. This magnificent cataract plummets about 80 feet to the beach within a shell-shaped cove of iridescent sea green water flanked by rocky cliffs. An ingenious terraced trail follows the cliff above the cove to a lookout opening out on a wide stretch of coastline. If you are seeking solitude, stay away from Pfeiffer Big Sur and Julia Pfeiffer Burns State Parks in summer or on weekends.

On the other hand, *Andrew Molera State Park* remains an adventurer's hideaway within easy reach of the main road, about 5 miles north of Big Sur proper. The park rises from the oceanfront and hugs the Big Sur River at about 3,400 feet above sea level. Within its 5,000 acres of cottonwood, oak, and redwood forests is a network of more than 20 miles of hiking and equestrian trails. To the delight of most visitors, the only thing missing is a road. People come for the excellent hiking, and the trails traverse the beachfront, bluffs, meadows, and banks of the Big Sur River. You might spot harbor seals and sea lions at the shore or mule deer and bobcat farther inland. One of the better trails follows the river to the lagoon for about a mile, emerging on a rocky beach watched over by egrets, gulls, surf scoters, and black oyster catchers. The stables within the park offer rides to the beach from morning until sunset. Contact Molera Horseback Tours at (831) 625-5486 or go to www.molerahorsebacktours.com.

After whetting your appetite for adventure, it's time to take on nearby *Ventana Wilderness.* This 167,000-acre refuge forms part of the vast Los Padres National Forest and represents the southernmost realm of the coastal redwoods. Wild boar, mountain lion, raccoon, California condor, and dozens of other species call it home. Within its rugged, chaparral-covered confines are 237 miles of hiking trails, such as Botchers Gap–Devil's Peak Trail, a steep, 4 mile hike offering spectacular views of the coast. For overnighters, Andrew Molera has twenty-four campsites available on a first-come basis. For information call (831) 667-2315.

Inland Valleys

One route for the adventurous leaves Highway 1 near Lucia, south of Big Sur. Scenic Nacimiento Road switchbacks over the rugged coastal mountains all the way to bucolic San Antonio de Padua Mission near Jolon. You are more likely, however, to enter the coast's interior valleys on US 101. If arriving from the north, you will leave the Bay Area outside of San Jose, then pass Gilroy, famous for its annual Garlic Festival. Just about anything related to "the stinking rose" can be found at *Garlic World*—braids, gifts, souvenirs, and gourmet items like garlic ice cream. It's located off US 101 at 4800 Monterey Highway, about 3 miles south of Gilroy; call (800) 537-6122 for more information.

Gilroy's agricultural roots are in full bloom at *Gilroy Gardens Family Theme Park.* There's a steam train and Quicksilver Express Mine Coaster, the Pinnacles Rock Maze, and a fistful of rides like the Mushroom Swing, Artichoke Dip, and Garlic Twirl (similar to Disney's teacups but with giant garlic bulbs doing the spinning). It's all set in a lush horticultural wonderland that includes a vast greenhouse called Monarch Garden and the park's highlight: nineteen bizarrely woven and sculpted sycamores called "circus trees." Gilroy Gardens Family Theme Park is open March through November and daily in summer; call (408) 840-7100 and check www.gilroygardens.org for further information.

You are leaving the Santa Clara Valley and entering San Benito County; follow US 101 south to Highway 156 and take it 2 miles east to *San Juan Bautista.* The town is a quiet place, with the feel of an old frontier community that time passed by. This tranquility belies the fact that San Juan, as locals call it, sits smack on the San Andreas Fault. At least one tremor a week rattles residents, with a good jolt several times a year.

The town's site, on an escarpment overlooking the San Benito River Valley, was handpicked by Franciscan missionary Fermin de Lausen on the feast day of John the Baptist, June 24, 1797. San Juan is alive with the dreamy feel of Old California, with a nicely restored mission, a main square where Mexican soldiers used to drill, and the Yankee town that later grew up around it. Before Spaniards arrived the valley was home to the Mutsun Indians, but despite the missionaries' efforts to "civilize" them, the natives were wiped out. The last full-blooded Mutsun died in 1930 and lies buried in the mission cemetery, along with about 4,000 other Native Americans, mostly in unmarked graves.

trivia

The sapphire blue gemstone called benitoite, a form of crystal, is found at only one place in the world: the Diablo range of San Benito County.

The mission's spacious church features a double row of arches, somber religious art, and flickering candles. Particularly noteworthy are the 40-foot-high altar paintings (called *reredos*) done by one Thomas Doakin 1816. This Boston sailor had jumped ship to become the first American to settle in California.

Now the fading paintings are lit dramatically and spruced up with some scarlet curtains and statues. San Juan boasts the only mission church open continuously since its founding, and the original chapel bells still call parishioners to Mass. The museum displays the standard collection of worn-out vestments, kettles, rawhide thongs, and such curiosities as gaming sticks used by local Indians. The mission, at 406 Second Street, is open daily from 9:30 a.m. to 4:30 p.m.; call (831) 623-4528 or check www.oldmissionsjb.org for details.

After Mexico lost California in 1846, San Juan Bautista became a trading center for livestock, and hotels, saloons, and stables sprouted up. It was also a key stop on the old stagecoach lines, with as many as a dozen stages a day trundling in and out of town on the San Francisco–Los Angeles run. Weary travelers would stay the night at *Angelo Zanetta's Plaza Hotel,* converted from soldiers' barracks. It was supposed to be a refined place (the future general William T. Sherman slept there), but two men died of gunshot wounds in the bar. A self-guided tour of the two-story hotel costs $1. You'll see a table set for dinner, a portrait of nefarious local outlaw Tiburcio Vasquez, and a marvelous old barroom complete with card tables and spittoons. It can still be the liveliest place in town whenever a group puts on a show.

Right next door sits the *Castro-Breen House,* built by the prefect of northern Alta California, a man who even changed the town's name briefly to San Juan de Castro. The house is completely furnished, down to the kerosene lamps and chamber pots, just as it was when the Breen family resided there. This remarkable bunch (the parents and seven kids) were stranded in the high Sierra with the infamous Donner party for 111 days, but all of them miraculously (or suspiciously) managed to survive. After being rescued, they made a fortune in the goldfields and settled in San Juan Bautista.

Across the square is Plaza Stable, a hive of activity in the old stagecoach days. On display are numerous carriages and wagons, including a fringed surrey and an elegant black barouche. Out back is the blacksmith's shop, and next door you'll find a fourth historic building—Plaza Hall, once used as a dormitory by Indian maidens. The San Juan Bautista Historic Park is open daily from 10:00 a.m. to 4:30 p.m.; call (831) 623-4526 or (831) 623-2454 for further information.

The *Salinas Valley,* one of the world's richest farming regions, lies to the southeast. Sometimes called "the Salad Bowl of the Nation," this 85-mile-long valley grows an astounding 60 percent of America's fresh vegetables. The town of Salinas, about 20 miles east of Monterey, has another claim to fame as birthplace of novelist John Steinbeck. Though largely scandalized by his writings at the time, now the town embraces the Steinbeck legacy with passion—understandably, as few places can claim a Nobel Prize winner as a native son.

One reason for the outrage was that Steinbeck borrowed liberally from the people and places encountered in his youth, and they often reappeared as thinly disguised fiction. The town was definitely the setting for *East of Eden.* One passage reads: "It was an immaculate and friendly house, grand enough but not pretentious, and it sat inside its white fence surrounded by a clipped lawn and roses." Steinbeck was describing his own house, the two-story Victorian where he was born in 1902 and spent his first eighteen years.

At present the prim ladies of a local society have taken over the **Steinbeck House** and run it as a restaurant, serving luncheon amid turn-of-the-twentieth-century furnishings. The front bedroom, where the author was born, is now a reception area. Steinbeck later occupied an upstairs bedroom and lived at home until after graduation from Salinas High School. The Steinbeck House Restaurant, at 132 Central Street, offers lunch Tuesday through Saturday and is available for private parties. Check the menu at www.steinbeckhouse.com and call (831) 424-2735 for reservations.

Steinbeck died in 1968, and his remains rest in the Garden of Memories at 768 Abbott Street. After much heated discussion, the town named its main library in his memory. Outside is an odd statue of the author smoking a cigarette (which vandals keep breaking off).

Just 2 blocks from his birthplace, the **National Steinbeck Center,** a museum filled with ingenious interactive exhibits and an archive, encapsulates just how creative contemporary museums have become. Ironically, the center sits facing Old Town Salinas and its tree-lined Main Street, where *The Grapes of Wrath* was publicly burned by local prudes shortly after publication. A stroll through the museum is like an intimate journey into the author's life and work, which were often interchangeable. But the collection is not merely for loyal readers or professors; complete novices will come away entertained and informed.

trivia

Almost 250,000 tons of sardines were processed on Cannery Row in 1945, the year John Steinbeck's novel of the same name was published.

The self-guided tour through a series of vignettes begins with the Growing Up East of Eden Room, which evokes the feel of turn-of-the-twentieth-century Salinas, including Steinbeck's attic room with books he read as a child. You feel the cool air coming from a boxcar for lettuce (which figures prominently in the Eden novel), a reminder that young Steinbeck worked in the valley's fields and factories. The Grapes of Wrath Room features migrant workers' cabins, and you can try your hand at washing laundry amid the sound of Woody

Guthrie tunes. Monterey's Cannery Row is re-created in precise detail, right down to the smell of sardines piped in from above.

If all this sounds kitschy, somehow it works, and visitors who might never dream of picking up a Steinbeck book could be inspired to do so. The writer's oeuvre was widely popular in his day and adapted by Hollywood, and film clips flicker among the various exhibits. You can sit on a bale of hay and watch *Of Mice and Men* or see Henry Fonda acting his heart out in *The Grapes of Wrath*. Steinbeck himself wrote a few scripts, including the highly successful *Viva Zapata!,* which is screened here in an ersatz Mexican plaza. Seven theaters also show clips of classics such as Cannery Row, East of Eden, and The Grapes of Wrath.

In another room you hear the author's moving Nobel Prize acceptance speech and see the actual camper-truck, nicknamed "Rocinante" (for Don

Padre with a Mission

Father Junípero Serra was the George Washington of the California missions, founding the first several in a chain of twenty-one along El Camino Real ("the royal road") from San Diego to Sonoma. He was a daring man of steadfast convictions, yet he is surrounded by controversy; some people want him canonized as a saint, while others say he helped destroy the California Indians.

Serra was born on the Spanish island of Mallorca in 1713 and became a Franciscan priest at a young age. In 1749 he went to Mexico as a missionary and was so successful he was put in charge of a new project to explore and convert the inhabitants of distant California. He established the first mission at San Diego in 1769 and, a year later, sailed to Monterey. Here he founded Mission San Carlos Borromeo del Rio Carmelo near the banks of the Carmel River. Serra settled down at Carmel. Thousands of Indians were baptized in the mission chapel, and they provided cheap labor for a thriving mission economy.

A statue of Serra presides serenely over a shaded garden of the old adobe building. Next to the church in a separate gallery is a memorial to the padre. The Convento Museum has a replica of his living quarters with a simple plank bed and other furniture, as well as a leather thong he used to tame temptations of the flesh through self-flagellation. On a wooden table is a reliquary containing some splintered remains from his original coffin.

Father Serra, who died in 1784, lies buried inside the mission beside his colleagues. Within fifty years of his death, mission life was gone forever, and the native population was decimated by disease and cultural trauma.

In 1988 Serra was beatified by the Catholic Church and awaits the highest of all honors—sainthood. Yet opponents say that while his motives may have been sincere, his ultimate legacy was disastrous.

Quixote's horse), that Steinbeck used to tour America for his book *Travels with Charley.* Another prized item is the original manuscript of his novelette *The Pearl,* just one of more than 30,000 items housed in the archival collection. These include letters, personal artifacts, oral histories (interviews), galley proofs with handwritten corrections, movie posters and scripts, and rare first editions. Steinbeck called Salinas "the Valley of the World," and the Valley of the World Agricultural History and Education Center explores this phenomenon. If farming is your thing, you can examine unique tools or take part in interactive activities like designing your own crate labels or "design vegetable shipping crate labels."

The National Steinbeck Center, 1 Main Street, Salinas, is open daily in summer from 10:00 a.m. to 5:00 p.m. and from Tuesday through Saturday the rest of the year; admission charged. For details call (831) 796-3833 or visit www .steinbeck.org.

The **Steinbeck Festival,** a four-day event held each August, celebrates the author with speakers, films, special events, and tours; call (831) 775-4724 for more information. Another good month to visit Salinas is July, when California's largest rodeo erupts in a fury of bucking bulls and broncos, and cowboys roping calves, wrestling steers, and racing around barrels. For further information contact the rodeo at (800) 771-8807 and www.carodeo.com, or the Salinas Valley Chamber of Commerce, 119 East Alisal Street, Salinas, CA 93902; (831) 751-7725; www.salinaschamber.com.

To continue south through the valley, an idyllic alternate route along the **River Road** takes you by fields of vegetables and grapevines. This scenic trip starts about 5 miles west of Salinas off Highway 68 and follows the course of the Salinas River south to Soledad. Historic sites along the way include farmhouses, an early mission (at Soledad), and hot springs.

Monterey County, and the Salinas Valley in particular, has emerged as the country's leading wine-grape–growing region, with about 40,000 acres under cultivation. The valley owns the distinction of being the world's first premium grape-growing region developed through scientific study. Back in the 1930s, two University of California professors found that parts of it exactly matched the climate of prime growing regions in Europe. But not until the 1960s was the potential realized. Now there are about a dozen **Salinas Valley wineries,** with many offering tastings and tours. Look for River Road wine route signposts.

One pleasant detour from the River Road is to the **Blackstone Winery** in Gonzales, at 800 South Alta Road, open daily for wine tasting from 11:00 a.m. to 4:00 p.m.; call (831) 675-5341 for information.

There are other outstanding wineries in the valley. **Hahn Estates/Smith & Hook Winery** near Soledad overlooks the spot where missionaries planted the first grapes. Tasting is offered daily from 11:00 a.m. to 4:00 p.m., and to 5:00 p.m. on weekends; call (831) 678-4555 for information. (A stop at this winery and Soledad Mission makes a nice conclusion to the River Road tour.) *Chalone Vineyard,* the patriarch of Monterey wineries, bottles some of the most respected American wines. Tastings on weekends are from 11:30 a.m. to 5:00 p.m., weekdays by appointment; call (831) 678-1717 for further details.

Chalone Vineyard lies near *Pinnacles National Monument,* whose western side is reached via Highway 146 (east from US 101) at Soledad. An alternate route to the Pinnacles' eastern side is via Highway 25 through Hollister and the San Benito Valley. The route dips and rolls through fields and vineyards, passing sleepy hamlets like Tres Pinos and Paicines. This is ranch and farm country free from urban blights, the air scented with a strange mixture of flowers and fertilizer—a place where things are grown rather than made.

English explorer George Vancouver discovered this incredible geological showcase back in 1794, long inhabited intermittently by Chalone and Mutsen Native Americans. The Pinnacles are one of America's first national monuments the remnants of an ancient volcano, carved and hammered by the elements over eons of time into jagged stone spires.

Rocky peaks and solitary minarets rise against the sky to 1,200 feet above a canyon floor, pockmarked with talus caves and deep clefts cut by seasonal streams. The starkly angular shapes in a barren, craggy landscape form a striking contrast with the soft rolling hills of the Gabilan range, making the place seem otherworldly. But the Pinnacles has another side—spring wildflowers sprouting in the crevices, golden eagles and prairie falcons wheeling across the sky, miles of superb hiking trails through awe-inspiring terrain. It's a place that challenges the spirit as well as the body.

Incredibly, the Pinnacles sits about 200 miles north of its original location. About twenty-three million years ago, a volcano in what is now Southern California spewed forth countless tons of rock and lava through fissures in the surface. California straddles the

trivia

The Monterey area has provided the backdrop for almost 200 movies, among them *East of Eden, Treasure Island,* and *Play Misty for Me,* which was filmed not far from Clint Eastwood's real home.

600-mile-long San Andreas Fault, a juncture of two large sections of the earth's crust. The Pacific Plate, moving north about 2 inches per year, has carried half of this lava flow with it. The Pinnacles' geological twin east of the fault remains where it was originally formed, buried beneath some hills near Lancaster in the south.

One reason the 4-by-6-mile park remains so wild is that it is not crossed by any road. Entry is from the west side at Chaparral Ranger Station or from the east, where park headquarters is located. Each side has its own personality and attractions: The west is better for basic camping or one-day visits. The more developed eastern side has a visitor center, as well as a private RV park and a small store. Both sides provide picnic sites and restrooms but don't allow pets on trails.

A series of scenic trails link the two sides of the Pinnacles. Hiking and rock climbing are extremely popular, and trails of all skill levels lead you through some inspiring scenery. Bear Gulch Caves, for example, are rimmed with red cliffs splashed with green lichens. The popular caves are actually narrow canyons roofed over by fallen boulders. Balconies Cave, on the west side, was similarly formed, and you'll have to crawl, duck, and squeeze in pitch black along a few hundred feet of the trail (flashlight required). Watch out for Townsend's big-eared bats in Bear Gulch Cave, which is closed from mid-May to Mid July while mothers nurture their young! Among the many good hiking prospects on the east side are Bench Trail and Six Bridges Nature Walk through stands of buckeye trees, live oaks, and giant chain ferns. More challenging trails to the high peaks leave from both sides and converge beneath North Chalone Peak at 3,304 feet.

You will likely spot animals common to the dense chaparral-brush habitat, such as black-tailed deer, and, if you're lucky, prowling bobcats or wild boars scavenging for acorns. The Ventura Wildlife Society has released condors into the Pinnacles.

Be sure to bring water; you can work up quite a thirst in this desiccated country. Late fall through spring is the best time to visit, because summer heat can be brutal. For more information contact the park rangers at (831) 389-4485 or visit www.nps.gov/pinn.

One final treat awaits adventurous travelers: ***Mission San Antonio de Padua,*** near King City, marooned in the nineteenth century as if history and modern California had passed it by. Other missions in the string of Spanish colonial outposts may be prettier, but here a sense of isolation is pervasive, as it must have been when Father Serra founded it back in 1771. One good reason why the mission seems so cut off from the world: It sits completely surrounded by a U.S. Army base, Fort Hunter-Liggett. In fact, you will have to pass through a military police checkpoint to enter the mission lands.

This splendid valley, leeward of the Santa Lucia Range, is well watered and filled with grassy, oak-dotted hills. By the year 1800, Mission San Antonio was known for its wheat and livestock, with thousands of head of cattle, sheep, and horses. Some 1,300 Indians worked the fields under the watchful eyes of the Catholic padres.

Sitting on a piece of flat ground, the nicely restored mission (with some of its original roof tiles) looks as if its inhabitants simply walked away one day. A small chapel anchors one corner of the compound, its three-bell campanario reaching skyward as if in prayer. The adjacent quadrangle includes a museum, guest rooms for the occasional religious retreat, and narrow passageways musty with the smell of bat droppings.

In the museum you can wander through several dark rooms displaying the best of mission life: handmade hymnals on sheepskin parchment, irons used to press the hosts for Holy Communion, and simple musical instruments that the padres taught their wards to play. Outside is further evidence that civilization passed this way: remains of an aqueduct, a water-powered gristmill, tanning pits, an oak stump for slaughtering livestock, and the original oak wine vat.

Mission San Antonio de Padua, located near the town of Jolon, is reached via County Roads G14 (north) or G18 (south) about 20 miles off US 101. It is open daily from 8:00 a.m. to 5:00 p.m., with a small admission charged. For more information and to confirm hours, call (831) 385-4478 and check www .missionsanantonio.net.

Places to Stay on the South Coast

SAN MATEO/SANTA CRUZ COAST

Beach House at Half Moon Bay
4100 North Cabrillo Highway
Half Moon Bay
(800) 315-9366

Costanoa Coastal Lodge
2001 Rossi Road
Pescadero
(650) 879-1100

The Darling House
314 West Cliff Drive
Santa Cruz
(831) 458-1958

Harbor View Inn
51 Avenue Alhambra
El Granada
(800) 886-6997

Old Thyme Inn
779 Main Street
Half Moon Bay
(650) 726-1616

Pescadero Creek Inn
393 Stage Road
Pescadero
(888) 307-1898

MONTEREY PENINSULA/ BIG SUR

Artichoke Inn
10341 Merritt Street
Castroville
(831) 633-3300

Bay Park Hotel
1425 Munras Avenue
Monterey
(800) 338-3564

Best Western Victorian Inn
487 Foam Street
Monterey
(800) 232-4141

Big Sur Lodge
47225 Highway 1
Pfeiffer Big Sur State Park
Big Sur
(800) 424-4787

Blue Sky Lodge
10 Flight Road
Carmel Valley
(831) 659-2256

Carmel Mission Inn
3665 Rio Road
Carmel
(800) 348-9090

WORTH SEEING/DOING ON THE SOUTH COAST

17-Mile Drive, Carmel

Año Nuevo State Natural Reserve,
San Mateo Coast

Cannery Row, Monterey

Fisherman's Wharf, Monterey

Monterey Bay Aquarium

Mystery Spot, Santa Cruz

Pebble Beach Golf Courses

Santa Cruz Beach Boardwalk

Carmel Valley Lodge
Carmel Valley Road/Ford
Road
Carmel Valley
(800) 641-4646

Casa Munras
700 Munras Avenue
Monterey
(800) 222-2446

Colton Inn
707 Pacific Street
Monterey
(831) 649-6500

Hotel Pacific
300 Pacific Street
Monterey
(831) 373-5700

La Playa Hotel
Camino Real at Eighth
Carmel-by-the-Sea
(800) 582-8900

Monterey Peninsula Inns
1100 Lighthouse Avenue
Pacific Grove
(800) 575-1805

Pine Inn
Ocean Avenue and Monte
Verde
Carmel-by-the-Sea
(800) 228-3851

Ventana Inn & Spa
Highway 1 South
Big Sur
(800) 628-6500

INLAND VALLEYS

**Casa de Fruta
Peacock Inn and
RV Orchard Resort,**
10021 Pacheco Pass
Highway
Hollister
(800) 548-3813

Good Nite Inn
545 Work Street
Salinas
(831) 758-6483

Hilton Garden Inn
6070 Monterey Road
Gilroy
(408) 840-7000

Inn at the Pinnacles
32025 Stonewell Canyon
Road
Soledad
(831) 678-2400

Keefer's Inn
615 Canal Street
King City
(831) 385-4843

Laurel Inn Motel
801 West Laurel Drive
Salinas
(831) 449-2474

Posada de San Juan
310 Fourth Street
San Juan Bautista
(831) 623-4030

San Juan Inn
410 The Alameda
San Juan Bautista
(831) 623-4380

Places to Eat on the South Coast

**SAN MATEO/SANTA
CRUZ COAST**

**Casa Blanca Restaurant
(Continental),**
101 Main Street at Beach
Santa Cruz
(831) 426-9063

Malabar Cafe (Sri Lankan)
514 Front Street
Santa Cruz
(831) 423-7906

Miramar Beach
Restaurant (American)
131 Mirada Road
Half Moon Bay
(650) 726-9053

Moss Beach Distillery
(seafood)
140 Beach Way
Moss Beach
(650) 728-5595

Pasta Moon (Italian)
315 Main Street
Half Moon Bay
(650) 726-5125

Sam's Chowder House
(seafood)
4210 North Cabrillo
Highway
Half Moon Bay
(650) 712-0245

Sanderlings (Continental)
1 Seascape Resort Drive
Aptos
(831) 662-7120

Stagnaro Brothers
Seafood
Municipal Wharf
Santa Cruz
(831) 423-1188

**MONTEREY PENINSULA/
BIG SUR**

Domenico's on the Wharf
(seafood)
50 Fisherman's Wharf
Monterey
(831) 372-3655

Fandango (seafood)
223 Seventeenth Street
Pacific Grove
(831) 372-3456

Il Fornaio (Italian)
Ocean Avenue and Monte
Verde
Carmel
(831) 622-5100

Jose's Mexican
Bar & Grill (Mexican)
638 Wave Street
Monterey
(831) 655-4419

La Bicyclette (French)
Dolores Street at 7th
Avenue
Carmel
(831) 622-9899

Lugano Swiss Bistro
(Swiss/Continental)
3670 The Barnyard
Carmel
(831) 626-3779

HELPFUL WEB SITES ON THE SOUTH COAST

Big Sur Chamber of Commerce: www
.bigsurcalifornia.org

Carmel Valley Chamber of Commerce:
www.carmelvalleychamber.com

Carmel Walks: www.carmelwalks.com

Half Moon Bay Coastside Chamber of
Commerce & Visitors Bureau:
www.halfmoonbaychamber.org

Monterey Bay Aquarium:
www.mbayaq.org

Monterey County Convention &
Visitors Bureau: www.montereyinfo.org

Moss Landing Chamber of Commerce:
www.mosslandingchamber.com

Pacific Grove Chamber of Commerce:
www.pacificgrove.org

Salinas Valley Chamber of
Commerce: www.salinaschamber.com

San Benito County Chamber of
Commerce:
www.sanbenitocountychamber.com

San Mateo County Convention
&Visitors Bureau:
www.sanmateocountycvb.com

Santa Cruz County Conference and
Visitors Council: www.scccvc.org

Massaro & Santos (seafood)
32 Cannery Row
Monterey
(831) 649-6700

Mission Ranch Restaurant (American)
26270 Dolores Street
Carmel-by-the-Sea
(800) 538-8221

Moss Landing Cafe (American)
421 Moss Landing Road,
Moss Landing
(831) 633-3355

The Mucky Duck (British pub)
479 Alvarado Street,
Monterey
(831) 655-3031

Nepenthe (American)
Pacific Coast Highway,
Big Sur
(831) 667-2345

Passionfish (seafood)
701 Lighthouse Avenue,
Pacific Grove
(831) 655-3311

Rappa's Restaurant (seafood)
101 Fisherman's Wharf,
Monterey
(831) 372-7562

Running Iron Restaurant (American)
24 East Carmel Valley
Road
Carmel Valley
(831) 659-4633

Stokes Restaurant & Bar (Californian-Mediterranean/seafood)
500 Hartnell Street,
Monterey
(831) 373-1110

INLAND VALLEYS

The Elegant Touch (American)
601-A San Benito Street
Hollister
(831) 637-6246

Jardines de San Juan (Mexican)
115 Third Street
San Juan Bautista
(831) 623-4466

Salinas Valley Fish House (seafood)
172 Main Street
Salinas
(831) 775-0175

The Steinbeck House (American)
132 Central Avenue
Salinas
(831) 424-2735

NORTH COAST

The North Coast stretches almost 400 miles from Marin County to the Oregon border. Within this huge domain, nicknamed the Redwood Empire, you will find some of California's outstanding scenery—sheer cliffs and craggy coastline, weathered fishing villages and square-jawed lumber ports, wine-country vineyards, and groves of redwoods as majestic as Gothic cathedrals.

You reach the North Coast via the twisting, incredibly picturesque Highway 1, or the faster and less scenic U.S. Highway 101. Numerous country roads connect the two before they join at Leggett in the heart of redwood country. Linking both roads makes a loop tour taking in the lion's share of the scenic wonders.

Marin County

To reach the North Coast, take US 101 north from the Golden Gate Bridge and exit at Mill Valley/Stinson Beach (Highway 1). After reaching Muir Beach proceed 8 miles north to *Audubon Canyon Ranch,* which shelters a rookery of great egrets and great blue herons, huge birds with wingspans of up to 6

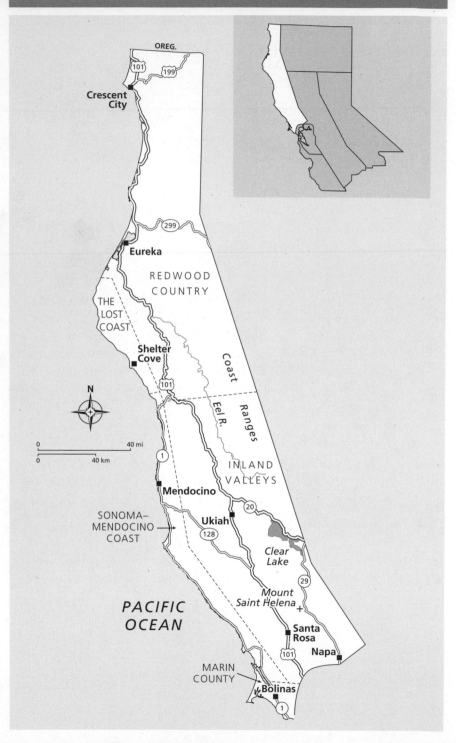

OREG.

101

199

Crescent City

299

Eureka

REDWOOD COUNTRY

THE LOST COAST

Coast

Shelter Cove

101

Ranges

Eel R.

N

0   40 mi
0   40 km

1

INLAND VALLEYS

Mendocino

20

SONOMA– MENDOCINO COAST

Ukiah

128

Clear Lake

PACIFIC OCEAN

29

Mount Saint Helena

Santa Rosa

101

Napa

MARIN COUNTY

1

Bolinas

feet. It's considered the best place on the Pacific coast to view these birds. The sanctuary is open mid-March to mid-July from 10:00 a.m. to 4:00 p.m. on weekends, and by appointment from Tuesday through Friday. Call (415) 868-9244 and consult www.egret.org for details.

Audubon Canyon Ranch sits on the east shore of Bolinas Lagoon, a shallow sheet of water enclosed by a sandpit that is home to an abundance of bird and marine life. On the inlet's other side is the curious village of *Bolinas,* 2 miles west of the highway at the end of Olema–Bolinas Road. But don't look for a sign pointing the way; reclusive residents keep tearing it down to confuse would-be visitors.

At the turn of the twentieth century, *Bolinas* was filled with hotels and saloons, then later declined. During the 1960s hippies flocked here, and many stayed; you can see their legacy in funky shops such as Kaleidoscope, redolent with incense, and Bolinas People's Store, featuring organic foods. Artists and craftspeople abound, and their work appears at a tiny museum at 48 Wharf Road, open Friday through Sunday afternoons. Call the Bolinas Museum at (415) 868-0330 or preview exhibitions at www.bolinasmuseum.org.

This main street also features a couple of good places to eat, including the Coast Cafe (46 Wharf Road; 415-868-2298; www.bolinascafe.com). Smiley's Schooner Saloon, down the block at 41 Wharf Road, is a local hangout with live music on weekends. You can also stay at the adjacent six-room hotel (415-868-1311; www.coastalpost.com/smileys). Some wealthy retirees live here, too, and there's an impressive collection of clapboard homes along Brighton Avenue, which leads down to the ocean past Calvary Church (1874).

According to U.S. Weather Bureau statistics, the Point Reyes Peninsula ranks as the foggiest and windiest spot on the entire Pacific Coast. Although Point Reyes lies in Marin County, only about 40 miles from San Francisco, it seems completely separated from the Bay Area. And even though visitors love

AUTHOR'S TOP TEN ON THE NORTH COAST

Point Reyes National Seashore	Redwood National and State Parks
Fort Ross State Historic Park	Boonville
Mendocino coast	Sonoma Plaza
The Lost Coast	Jack London State Historic Park
Ferndale	Mount Saint Helena

the peninsula, it is large enough and wild enough to offer miles of untouched beaches and hundreds of hideaways. Most of the roughly triangular landmass belongs to one of **Point Reyes National Seashore**'s two distinct areas: the wind-lashed beaches, treeless hills, and dairy farms to the north, or the forested slopes of Bear Valley to the south (near Olema and park headquarters).

La punta de los reyes (kings' point) owes its name to Spaniard Sebastian Vizcaino, who sailed past on January 6, 1603, the Feast of the Three Kings.

Searching for Nova Albion

In the summer of 1579, Sir Francis Drake anchored his ship *The Golden Hinde* somewhere along the coast of Northern California. This rollicking English buccaneer, who served Queen Elizabeth I, had been raiding Spanish American outposts, and his leaking vessel was overloaded with treasure and in need of repairs. Upon disembarking he named the land *Nova Albion* and claimed it for England a full forty-one years before the first Pilgrims landed at Plymouth Rock.

The exact site of Drake's landfall is uncertain and is hotly debated by local historians and mariners. Unfortunately, the ship's logs describing important details were lost after being turned over to the queen. According to the journal of Chaplain Fletcher, a landing party went ashore and set up tents along the beach as curious Indians watched. One man hammered out a metal plate detailing Drake's claims, which was nailed to a post stuck in the sand and, by the logic of the day, "this kingdome . . . Nova Albion" became property of England.

The brass plate Drake left behind was found in 1936 and authenticated, but it turned up at an inland site, obviously moved during the ensuing centuries and of questionable origin. The puzzle is further complicated by a confusing chart of *The Golden Hinde*'s landing site drawn by a Dutch cartographer. It seems to be a treasure map, recording the site of several tons of silver bars buried by Drake and his men. Several later expeditions failed to recover the buried treasure due to the faulty records. (According to another theory, one ship did find it around 1600, but it sank under the weight off Duxbury Point Reef nearby.)

Now a historical marker honoring the landing sits above the beach at Drake's Estero, a small estuary within Drake's Bay at the southern end of Point Reyes National Seashore. Along its leeward curve, white cliffs, much like those in Dover, England, protect the bay, and these may have inspired the name New Albion. Enthusiasts of the local Drake Navigators' Guild also claim that shards of Chinese porcelain found here (taken as booty) pinpoint the exact spot of Drake's camp at the entrance to the estuary.

But other people challenge the claim, proposing alternate sites like Agate Beach in Bolinas, 10 miles to the south. Here black rock ballast and stone cannonballs, along with a mariner's dial and other artifacts, have surfaced. Some other people say the landing took place within San Francisco Bay or as far south as Half Moon Bay. So until more evidence is unearthed, the debate will rage on.

But even he was a Johnny-come-lately—more than twenty years earlier, Sir Francis Drake had arrived aboard *The Golden Hinde* and claimed these lands for Queen Elizabeth. According to legend the rollicking seafarer nailed a brass plaque to a tree near the inlet we now call Drake's Bay.

History of quite another sort created Point Reyes. The infamous San Andreas Fault splits Olema Valley and Tomales Bay, geologically separating the peninsula from the mainland. Point Reyes sits perched on the Pacific Plate, which is moving about 2 to 3 inches northward per year and has its own distinctive plant life and minerals. For example, redwoods thrive on Bolinas Ridge to the east, but not on the peninsula.

Near the national seashore's visitor center you can walk the Earthquake Trail and see where the 1906 San Francisco earthquake moved a wooden fence 16 feet. (The only casualty was a cow that fell into a gash in the earth and had to be pulled out by its tail.)

Also near the visitor center is Kule Loklo, a re-created **Coast Miwok Indian Village.** Sitting in a quiet meadow, the settlement consists of huts made tepee-style from rough planks or thatched reeds, a granary for storing acorns, a ceremonial dance house, and a sweat house—all built using aboriginal tools and methods.

Bear Valley Trail (named for the once numerous grizzlies) cuts through Inverness Ridge from the visitor center to the ocean. The 4.4-mile path is the park's most popular, passing through woods and meadows to an agate-strewn beach, tide pools, and Arch Rock—carved by crashing Pacific waves. Here begins a breathtaking 11-mile hike called the Coast Trail, with exceptional rock formations, tide pools, and even a waterfall.

But Point Reyes is not only for hikers. You can drive through the little town of Inverness, founded by a judge who noted the area's resemblance to the Scottish Highlands, or out Limantour Road to a long, sandy spit. Facing almost due south, Drake's Bay has a flat, sandy beach abutting sandstone bluffs.

The most popular drive winds 21.5 miles out to **Point Reyes Lighthouse,** cowering from the elements at the southwestern corner of the peninsula. A winter shuttle bus circles from Drakes Beach to the Lighthouse and Chimney Rock (see www.nps.gov/pore/planyourvisit/shuttle.htm). Before the lighthouse went up in 1870, about forty ships had been smashed into kindling against the rocks here. To keep below the fog ceiling, the lighthouse sits at 294 feet above sea level and is reached from an even higher platform via a vertiginous staircase of 308 steps.

A catwalk and railing around the lighthouse provide an outstanding vantage point for whale watching in season. The big gray ones (*Eschrichtius*

TOP ANNUAL EVENTS ON THE NORTH COAST

Napa Valley Mustard Festival
(February–March)

Mendocino Coast Whale Festivals,
Mendocino/Fort Bragg (March)

Redwood Coast Jazz Festival, Eureka
(March)

Aleutian Goose Festival, Crescent City
(late March)

Kinetic Grand Championship, Arcata
to Ferndale (Late May)

Arcata Bay Oyster Festival (June)

World's Largest Salmon Barbecue,
Noyo Harbor, Fort Bragg (July)

Fort Ross Cultural Heritage Day
(late July)

Wildwood Days, Rio Dell (July–August)

Paul Bunyan Days, Fort Bragg
(early September)

**Mendocino County Fair and Apple
Show,** Boonville (September)

Festival of Lights, Yountville
(December)

robustus)—as many as eighty a day during the mid-January peak—can pass within a few hundred yards. It's fortunate for whale watchers that there's nothing to see in summer, when this spot becomes the foggiest in the United States. The only time you can see anything is when the winds are so strong you may get blown out to sea; gusts up to 133 miles per hour have been recorded. The lighthouse is open Thursday through Monday from 10:00 a.m. to 4:00 p.m., but it may be closed during high winds.

Point Reyes is packed with sightseeing options, but one highlight is the **Tule Elk Preserve** at the northern end of the Tomales Peninsula, reached by a jaw-dropping drive along a wooded ridge top. Then take the Pierce Ranch Trail for a closer look. Elk calves and young bulls begin to appear in May, and by late summer the dominant males start to gather their harems for breeding. Sometimes the bulls battle by locking horns to secure their territory and favorite females. There are about 400 elks in the herd.

For further information about activities and camping throughout the park, call the Bear Valley Visitor Center at (415) 464-5100 or check the national seashore web site at www.nps.gov/pore. The entire Point Reyes area enjoys an abundance of atmospheric hotels and bed-and-breakfast inns, though they tend to be pricey. The Blackthorne Inn in Inverness (415-663-8621; www .blackthorneinn.com) floats among the trees like a sailing ship, and one room called the Eagle's Nest is reached by climbing a narrow spiral staircase. Among other choices are the Olema Inn (Olema; 415-663-9559; www.theolemainn .com), Ten Inverness Way (Inverness; 415-669-1648; www.teninvernessway

.com), and the Holly Tree Inn & Cottages (Point Reyes Station; 800-286-4655; www.hollytreeinn.com). Contact Point Reyes Lodging for a partial list of area hostelries at (800) 539-1872; www.ptreyes.com.

Due to its shallow inlets and cool water, this area is ideal for raising oysters, which feed on the abundant plankton found here. At special **oyster farms** they are strung together and hung on racks in the bay to grow into mature clusters ready for harvest. A pioneer of this technique is the Drake's Bay Oyster Company on Drake's Estero, located within the national seashore, just off Sir Francis Drake Boulevard—but check before arriving because the National Park Service may require a relocation of the company's operations to protect the seashore wilderness designation. Oysters are rough on the outside but tasty inside, and here you can buy them shucked or in the shell to eat on the spot or take home. Open daily from 8:00 a.m. to 4:30 p.m.; call (415) 669-1149 or consult http://drakesbayfamilyfarms.com for more information.

Tomales Bay tends to be warmer and less windy than the peninsula, and the eastern shoreline along Highway 1 is home to several more oyster farms. Best of the bunch may be Hog Island Oyster Company in the historic town of Marshall (20215 Highway 1; 415-663-9218; www.hogislandoysters.com). Here, or at Hog Island Bar in San Francisco's Ferry Building, feast on oysters live in the shell or barbecued (bring your own sauce and napkins) as well as clams and mussels.

Sonoma–Mendocino Coast

Highway 1 between Bodega Bay and Fort Bragg offers stunning seaside scenery as well as nineteen state and county parks with delightful opportunities for hikers, campers, anglers, and photographers. The stretch south of Jenner, at the mouth of the Russian River, traverses a gentle shelf fringed by sandy beaches, then bucks and snakes through a landscape of sheer cliffs and pounding waves.

A recommended side trip from the coast starts at the village of **Bodega,** the setting for Hitchcock's thriller *The Birds* (you can see the old Potter School used in the film). Farther east along Highway 12 is Freestone, where you can partake of a unique Japanese-style cedar enzyme bath and massage at a spa called Osmosis; call (707) 823-8231 or review www.osmosis.com for more information. Turn north here onto the Bohemian Highway to reach the town of **Occidental,** following an old railroad route through thick stands of redwood trees. Area residents flock here for the scenic location and collection of family-style restaurants, coffeehouses, and shops. Particularly appealing for an outdoor lunch is the patio restaurant at the Union Hotel (707-874-3444; www

.unionhotel.com). Continue north 6 miles to the Russian River and turn west on Highway 116 toward a small settlement called ***Duncans Mills.*** Several historic buildings, including the Northwest Pacific Rail Depot, and railway cars house the Duncans Mills Museum, at one time the last stop on the Russian River line from San Francisco, 77 miles to the south. Good places to eat include Gold Coast Coffee (707-865-1441) and Cape Fear Café (707-865-9246), and an interesting shop to browse in is called Worldly Goods (707-865-3025). Return to the coast and the town of Jenner at the mouth of the Russian River by driving west on Highway 116.

The Russians were here! The Russians were here! ***Fort Ross State Historic Park,*** sitting on a bluff overlooking the Pacific, re-creates the substantial Russian colony located here in California's early days. The setting, about 12 miles north of Jenner in Sonoma County, is a dramatic one—a weathered gray fortress with the sea at its feet and a backdrop of forested hills. Fort Ross was the largest Russian settlement outside Alaska and caused the Spanish much heartburn about the safety of Alta California. But in the end, neither nation would control this rich land.

In 1812 Ivan Kuskov and a shipload of colonists landed to establish a beachhead on the Pacific coast for the powerful Russian American Trading Company. Raising food was one objective, but most of the Russians and Native Alaskans arrived eager to exploit the lucrative sea otter pelt trade. Over the next few years, the outsiders, using two-man kayaks and harpoons, slaughtered the otters nearly to the point of extinction.

The Russians remained almost thirty years, and Fort Ross became the centerpiece of a sizable community during its heyday. Despite intense rivalry, a lively trade developed with the Spanish, and products from Fort Ross were highly prized by *Californios.*

Fort Ross has been carefully reconstructed with some intact original elements, such as the Rotchev House, home of the last commandant and his gracious wife, Princess Helena. The domed chapel is the most interesting building architecturally; built in 1824, it was completely destroyed by a fire in 1970. One of the original bells, which melted in the blaze, was recast for display outside the church. Inside, where the Russians once prayed, are religious icons and flickering candles.

But the Russian experiment did not last. By the 1830s, sea otters were thought to be extinct, and gophers were destroying the crops. In 1841 the colonists tried unsuccessfully to sell the fort to Mexico. Later it was unloaded for $30,000 to none other than John Sutter of Sacramento, who would have his own rendezvous with history several years later when he discovered gold. In a few months the Russians were gone, and the future of California changed course.

Fort Ross State Historic Park is open daily from 10:00 a.m. to 4:30 p.m.; entry fee is $7 per car. For information call (707) 847-3286.

One final sight before leaving Sonoma County, 29 miles north of Jenner, is the **Sea Ranch,** a high-end residential and vacation development famed for its innovative architecture: highly modern yet clad in sea-weathered wood. Back in the 1960s developers purchased 5,000 acres, a 10-mile stretch of coastline, and began to build amid some controversy. Yet the final product is a fine example of low-impact development. There is a luxury hotel, golf course, and even a chapel, to supplement incredible ocean views.

The **Mendocino coast** is steeped in a kind of sleepy beauty—with emerald forests cooled by ocean mists, the blue green water and white surf of the Pacific, and weathered redwood barns and fences. Sheep graze languidly on the hillsides while seals splash offshore. The whole coast is so scenic that television and movie crews flock to places like Mendocino (used to simulate New England for the TV series *Murder, She Wrote*).

Highway 1 enters Mendocino County at **Gualala** (pronounced wa-LA-la), a relatively balmy village where the wealthy and famous have been known to hang out. To the north sits stately **Point Arena Lighthouse,** and you can huff and puff up the 115-foot tower to eye-popping views of the coastline. It's open daily from 10:00 a.m. to 3:30 p.m.; $5 admission. Call (877) 725-4448 or check lighthouse, keeper home accommodations, and area information at www .pointarenalighthouse.com. Manchester State Beach, a 5-mile sweep of sand and surf, is the first in a string of fine state parks along this magical coast.

trivia

Noyo Harbor north of Mendocino near Fort Bragg was used to film the wild boat ride of Jack Nicholson and other crazy inmates in the classic 1970s movie *One Flew Over the Cuckoo's Nest.*

Lumber profoundly shaped Mendocino's modern history. In 1850 an expedition seeking a foundered ship brought back reports of vast redwood forests—just the kind of news needed by the lumber-hungry boomtown of San Francisco. Wherever a river or stream met the ocean, a mill and small town sprouted, each with a doghole port just large enough for a ship to anchor.

Though most mills shut down by the 1960s, there are still remnants of docks and piers running out into cramped coves. The Victorian village of **Elk,** about 15 miles south of Mendocino, is a classic doghole port town, sprawling on a high bluff overlooking a rock-strewn cove where lumber was once king. Now it offers solitude and fabulous views.

Little River is another photogenic coastal hamlet with its fair share of country-style inns. Among them is the Inn at Schoolhouse Creek (800-731-

5525; www.schoolhousecreek.com) on the site of a former Coast Guard look-out station. Just opposite Little River Cove a few miles south of Mendocino lies *Van Damme State Park,* where nature is practicing its own curious form of bonsai with the native cypresses and pines. In the Pygmy Forest, fully mature trees range from just 6 inches to a few feet in height, stunted by shallow root penetration, a lack of nutrients, and the world's most acidic soil. The contrast with the giant stands of redwoods nearby is unnerving. Van Damme also offers a delightful 5-mile round-trip hike up to Fern Canyon, where a junglelike pro-fusion of lush foliage crowds the banks of Little River. The park is open daily from dawn till dusk for a $6 per car day-use fee; for information call (707) 937-5804.

Another nearby park is definitely worth a stop. *Jug Handle State Natural Reserve* offers a special nature trail called the Ecological Staircase on which hikers can trace half a million years of geological history along five wave-cut terraces. Going from the shoreline inland, each one is 100 feet higher and 100,000 years older and features different rock formations and flora.

The town of *Mendocino* is a real charmer, with a white-steepled church and clapboard houses, unique shops (like one selling only local jams and preserves) and cozy country inns. The town sits next to scenic Mendocino Headlands. Downtown offers an intriguing collection of galleries, some selling crafts and others, like the Highlight Gallery (45052 Main Street; 707-937-3132; www.thehighlightgallery.com), offering sophisticated fine art. Pour a Guinness and sample pub grub at Patterson's (10485 Lansing Street; 707-937-4782; www.pattersonspub.com) or dine out in style at one of several gourmet restaurants. For all of these reasons, on weekends Mendocino can become overrun with tourists, so try to come during the week. Even though everyone talks about how it looks "just like" a New England fishing village, it really does not. The streets are too wide and straight, and the houses are set too far apart and don't have shutters.

trivia

The tallest totem pole in the United States (160 feet) is found at McKinleyville in Humboldt County.

Rough-and-tumble *Noyo Harbor,* on the other hand, could have been lifted from the Maine coast. This little fishing port just south of Fort Bragg is chockablock with trollers, drag boats, and Boston whalers tied up two and three deep along the wharves. Weathered canneries, warehouses, and salty-dog restaurants jostle for position along the waterfront with marine hardware stores and fish markets. A handful of shops sell things like smoked salmon and burl art, a world apart from Mendocino.

Quaintness comes hard in Noyo. This is a place of scavenging gulls and marine shortwaves, cannery workers in rubber boots and derelict trailers, battered pickups and rotting nets. A sign on the door of the local grocery says it all: ABSOLUTELY NO WETSUITS OR MUDDY FEET! Many of the muddy feet come from divers for sea urchins, those spiny purple creatures whose private parts are in great demand for Japanese sushi. But there are no sushi bars in Noyo, nor does fish come served with delicate sauces of garlic and herbs; most likely it will arrive breaded and deep-fried, served in a basket with tartar sauce and fries. For good food try the outside view of harbor traffic at Sharon's By the Sea (707-962-0680; www.sharonsbythesea .com) or Cap'n Flints (707-964-9447). Noyo also claims the World's Largest Salmon Barbecue, a giant fish feed every Fourth of July weekend.

To catch your own, try one of several charter boat services, which also do

trivia

Less than 5 percent of old-growth redwood forest remains unlogged and protected from commercial development.

whale-watching trips in season. There are shops to outfit you for the trip, and others to freeze, can, or smoke your catch. Noyo Harbor lies 1 mile south of Fort Bragg at the end of North Harbor Drive.

Fort Bragg got its start as part of the Mendocino Indian Reservation and later became a military post. Charles Russell Johnson, who built the first mill in 1885, launched the Skunk Railroad (named for the smell of its original gas engines), Fort Bragg's number-one visitor attraction. From a frontier-style depot, the train, powered by a mint-condition 1924 Baldwin steam engine, takes visitors on an inspiring trip to Willits on the other side of the densely forested coastal mountains. The Skunk Train departs Fort Bragg daily from April to October and weekends in March and November. Call (866) 457-5865 or check www.theskunktrain.com. Lumber has always counted here, and the town puts on its best face for events like Paul Bunyan Days on Labor Day weekend, when big crowds gather to watch loggers throwing axes, climbing poles, and rolling logs. The history of this lumber and fishing town is well told at the Guest House Museum, 343 North Main Street (707-964-4251).

Fort Bragg's historic downtown section along Main and Franklin Streets has antiques shops, art galleries, restaurants, and hostelries. The North Coast Brewing Company has taken over the 400 block of North Main Street with towering vats, a store, and a restaurant; brewery tours are available. For more information call (707) 964-2739 or consult www.northcoastbrewing.com.

Several miles of beachfront north of Fort Bragg belong to MacKerricher State Park, which offers the rare chance to explore pristine coast with large sand dunes and crashing waves. It's open without day-use fee to picnickers, beachcombers, and horseback riders.

For further area information contact the Mendocino Coast Chamber of Commerce at (800) 726-2780 or go to www.mendocinocoast.com.

The Lost Coast

After Rockport, 28 miles north of Fort Bragg, Highway 1 turns inland, merging with US 101 at Leggett. The reason is simple—coastal mountains called the *King Range* thrust out to sea like a clenched fist, rising from sea level to 4,000 feet in just 3 miles. This precipitous climb caused construction engineers to shake their heads and change direction, and the resulting slice of highway-free terrain (about 50 miles long) is called the *Lost Coast.*

> trivia
>
> The King Range is one of the most geologically active ranges in the United States. It has risen 66 feet over the last 6,000 years.

Adventurous travelers can explore some of California's wildest landscapes—wave-battered sea stacks and wrecked steamers, jagged cliffs and talus piles—and see an abundance of wildlife including mink, deer, river otter, and black bear. The King Range is one of the wettest spots on the Pacific coast, with about 100 inches annually (mostly between October and April) and almost twice that amount in a really wet year.

The heart of the Lost Coast is the *Sinkyone Wilderness,* one of the most remote pockets in the nation. Usal Road, north of Rockport (at milepost 90.88), is the unpaved route into this area, and it continues in a generally northward direction along the top of a steep ridge. From the crest you can catch glimpses of the uninhabited coast, with its tiny "ghost ports," such as Wheeler at the mouth of Jackass Creek, now just a pile of bleached timbers. There are also some rugged trails and camping facilities for the backpacking set. For more about Sinkyone Wilderness State Park, call (707) 986-7711.

The quiet village of *Shelter Cove* nestles on a small bay between the two main wilderness areas comprising the Lost Coast. Reached by a tortuous, 24-mile road from Garberville (on US 101), or private plane (!), it is a special place with a palpable sense of isolation and a rare black-sand beach. At one time a vital shipping point, Shelter Cove now draws campers, whale watchers, and fishermen. Nearby are miles of pristine beaches and

> trivia
>
> Some 90 percent of the oysters produced in California are harvested from Humboldt Bay.

small parks, perfect for a getaway picnic, and the shoreline offers an abundance of crab, shellfish, and driftwood.

Much of the Lost Coast belongs to the *King Range National Conservation Area,* stretching north of Shelter Cove about 25 miles to the mouth of the Mattole River. There are a handful of drivable roads and a leg-stretching trail leading to the summit of King Peak. Serious hikers rate the Lost Coast Trail as outstanding. It's primarily a beach route, passing waterfalls, relics of early shipwrecks, an abandoned lighthouse, Indian shell mounds, and abundant marine life. (Be careful; rattlesnakes often hide in piles of driftwood.)

A Whale of a Show

Each year more than 15,000 giant whales weighing up to forty tons—grays and other species—travel thousands of miles between the Bering Sea (Alaska) and warm lagoons in Baja California to mate and give birth to 15-foot calves. Along the craggy coast of Northern California, whale watchers gather to see the parade of these magnificent mammals, who often come close to the shore.

When: The trip south starts in late November and peaks in January; the return takes place in March and early April, by which time the calves have grown to 20 feet and more. The best viewing time is early morning with the sun at your back, when the water is calmest.

Where: The best observation sites are high on cliffs, where the land juts out and lighthouses often stand. Among the best spots (by county from south to north):

- Marin: Point Reyes National Seashore, especially the lighthouse and Drakes Bay

- Sonoma: Salt Point State Park near Jenner and Bodega Head in Sonoma Coast State Park

- Mendocino: Gualala Head, Point Arena Lighthouse, Noyo Harbor entrance, Mendocino Headlands State Park, Laguna Point in MacKerricher State Park, Point Cabrillo Light Station in Caspar

- Humboldt: Shelter Cove and Clam Beach (north of Eureka)

- Del Norte: Castle Rock and Endert's Beach in Redwood National and State Parks (south of Crescent City)

What: You may see just one mother and her calf or a hundred whales traveling in a pod, swimming (at 3 to 4 mph) and frolicking merrily. Among the behaviors to watch for: breathing (approaching the surface to take several breaths before diving); spy hopping (poking the head above the surface and holding the pose as if for a photo op); blowing (exhaling water and air through the top of the head in a V-shaped spout); sounding (diving at a steep angle so that the fluke, or tail, is thrust out of the water); and breaching (leaping from the water and twisting the entire body dramatically in the air). Experts are most puzzled by breaching, but many believe whales do it just for fun!

For information about the King Range National Conservation Area, contact the Bureau of Land Management, 1695 Heindon Road, Arcata, CA 95521 or call (707) 825-2300.

The easiest way to explore the north part of the Lost Coast is by taking a spectacular 70-mile detour from US 101. Mattole Road in Humboldt Redwoods State Park leads to wide-open country of wooded slopes and into the Mattole River Valley, where locals raise livestock, apples, and strange substances not currently considered legal. The hamlet of Honeydew consists of a gas station, post office, and a few refugees from the 1960s. Fifteen miles farther on is Petrolia, site of California's first oil strike and today a sleepy village with sleepy residents and a white-steepled church.

Follow the road a few more miles and the ocean suddenly leaps out in all its splendor. That huge pile of rocks to the north is ***Cape Mendocino,*** the most westerly point in California. Cattle and sheep graze on the hillsides and along the shore, where sand sprays the beach like shrapnel during storms. After about 3 miles the road takes a steep turn back into the mountains. (The approach is even more impressive coming down this grade from the direction of Ferndale.) It's a thrilling drive not to be missed.

Redwood Country

Although not really off the beaten path, a drive along the ***Avenue of the Giants*** in Humboldt Redwoods State Park forms an essential part of any visit to the Redwood Empire. This popular 31-mile scenic alternate runs generally parallel with US 101 and the South Fork of the Eel River, and it's a slow-down-and-look kind of road without any heavy trucks or high-speed traffic. The south entrance lies 6 miles north of Garberville, and the two-lane road then tunnels through several dozen different groves (the park was acquired piecemeal). An auto-tour brochure is available at either end of the avenue or can be printed out from http://avenueofthegiants.net.

trivia

At Humboldt Redwoods State Park is the Travel-log, a 1915 mobile home crafted from a single tree, in which impresario Charles Kellogg traveled the nation to preach the importance of preserving the redwood forests.

Numerous turnouts allow for neck craning, and trails lead to tranquil glens and riverbanks. The giant pillars of redwood form a green canopy overhead, penetrated only by solitary shafts of sunlight filtering down to a lush carpet of mosses and ferns clutching the forest floor.

California can claim two native giants—the mighty Sierra redwood, or giant sequoia, with a diameter up to 35 feet, and the taller, more slender Sequoia sempervirens, or coast redwood, found here. These are the blue-bloods of the tree world, whose ancestors date back to the dinosaur age—"ambassadors from another time," as John Steinbeck put it.

The victory of conservationists in saving the trees is honored at **Founders Grove** near Weott, where an inviting pathway takes you to Founders Tree, 346 feet tall and about 1,500 years old. Among the redwoods live other species such as Douglas fir, madrone, and tan oak, but mainly ferns or fernlike plants survive in the shadowy world below. The most abundant is the redwood sorrel, a cloverlike ground cover lining the pathways. This vegetation creates a kind of damp twilight mood whatever the time of day; the air is heavy and musty, and the only sounds you hear are the twitter of birds, the trickle of a small stream, or the crunch of humus beneath your feet.

You can exit the Avenue of the Giants at a number of spots within the state park, which is Northern California's largest. One detour goes to Rockefeller Forest, a vast expanse of virgin redwoods untouched by logging. That in itself is miraculous, because just one specimen, called the Tall Tree, would yield 235,000 board feet of lumber. Another, the Giant Tree, is one of the largest coast redwoods, with a height of 363 feet, circumference of 53 feet, and crown spread of 62 feet. There is an excellent visitor center near Founders Grove that provides details about out-of-the-way trails and attractions. For

trivia

Rockefeller Forest in Humboldt Redwoods State Park boasts ten of the sixteen tallest trees on earth.

further information contact Humboldt Redwoods State Park Visitors Center at (707) 946-2263 or www.humboldtredwoods.org; the center is open daily April through October from 9:00 a.m. to 5:00 p.m. and from 10:00 a.m. to 4:00 p.m. November through March.

If you want to see what Small Town U.S.A. ought to look like, stop by **Ferndale,** the best-preserved Victorian town in California. Throughout this picturesque village grand old wood-and-shingle ladies have been meticulously renovated and painted in outrageously bright color combinations. Naturally, all this provides a startling counterpoint to the wild Lost Coast immediately to the south and to every merely ordinary town.

Founded in 1852 by Seth Lewis Shaw, Ferndale sits snugly at the base of a forested ridge above the Eel River valley, 4 miles west of US 101. All around are dairy farms, with green pastures, red barns, and white farmhouses. There was a time when Ferndale was dubbed "Cream City," and successful local dairymen erected mansions known as "Butterfat Palaces," done up with gingerbread trim and surrounded by white picket fences. Farming still helps Ferndale to prosper, and nobody here wants subdivisions replacing open space and cows. But times do change, and Ferndale is now hoping to milk some of the tourist trade whizzing past on the way to redwood country.

trivia

More than 8,000 artists call Humboldt County home.

The town's top attraction is a perfect version of Main Street, with no parking meters or traffic lights and a fine collection of shops. Painted ladies stand cheek-by-jowl up and down the street, showing off their bay windows, cupolas, false fronts, and dazzling color combos. Except for the cars this could be a nineteenth-century American street.

There's plenty to see along Main Street, Ferndale: historic relics such as Danish Hall and the Hotel Ivanhoe (707-796-9000; www.ivanhoe-hotel.com), restored to its 1870s glory. There's a Rexall drugstore and shops galore, like the Ferndale Emporium (707-786-9877; www.ferndale-emporium.com), selling everything you never knew you wanted, from stained glass to antique dolls. By mid-morning the Palace Saloon (1890) should be doing a thriving trade again (it claims to be the most westerly in California), after a post-fire restoration undertaken in 2008. There's an abundance of unpretentious eating spots, including Curley's Bar & Grill (400 Ocean Avenue; 707-786-9696) and Cream City Cafe (543 Main Street; 707-786-4442).

Victoriana is hardly restricted to Main Street; one of Northern California's most photographed charmers, the **Gingerbread Mansion,** stands a couple of blocks away at 400 Berding Street. This yellow and peach fantasy of jigsawed woodwork, turrets, and gables belongs to the Queen Anne–Eastlake style. A prim and proper English garden adorns the exterior, and inside is one of the most highly rated bed-and-breakfast inns in Northern California,

trivia

Fern Canyon in Prairie Creek Redwood State Park was chosen by director Steven Spielberg as the primordial backdrop for his film *The Lost World: Jurassic Park.*

prettied up with lace curtains and floral wallpaper, ceiling mirrors, and old clawfoot bathtubs. Call (800) 952-4136 or look at www.gingerbread-mansion.com. Another Victorian charmer, complete with gazebo, is the Shaw House Inn Bed and Breakfast on Main Street (800-557-7429; www.shawhouse.com).

For the best overall view of this idyllic community, drive or walk to the top of the city cemetery, filled with moss-covered tombstones. A bit farther out on the same road lies Russ Park, a bird-watcher's dream, where you will find tranquility and, among Sitka spruce, the ubiquitous ferns whence Ferndale got its name. For information call the Ferndale Chamber of Commerce at (707) 786-4477, or go to www.victorianferndale.org/chamber.

Humboldt County seat **Eureka** makes a good base for exploring redwood country without roughing it. The spectacular **Carson Mansion** on Second Street is the ultimate Victorian. Its architect took all the design elements to their whimsical extremes and created a monument to pomposity (in the eyes of some), but it's the most-photographed building in town. Surprisingly, most of the "wood carving" is actually done with plaster. Today the Carson Mansion is a private club and cannot be visited without an invitation. Right across the street is another gem built for the Carson family. The Carter House is a remarkably good re-creation built using 1884 blueprints. It sits at the corner of Third and L Streets and is one of a group of four Carter House Inns.

Eureka's Old Town near the waterfront is a trove of Victorians, many restored to mint condition, including the Vance Hotel and Oberon Saloon. The new **Eureka Boardwalk** between C and M Streets provides splendid views of Woodley Island and Humboldt Bay, where pelicans dive and harbor seals frolic. Dotted with signal flags and nautical banners, it makes a great place for a stroll. The bay is a haven for wildlife, and a small ferry called *The Madaket* provides a narrated cruise. Operated by the Humboldt Bay Maritime Museum,

trivia

Eureka has more Victorian buildings per capita than any other city in California, including the most photographed of all: the Carson Mansion.

the boat has the smallest licensed bar in California. The ferry docks at the foot of F Street late May through September; for details call (707) 445-1910 or check www.humboldtbaymaritimemuseum.com.

The heart of Old Town is a gazebo at Second and F Streets, the site of many local cultural events such as Arts Alive on the first Saturday of each month. Eureka has become the arts capital of northwest California, with an abundance of working artists and many fine galleries and museums. The district's centerpiece is the **Morris Graves Museum of Art,** housed in a refurbished Carnegie Library at 636 F Street (707-442-0278; www.humboldtarts.org). It features exhibits in seven galleries and an innovative outdoor sculpture garden. Look for Humboldt County's arts guide, *The Palette,* for current details.

Want to find a wooden rain gutter or ornate balustrade for your house? For an inside look at how Victorians are restored, be sure to visit the **Blue Ox Millworks and Historic Park,** dedicated to preserving the skilled craftsmanship involved in transforming raw wood into fine architectural details. The mill features a collection of vintage machinery and human-powered tools that even the Smithsonian would salivate over, among them a bicycle-like velocipede and rare scroll saws and tenoners. This amazing complex of buildings and workshops is a thriving business, not just a museum, and a self-guided tour takes you to a lathe room, sawmill, blacksmith shop, and vintage print shop with the oldest press in California. Here Blue Ox's owner, the Bunyanesque Eric Hollenbeck, prints his own newspaper when not involved in countless other activities, from boatbuilding to making resins from tree sap. A true monument to American self-reliance, the Blue Ox is located at First and X Streets; for information call (800) 248-4259 or go to www.blueoxmill.com. Open daily except Sunday from 9:00 a.m. to 4:00 p.m. and weekdays until 5:00 p.m.; admission is charged.

trivia

The Trees of Mystery near Crescent City boasts the world's largest statue of Paul Bunyan (nearly five stories tall and weighing fifteen tons) as well as a gigantic Blue Ox Babe and an "upside-down tree."

Eureka has many gourmet restaurants, but for a different experience be sure to sniff out the **Samoa Cookhouse,** the last survivor of its kind in the West. Open for three meals a day, seven days a week, the cookhouse continues the two-fisted tradition of serving huge mounds of hearty food for a fixed price, lumber-camp style. For dinner your rosy-cheeked, well-scrubbed waitress might serve up soup and two salads, baked cod and roast beef, Spanish rice and green beans, apple or cherry pie, milk or juice, and buckets of steaming coffee. You reach the Cookhouse by taking Samoa Bridge across Humboldt Bay to Samoa, about five minutes from Eureka. Call (707) 442-1659 or check www.samoacookhouse.net.

The **Trinidad coast** 20 miles north of Eureka is especially beautiful, with a rocky shoreline, ocean bluffs, spruce forests, and even an agate beach. There's excellent hiking at Patrick's Point State Park, a couple of local inns, and even a restaurant, Seascape (707-677-3762), serving crab omelets.

Redwood National Park, about an hour's drive north, claims one of the world's tallest trees, as well as some fine scenic and recreational spots spread over 106,000 acres of prime forest and 33 miles of coastline. Park headquarters is located in Crescent City near the Oregon border, but the main visitor center lies to the south at Orick. Try not to get confused, but within the national park are three California state parks, each

trivia

The MV *Madaket,* the oldest surviving passenger-carrying commercial vessel in the United States (1910), still cruises Humboldt Bay.

Monarchs of the Forest

For millions of years before the last ice age, redwood trees stretched across the entire Northern Hemisphere, including Europe and Asia. Now they thrive exclusively in the mists of northern California. The coast redwood (*Sequoia sempervirens*) grows along a narrow coastal strip about 450 miles long by 25 miles wide from just north of the Oregon border to Big Sur. This belt is defined by a Pacific climate of mild, foggy summers and cool, wet winters, which is ideal for the trees.

A typical coast redwood lives several hundred years and can reach 2,000 years and more. Mature trees average 200 to 250 feet, but the tallest among them surpass 365 feet. That's twice the height of Niagara Falls. Though not as massive as their arboreal cousins, the giant sequoia of the southern Sierra Nevada, some coast redwoods grow up to 20 feet in diameter.

Despite these superlatives, however, redwoods are delicate in many ways. Their cones are quite small, and it takes more than 100,000 seeds to make one pound. Their root systems are broad and shallow, no more than 13 feet deep, which means they can be toppled by strong winds. (In 1991 this happened to the venerable Dyerville Giant in Humboldt Redwoods State Park.)

Yet redwood trees are strong. The soft, reddish bark, from 6 to 12 inches in thickness, acts like asbestos in protecting them from fire. Tannin in the bark makes them resistant to fungus and insects such as termites. For these reasons the heartwood, bright cherry to dark mahogany in color, has been highly prized in building since Americans first arrived. Of two million acres of original old-growth forest, fewer than 100,000 remain today.

Founded in 1918, the Save-the-Redwoods-League has been instrumental in protecting the species by purchasing large tracts of old-growth forest. At present the trees are sheltered in thirty-two California state parks in coordination with Redwood National and State Parks. For more information go to www.savetheredwoods.org.

floating in a sea of federal land. But no matter who's in charge, every corner of the vast expanse has something to offer, whether a Roosevelt elk weighing up to 1,200 pounds, a kayak trip along a mountain stream, or groves of redwood skyscrapers reaching to the heavens.

At **Orick** you learn why these Goliaths of the plant world can live more than two millennia. Unfortunately, the same things that make a redwood "everlasting" also make its lumber highly prized by the builders of cities. By 1940, about half of California's virgin forests were gone.

Nevertheless, here you can still recapture the feel of a primeval redwood forest. A lush green carpet of ferns and other small plants contributes to the almost fairyland quality found along many trails. Among the more popular are the Redwood Creek Trail to the Harry Cole Tree, an overachiever measuring

366.3 feet from crown to base, taller than a thirty-five-story building. (The grove, near Orick, is accessible year-round.)

Another exceptional stand is fog-drenched Lady Bird Johnson Grove, where a trail passes one tree hollowed out by fire and used as a goose pen. The Penthouse Tree, just a shattered hulk after a storm ripped through the area, now serves as fertile home for a plethora of forest life. Even the heavily damaged trunk sprouts tiny branches again, a noble testimony to the tenacity of redwoods.

trivia

Battery Point Lighthouse in Crescent City (1856) is the state's oldest working lighthouse.

Prairie Creek Redwoods State Park offers a spine-twanging excursion along 4 miles of gravel road to Gold Bluffs Beach, where you might spot an elk wading into the surf amid huge piles of driftwood. About 2,000 wild elks live here in the park; a small group is usually near the Elk Prairie Campground. Four miles farther on, Fern Canyon's nearly vertical walls, set just 15 feet apart in some places, are completely covered with ferns and other plants. Though not awe-inspiring like the redwoods, Fern Canyon provides a startling contrast in scale. (Exit at Davison Road from US 101; trailers are prohibited.)

The Thomas H. Kuchel Redwood Information Center in Orick is open from 9:00 a.m. to 5:00 p.m. daily, closing at 4:00 p.m. from November through February; for information call (707) -465-7765 and look at the parks' Web sites: www.nps.gov/redw and www.parks.ca.gov/?page_id=415.

U.S. Highway 199 north of Crescent City heads along the emerald green Smith River, which begins high in the Siskiyou Mountains and, uniquely in California, flows freely without a dam for the entire length,. This designated scenic byway/highway weaves through a few miles of coast redwoods before reaching soaring canyon walls, wild rapids, and the confluence of the South and Middle Forks of the Smith River. The route follows its course closely, and there are many turnouts for viewing and photography.

trivia

In 1964 a tsunami caused by a huge Alaska earthquake destroyed most of Crescent City's waterfront and downtown.

The **Smith River National Recreation Area** is a 305,000-acre (450-square-mile) preserve within Six Rivers National Forest, created to protect the area's special scenic value, wilderness, and wildlife. The lush natural environment, which is warmer than the coast and fairly dry May through September, is home to hundreds of plant and animal species. Along the river you will see otters, ducks, osprey, and kingfishers. Sport fishers flock here for trophy-sized salmon and steelhead, and rafters take on the 145 miles of navigable whitewater. For more information, call (707) 442-1721 or check the Six Rivers National Forest Web site at www.fs.fed.us/r5/sixrivers/recreation/smith-river.

Inland Valleys

As mentioned, Highway 1 is the more scenic choice for exploring the North Coast's lower regions. The **Redwood Highway** (US 101) is faster and more direct but by no means shabby in the scenery department. And its tributaries lead to one of the region's top draws—Wine Country. You can drive the highway as an alternative to the coastal route or combine the two in a loop; remember that they join at Leggett, about halfway to the Oregon border from San Francisco.

Heading north from Marin, your first stop should be **Petaluma Adobe State Historic Park** in Sonoma County. This was the heart of Vallejo Country—General Mariano Vallejo to be exact, whose rancho sprawled over 66,000 acres. The Mexican commandant founded Sonoma and lived part-time on his country estate, a portion of which forms the historic park.

Construction on the adobe house began in the mid-1830s and took a decade to complete. Bricks of adobe (water and straw mixed with clay and then sunbaked) went into 3-foot-thick walls surrounding a central courtyard. Today about 80 percent of the walls are original, and the two-story house has been restored to a working rancho, right down to the crowing roosters, grazing livestock, and hides hanging out to dry. You'll find a pit where adobe bricks are made, a horse-powered millstone, a cast-iron pot filled with bubbling paraffin for candles, a candle-dripping device, wooden looms, and clay ovens for baking bread.

The rancho's brief halcyon era was shattered with the American takeover of California in 1846 and the discovery of

> **trivia**
>
> The "burl art" capital of the world is the town of Orick, southern gateway to Redwood National Park.

gold two years later. Vallejo himself became a living symbol of the romantic days, reluctantly resigned to the inevitable changes. The park is open daily from 10:00 a.m. to 5:00 p.m.; admission is charged. For information call (707) 762-4871 or look online at www.petalumaadobe.com.

The town of **Petaluma** also merits a visit, if only to see the curious blend of ornate Victorians and silos. Bisected by a river and surrounded by rich farmland, Petaluma has been a dairy and poultry center ever since the incubator was perfected here. (There's still an annual Butter & Eggs Day celebration, not to mention the World Wrist Wrestling Championships.) In an earlier era the town was also one of the nation's foremost carriage-building centers, and all the prosperity left a 4-block core of historic structures that went unscathed by the 1906 earthquake. Parts of Petaluma were used in filming *American Graffiti*.

Northwest of Petaluma, the town of **Sebastopol** is the heart of Sonoma County's Gravenstein apple district. The sweet local variety is green-yellow in color with red streaks. According to one story, Russians from Fort Ross brought Gravensteins to Sonoma in the early 1800s. Another story has botanical wizard Luther Burbank planting them here about a century ago (he had a farm nearby). Sebastopol is one of few places growing them today, accounting for 90 percent of the entire U.S. crop. Tasty Gravensteins are like the Model T of apples, with thin skin and too short a shelf life for modern markets.

trivia

Future general and president Ulysses S. Grant served as an army captain during 1853 at Fort Humboldt, where he was known as "Sam Grant."

From US 101 follow Highway 116 (west) at Cotati. "The Gravenstein Highway" meanders through hilly countryside dotted with farms and orchards and crisscrossed by unpaved country lanes. Sebastopol lies about 10 miles west and is a pleasant enough town, with an abundance of antiques stores. But people come for the many farms and roadside fruit stands selling Gravensteins starting in late July and other varieties in autumn. Apple-A-Day Ratzlaf Ranch, Kozlowski Farms, Walker Apples, Twin Hill Ranch, and dozens more are listed on the **Sonoma Farm Trails Map,** available by calling (800) 207-9464 or by visiting www.farmtrails.org.

The season opens each spring with the Apple Blossom Festival. During Sebastopol's **Gravenstein Apple Fair** in mid-August, apple mania descends on the area as the fruit appears in every conceivable form: fresh and dried; in pies, cakes, bread, and apple butter; in jam, jelly, juice, and sauce; in apple wine and, of course, pure, delicious apple cider. From Sebastopol take Highway 12 northeast to **Santa Rosa,** a town with a nice historic district, especially around Railroad Square, and a couple of attractions from a time when the area, as described by Luther Burbank, was "the chosen spot of all the earth as far as

trivia

At least 370 species of birds have been spotted traveling the Pacific Flyway along the North Coast.

nature is concerned." The famous Massachusetts-born horticulturist lived here for more than fifty years and was buried next to his home.

The *Luther Burbank Home and Memorial Gardens* honors the genius who spent a lifetime trying to improve the quality of plants. Join a guided tour of the Burbank house, including a visit to a greenhouse, and stroll through the gardens.

Burbank's record is written in the hundreds of new plant varieties he developed (an estimated 800 fruits, vegetables, flowers, and grains) that now grow in almost every country on earth. Armed with elaborate scientific theories and an uncanny green thumb, the plant wizard startled contemporaries by creating, among many others, the Shasta daisy; the russet potato; a spineless cactus for animal fodder; an edible raspberry; large, modern varieties of rhubarb and corn on the cob; and the "plumcot," a cross between apricot and plum. Burbank was fond of grafting the branches of one tree to another, and you can see the elm he created to provide more shade and a single apple tree that produced thirty-six varieties of the fruit. Once challenged by a skeptic to make a white blackberry, he proceeded to do just that to prove it could be done!

trivia

Acres of Easter lily bulbs are planted annually between Smith River and Brookings, Oregon, and account for 90 percent of the Easter lilies sold nationwide.

The Burbank Home, on Santa Rosa and Sonoma Avenues, is open April through October, Tuesday through Sunday from 10:00 a.m. to 4:00 p.m.; admission is charged. The Memorial Gardens are open year-round from 8:00 a.m. to dusk at no charge. For information call (707) 524-5445.

Snoopy, Charlie Brown, and Lucy of the Peanuts comic strip are the stars of the *Charles M. Schulz Museum and Research Center.* Born in Minnesota, the humble genius who coined "Happiness is a warm puppy" and other such gems was a Santa Rosa resident for many years before his death in 2000. The museum is located across the street from the ice rink where he ate two meals a day, and it has the feeling of a large house.

Peanuts was the most widely circulated comic strip in history (read by 355 million people worldwide), inspired many TV specials, and is the only such feature given a retrospective at the Louvre in Paris. Yet it took time for the innovative concept to catch on: kids faced with the tribulations of childhood in ways every adult could identify with. The strip first appeared in 1950, and it met with some hostility (critical letters denouncing Peanuts as boring and stupid are on view). About one hundred original four-panel storyboards are on display from an archive of 7,000. The most remarkable exhibit is a mural in the

Great Hall made from 3,588 Peanuts strips reproduced on tiles, which forms a giant image of Charlie Brown and Lucy. Outside is the Snoopy Labyrinth, a winding path of grass and rocks shaped like a beagle's head. The Charles M. Schulz Museum, 2301 Hardies Lane, Santa Rosa, is open daily except Tuesday from September through Memorial Day. For hours and admission charges, call (707) 579-4452 or go to www.schulzmuseum.org.

North of Santa Rosa, shopping malls and tract homes give way to a rustic landscape of woods and vineyards interspersed with a few well-groomed villages like Healdsburg and Geyserville. One delightful side trip from the main highway takes you into bucolic Anderson Valley, which looks more like parts of Germany than tourist-poster California. Some residents still speak a strange local dialect called Boontling, created to confuse outsiders decades ago.

Heading west from Cloverdale take Highway 128, a road with a thousand curves that passes through deep green hills and pastureland, fruit orchards and vineyards. The road flattens out around the town of Boonville, a good place for a break at Anderson Valley Brewing Company (800-207-2337; www.avbc.com). From February through November, Friday through Sunday from 1:00 p.m. to 4:00 p.m., the *Anderson Valley Historical Museum,* housed in a little red schoolhouse, displays an unusual collection of bear traps and Indian baskets, loggers' saws and old gingham dresses. You'll find it at 12340 Highway 128, Boonville (707-895-3207; www.andersonvalleymuseum.org).

Boonville is the linguistic home of Boontling, which is a hodgepodge of English, Scottish, Pomo Indian, and made-up words, "a deliberately contrived jargon," according to one Cal State University professor, who has compiled a dictionary of the "language." For example, *bahl gorms* means "good eats," and a pay telephone is called a *bucky walter.* Spot signs on Main Street written in Boontling, like one for the cafe Horn of Zeese, which means a good "cup of coffee."

Cut by the Navarro River, 16-mile-long Anderson Valley was originally devoted to logging and livestock, but farmers soon discovered it was perfect for raising apples and wine grapes. There are about a dozen wineries with crowd-free tasting rooms along Highway 128. Among them are Roederer Estate (707-895-2288; www.roedererestate.com) near the hamlet of Philo and Navarro Vineyards (800-537-9463; www.navarrowine.com), which makes some of the best gewürztraminer outside Germany.

From here you can continue along Highway 128 to the Mendocino coast, about thirty minutes away, or double back to Boonville and take Highway

trivia

At the Featherbed Railroad on the shores of Clear Lake in Nice, California, you can sojourn in a renovated caboose.

235 northeast to the town of **Ukiah** to rejoin US 101. *Ukiah* is a Pomo Indian word meaning "deep valley," and is the Mendocino County seat about halfway between Santa Rosa and Leggett. The **Sun House,** a State Historic Landmark, and the adjacent **Grace Hudson Museum,** are devoted to the memory of this inspired artist.

In 1891, soon after Grace Carpenter married Dr. John Hudson, she painted a portrait of a Pomo Indian child called *National Thorn,* the first in a numbered series of 684 oils, mostly of Native American subjects. The Ukiah museum boasts only a few of the paintings. The collection derives chiefly from the work of Doctor John Hudson, who became so enchanted with the Pomos that he gave up his practice to gather artifacts. For the next forty years, he amassed such a large collection that both the Field Museum and the Smithsonian share part of it today, with plenty left for Ukiah. Included are superb basketry, flutes and clapper rattles, a mush paddle, a modern-looking handbag with abalone pendants, and the scalp of a black mallard. Other exhibits focus on the Hudsons' personal lives. The Sun House next door was the Hudsons' home.

> ## trivia
>
> The di Rosa Preserve in Napa is a unique art and nature preserve with 217 acres of protected fauna and flora, a huge lake, and an art collection featuring more than 800 Northern California artists.

Over the front door hangs the symbol of the Hopi Indian sun god, representing the eternal cycle of fertility and growth. Constructed in 1911, the house features solid, 18-square-inch redwood beams, overhanging eaves, and rough board-and-batten exterior. The Grace Hudson Museum and Sun House, 431 South Main Street, are open Wednesday through Sunday (707-467-2836; www .gracehudsonmuseum.org).

Rather than sticking to the Redwood Highway, you may wish to get a taste of Northern California's famed **Wine Country,** hundreds of vineyards and wineries in a three-county piece of paradise. Fame has its price, however, and the entire Napa Valley and much of the Sonoma area are awash in wine-sipping visitors.

One of the nicest spots in Wine Country is **Sonoma Plaza,** a large park lined with historical sites, shops, and restaurants right in the middle of town. Sonoma City Hall, built with huge sandstone blocks, sits on the plaza. This area was in the thick of things during the Spanish-Mexican period, evident by the old Mission San Francisco Solano de Sonoma (last in the original string), army barracks, and old adobe houses. A monument in the park honors those who proclaimed the "California Republic" here by raising the Bear Flag in 1846. Several of these old structures form Sonoma State Historic Park.

In addition to history, however, Sonoma's plaza has a wonderful mood about it, an unspoiled quality in the heart of so much tourism. Interesting shops are found in the Spanish-style El Paseo complex and on First Street. Sonoma Cheese Factory (707-996-1931; www.sonomacheesefactory.com) specializes in the local variety: Sonoma Jack. Several good restaurants line the square, including the Swiss Hotel (707-938-2884; www.swisshotelsonoma.com) and Taste of the Himalayas (707-996-1161).

trivia

California's fabled Wine Country and its multibillion-dollar industry got its start near Sonoma Plaza, when Franciscan priests founded a mission and planted the first grapes in 1823. The first commercial winery was opened three decades later by a Hungarian nobleman.

Jack London State Historic Park lies slightly off the beaten path, 8 miles north of Sonoma in the Valley of the Moon. You reach it by taking Highway 12 through a rural landscape of meadows and creeks to the pocket-size community of Glen Ellen. London Ranch Road leads to the park, located on part of the ranch the illustrious author carved out of "the most beautiful, primitive land to be found in California."

Jack London fought his way up from the grimy factories and waterfront dives of Oakland to become one of the most popular and highest-paid writers nationwide. He became widely known for his personal exploits and travels and was considered the rugged individualist incarnate (ironic, given his socialist beliefs).

Weary of roaming, at least for the time, London arrived here with royalties from the sale of *The Call of the Wild;* with the money he purchased 129 acres of land. For the next few years, he pursued a furious pace of living life to the fullest, including a daily writing stint, building and managing the ranch, riding his horse around the property, and entertaining a steady stream of guests—from fellow writers to passing tramps.

Wander the sad remains of one of London's most cherished projects—the grandiose *Wolf House,* a sprawling four-story home built with volcanic boulders, redwood logs, and Spanish tiles. Plans called for twenty-six rooms, including a dining room for fifty, nine fireplaces, and a fireproof manuscript vault. The author predicted that Wolf House would stand a thousand years, but soon after construction ended, word reached London and his wife that their dream home was on fire. Except for the foundation and stone walls, the house was destroyed, and the stark skeletal ruins stand as a tragic reminder of the disaster.

Although London vowed to rebuild, the forty-year-old died just three years later, in 1916. The author's ashes lie beneath a reddish lava boulder on a weedy plot near the trail to the ruins.

The House of Happy Walls, built by his widow, Charmian, is steeped in London memorabilia. His study has been re-created with its big rolltop desk, Dictaphone, and other authentic pieces. The museum also contains some of the 600 rejection slips London received from publishers before success came, and copies of stories filed during his stints as a war correspondent. Boxing gloves and fencing gear attest to London's combative spirit. Don't overlook the South Seas collection upstairs, which includes a photo of Jack wearing a costume made from human hair.

Jack London State Historic Park, 2400 London Ranch Road, is open daily with an admission charged. For further information call (707) 938-5216 or go to www.jacklondonpark.com.

Glen Ellen is a delightful little town to browse around in. Here, too, is an unusual place to do some "tasting"—not wine but local olive oil of exceptionally high quality. During the olive season (October through March) the press is in operation daily, churning out extra virgin oil of low acidity and distinctive taste. You can sample several varieties of oil with bread cubes amid the heady scent of crushed olives. The Olive Press tasting bar is located at 14301 Arnold Drive, Glen Ellen. It's open 10:00 a.m. to 5:30 p.m. daily; call (707) 939-8900 for more information or consult www.theolivepress.com.

From Glen Ellen, a delightful 11-mile drive via *Oakville–Trinity Road* snakes over the hills into Napa Valley. You pick it up just north of town and continue about 8 miles before getting your first view of the vineyards from atop a ridge, near a Carmelite monastery. The panorama here is so engaging that the monks must sometimes think they've died and gone to heaven! If you hate crowds, however, rather than dawdling in the valley, head northeast to visit an unusual town.

Just north of St. Helena, Deer Park Road heads east into the wooded foothills rising from Napa Valley. After a few miles you reach *Angwin,* a town inhabited largely by Seventh-day Adventists since the founding of Pacific Union College back in 1909. Here the students are different from those at, say, Berkeley, and tune into a campus radio station playing the "inspirational top forty." Despite living amid the temptations of Wine Country, Adventists shun alcohol and likewise abstain from tobacco and meat. The local supermarket offers an astounding variety of vegetarian and alternative foods; only the pet food section contains meat products.

Down the road from Angwin lies *Elmshaven,* a stately Victorian home deemed a National Historic Landmark. Here Ellen G. White, who cofounded the Seventh-day Adventists, wrote numerous books inspired by hundreds of angelic visions. Open daily; call (707) 963-9039 or check www.elmshaven.org for information on scheduled tours.

Four twisting miles over the hill from Angwin along Howell Mountain Road lies arcadian **Pope Valley,** which looks like Napa or Sonoma must have decades ago. Yet, the biggest attraction here is a bizarre monument to modern technology and one man's obsession: **Litto's Hubcap Ranch.** For thirty years Emanuele "Litto" Damonte amassed a personal collection of thousands of automobile hubcaps from every known make and model. He carefully arranged these—along with tractor tires, bottles, wooden ducks, and rosebushes—into clever and artistic configurations around his house.

Damonte passed away in 1985, but his family maintains the site, now a registered state landmark, proclaiming that "Litto, the Pope Valley Hubcap King, was here." Located 3 miles north of Pope Valley village, the site has no regular hours, and no admission is charged.

Returning to the Napa Valley, take the Silverado Trail north to **Calistoga,** a historic spa/resort deemed "California's Saratoga" by gold rush entrepreneur Sam Brannan. Local geothermal activity created a spouting geyser, a subterranean river, and huge pools of natural mineral water used in the town's numerous mud baths and hydrotherapy clinics, as well as Calistoga brand bottled water.

Natural turmoil likewise created an interesting nearby attraction called the **Petrified Forest,** which has been attracting visitors since Robert Louis Stevenson wrote about it in 1883. Volcanic eruptions 3.4 million years ago covered the original redwood forest with lava and ash, and over millennia, water laden with silicates seeped into the tree fibers and transformed the wood into stone.

A shaded trail leads past the world's largest petrified trees, most with their original bark. Among them are the Giant, a 60-foot-long tree already 3,000 years old when it was buried. A shop displays petrified worms, snails, clams, nuts, and coral, plus opalized wood and fossilized insects.

Located about 5 miles from Calistoga on Petrified Forest Road, it is open daily; admission is charged. Call (707) 942-6667 or check www.petrifiedforest .org for information about hours.

Seven miles to the northeast, **Mount Saint Helena** is the tallest of all "Bay Area" peaks at 4,343 feet. The view is almost as good as from Mount Diablo (see the Bay Area chapter) but much less crowded because cars can't drive to the top. After a fairly rigorous 5-mile hike through chaparral and pine, you peer out on the entire Wine Country and beyond—to the emerald vineyards of Napa and Sonoma, the oak-studded hills of the Valley of the Moon, the vast

Dipping in the Mud

I enter the room with some trepidation. This is my first mud bath, and I pause momentarily at the eerie scene: three seemingly disembodied heads floating in vats of bubbling black mud. In an instant my towel is removed by a no-nonsense attendant, and I'm politely but firmly ushered to a cement tub to wallow in the mire.

I roll over into the hot stuff and am immediately surprised—I don't sink. This is normal, because the mud—a mixture of scalding geyser water, volcanic ash, and peat moss—has the consistency of wet cement, dense and not slimy at all. The attendant scoops 100-degree black muck over me as I lie prone, and he warns me not to stand up because of the intense heat down below. Soon I'm immersed up to my Adam's apple and surprised by how heavy the mud feels as I lie motionless and seemingly weightless. My face is pouring sweat, and a cool cloth placed on my forehead feels wonderful. Soon my body seems to glow, and I feel deeply relaxed.

Situated at the north end of Napa Valley, Calistoga's medicinal water and mud baths, including my choice—Indian Springs on Lincoln Avenue—have attracted visitors for more than a century. At first people came to alleviate rheumatic ailments, but now it's stress, along with "exfoliation" of toxins. And, of course, there are the merely curious, like me. Most spas here sit atop a gigantic natural teakettle of boiling mineral water and offer comparable treatments for about $85.

After twenty minutes I roll out of the tub, and the attendant scrapes off most of the mud before I leap into a much-needed shower. Next I enter a claw-foot porcelain tub filled with steaming mineral water for a good scrub and more relaxation. With all the perspiring there's a danger of dehydration; however, I'm treated to an endless supply of chilled cucumber-lemon water and cool facial towels. Next comes a eucalyptus-scented sauna for more heat and steam, and on to a cooling-off room and towel wrap. I drink more water and slices of cucumber are placed on my eyes.

By now I feel as if I'm floating on a cloud of mist, almost tipsy, and a strange sort of euphoria has taken over my body and mind. I ponder my options—a massage or facial, perhaps, or a dip in the heated outdoor pool. I wonder if someone will have to cart me away in a wheelbarrow, but I don't really care. Right now worries seem to belong to another place, another lifetime.

Santa Rosa Plain, and redwood groves near the Russian River. On exceptionally clear days, you can see Mount Shasta, 192 miles away.

With a little imagination you can also conjure up much of the area's history. Among a Russian party that scaled the mountain in 1841 was Princess Helena, the beautiful wife of Alexander Rotchev, last commander at Fort Ross. The peak was named after her patron saint. Later, mountain man George Yount—having been offered a land grant by General Vallejo—stood on the same summit and picked out his Napa Valley domain, present-day Yountville. He went on to plant the first vineyard here in the spicy volcanic soil that proved perfect for growing grapes.

In 1880 young Scottish writer Robert Louis Stevenson brought his bride, Fannie, to the mountain for their honeymoon, and they lived in an abandoned bunkhouse at the Silverado Mine. They spent much time exploring the area and sampling local wines, which Stevenson fondly called "bottled poetry."

At present, rustic **Robert Louis Stevenson State Park,** along Highway 29 from Calistoga, takes in about 4,000 acres of the mountain. About a mile up the trail, a granite monument is inscribed with a quotation from the author, who "came and stayed and went, nor ever ceased to smile." The mountain provides a wonderful getaway from the often frenetic activity of the Napa Valley below. The park is open daily from dawn till dusk. For information call (707) 942-4575.

A collection devoted to the author's life is located in the pretty and trendy town of St. Helena in Napa Valley. The **Robert Louis Stevenson Silverado Museum** honors the author of *Treasure Island, Kidnapped,* and *Dr. Jekyll and Mr. Hyde* with displays of personal items such as a writing desk, a hammock, and an inkwell. Among the collection are rare first editions (including an autographed copy of *A Child's Garden of Verses*), original manuscripts, letters, photographs, and memorabilia. There's even a lock of the infant Stevenson's hair! The museum is open Wednesday to Sunday from noon to 4:00 p.m. Call (707) 963-3757 for further information or go to www.silveradomuseum.org.

trivia

Safari West Wildlife Preserve near Santa Rosa is a blend of wildlife sanctuary (some 80 species including giraffes and lemurs) and posh inn (where tents go for $200 a night and up).

Lake County lies to the north of the Napa Valley and is, aside from the highly visited Clear Lake area, largely overlooked. Yet it boasts a large number of vineyards and wineries and claims to have California's cleanest air. There's also a unique side trip. Continuing north on Highway 29 past Mount Saint Helena, you reach **Middletown** (about halfway between Calistoga and Clear Lake) in the heart of the Mayacamas Mountains.

The big attraction here is a 30-square-mile area of geothermal energy called **The Geysers.** Twenty-one power plants produce clean energy, and a company called Calpine operates a Geothermal Visitor Center in Middletown. Here you can see exhibits about the labyrinth of pipes and wires, turbines and flashing controls. This is a serious operation: Wells are drilled up to 2 miles deep to tap the steam and create electricity. Located at 15500 Central Park Road, the center is open Wednesday through Saturday from 10:00 a.m. to 4:00 p.m.; admission is free. Check www.geysers.com or call (866) 439-7377 for more information.

A very different use for this same thermal energy is found at ***Harbin Hot Springs,*** a "clothing optional" membership-required retreat resort a few miles north of town. Its seven natural springs produce medicinal waters that visitors claim work miracles. Native Americans came here long before white settlers came, and taking the waters became the rage for stagecoach arrivals in the 1880s. New Age flavor has arrived, with yoga, tantra, watsu, and a whole range of self-improvement seminars and workshops. For information about Harbin Hot Springs, call (800) 622-2477 or check www.harbin.org.

Places to Stay on the North Coast

ALONG HIGHWAY 1 (MARIN–SONOMA–MENDOCINO)

Breakers Inn
39300 South Highway 1
Gualala, CA
(707) 884-3200

Elk Cove Inn
6300 South Highway 1
Elk
(800) 275-2967

Greenwood Pier Inn
5928 South Highway 1
Elk
(707) 877-9997

The Hotel at St. Orres
36601 Coast Highway 1
Gualala
(707) 884-3303

The Inn at Occidental
3657 Church Street
Occidental
(800) 522-6324

The Inn at Schoolhouse Creek
7051 North Highway 1
Little River (Mendocino)
(800) 731-5525

Jenner Inn
10400 Highway 1
Jenner
(707) 865-2377

John Dougherty House
571 Ukiah Street
Mendocino
(800) 486-2104

The Lodge at Noyo River
500 Casa del Noyo Drive
Noyo Harbor, Fort Bragg
(800) 628-1126

MacCallum House Inn
45020 Albion Street
Mendocino
(800) 609-0492

Point Reyes Seashore Lodge
10021 Highway 1
Olema
(415) 663-9000

Smiley's Saloon & Hotel
41 Wharf Road
Bolinas
(415) 868-1311

Stanford Inn by the Sea
Coast Highway and
Comptche Ukiah Road
Mendocino
(800) 331-8884

LOST COAST/REDWOOD COUNTRY

Abigail's Elegant Victorian Mansion B&B
1406 C Street
Eureka
(707) 444-3144

Bayview Inn
310 Highway 101 South
Crescent City
(800) 446-0583

WORTH SEEING/DOING ON THE NORTH COAST

Arcata Marsh and Wildlife Sanctuary

Clear Lake

Napa Valley Wineries

Old Faithful Geyser, Calistoga

Russian River

Skunk Train, Fort Bragg

Stinson Beach, Marin

Trees of Mystery, Klamath

Beachcomber Inn
245 Machi Road
Shelter Cove
(707) 986-7551

Benbow Inn
445 Lake Benbow Drive
Garberville
(800) 355-3301

Best Western Humboldt Bay Inn
232 West Fifth Street
Eureka
(800) 521-6996

Carter House Inns
301 L Street
Eureka
(800) 404-1390

Curly Redwood Lodge
701 Redwood Highway
South
Crescent City
(707) 464-2137

Daly Inn
1125 H Street
Eureka
(707) 445-3638

Lady Anne B&B
902 Fourteenth Street
Arcata
(707) 822-2797

Requa Inn Bed & Breakfast
451 Requa Road
Klamath
(866) 800-8777

Shaw House Inn
703 Main Street
Ferndale
(800) 557-7429

Stonegate Villas
65260 Drive–Thru Tree Road
Leggett
(707) 925-6226

ALONG U.S. HIGHWAY 101 CORRIDOR/WINE COUNTRY

Beltane Ranch
11775 Sonoma Highway
(Highway 12)
Glen Ellen
(707) 996-6501

Cottage Grove Inn
1711 Lincoln Avenue
Calistoga
(707) 942-8400

El Dorado Hotel
405 First Street West
Sonoma
(800) 289-3031

Gaige House Inn
13540 Arnold Drive
Glen Ellen
(800) 935-0237

Hotel La Rose
308 Wilson Street
Santa Rosa
(800) 527-6738

Sanford House Bed & Breakfast
306 South Pine Street
Ukiah
(707) 462-1653

Sebastopol Inn
6751 Sebastopol Avenue
Sebastopol
(800) 653-1082

Sonoma Creek Inn
239 Boyes Boulevard
Sonoma
(888) 712-1289

Sonoma Hotel
110 West Spain Street
Sonoma
(800) 468-6016

Swiss Hotel
18 West Spain Street
Sonoma
(707) 938-2884

Places to Eat on the North Coast

ALONG HIGHWAY 1

Bovine Bakery (American)
11315 Main Street
(Highway 1)
Point Reyes Station
(415) 663-9420

Cafe Beaujolais (French)
961 Ukiah Street
Mendocino
(707) 937-5614

Eggheads (American)
326 North Main Street
Fort Bragg
(707) 964-5005

Home Style Cafe (American)
790 South Main Street
(Highway 1)
Fort Bragg
(707) 964-6106

MacCallum House Restaurant (American)
45020 Albion Street
Mendocino
(707) 937-0289

Olema Farm House (American)
10005 Highway 1
Olema
(415) 663-1264

Pangaea (Californian)
39165 Highway 1
Gualala
(707) 884-9669

Rivers End (seafood)
11048 Highway 1
Jenner
(707) 865-2484

The Station House Cafe (American)
11180 Highway 1
Point Reyes Station
(415) 663-1515

Silvers at the Wharf (American)
32260 North Harbor Drive
Fort Bragg
(707) 964-4283

LOST COAST/REDWOOD COUNTRY

Cafe Waterfront (seafood)
102 F Street
Eureka
(707) 443-9190

HELPFUL WEB SITES ON THE NORTH COAST

Anderson Valley:
www.andersonvalleychamber.com

Crescent City–Del Norte County Chamber of Commerce:
www.northerncalifornia.net

Humboldt County Convention and Visitors Bureau: http://redwoods.info

Lake County Marketing Program:
www.lakecounty.com

Marin County Visitors Bureau:
www.visitmarin.org

Mendocino County Alliance:
www.gomendo.com

Napa Valley Conference & Visitors Bureau: www.napavalley.com

Petaluma Visitor Center:
www.visitpetaluma.com

Point Reyes National Seashore:
www.nps.gov/pore

Redwood Coast Chamber of Commerce:
www.redwoodcoastchamber.com:

Russian River Chamber of Commerce: www.russianriver.com

Sebastopol Area Chamber of Commerce: www.sebastopol.org

Sonoma County Tourism Bureau:
www.sonomacounty.com

Greater Ukiah Chamber of Commerce: www.ukiahchamber.com

Curley's Grill (American)
400 Ocean Avenue
Ferndale
(707) 786-9696

Lost Coast Brewery & Cafe
617 4th Street
Eureka
(707) 445-4480

Restaurant 301 (Continental)
301 L Street
Eureka
(707) 444-8062

HIGHWAY 101 CORRIDOR/WINE COUNTRY

Della Santina's (Italian)
133 East Napa Street
Sonoma
(707) 935-0576

Garden Court Cafe & Bakery (American)
13647 Arnold Drive
Glen Ellen
(707) 935-1565
Hopland Brewery

John Ash & Co. (Californian)
4330 Barnes Road
Santa Rosa
(707) 527-7687

LaSalette Restaurant (Portuguese)
452 First Street East
Sonoma
(707) 938-1927

Madrona Manor Restaurant (Californian)
1001 Westside Road
Healdsburg
(800) 258-4003

McNears Saloon & Dining House (American)
23 Petaluma Boulevard
North
Petaluma
(707) 765-2121

Mount View Hotel Restaurant (Californian)
1457 Lincoln Avenue
Calistoga
(707) 942-6877

Redwood Valley Cafe (American)
9621 North State Street
Ukiah
(707) 485-5307

Tavern and Restaurant (American)
13351 South
Highway 101
Hopland
(707) 744-1361

CENTRAL VALLEY

When mountain man Jedediah Smith first entered the Central Valley in 1828, he encountered great expanses of grassland, lakes that spread like pancakes in spring floods, vast herds of tule elks, and peaceful Indian tribes that had lived here for millennia. A century or so later, this same valley was the California first seen by dust-bowl families searching for a better life, drawn by the rich soil and bountiful farms.

Lying between the Sierra Nevada and the Coastal Range, the valley contains the world's most productive farmland, which yields an incredible one-quarter of America's table food. Some 450 miles long and 50 miles wide (larger than England), the Central Valley encompasses the two valleys of the Sacramento and San Joaquin Rivers, which flow into the California Delta southwest of Sacramento. This delightful capital city is an inland port with ocean access, as is workaday Stockton to the south.

The Central Valley is a part of California little known to visitors and ignored by most coastal residents, who tend to think of it as an alternately hot and foggy, painfully boring stretch crossed on the way to somewhere else. Driving the valley is sure to involve either the speedy, ramrod straight

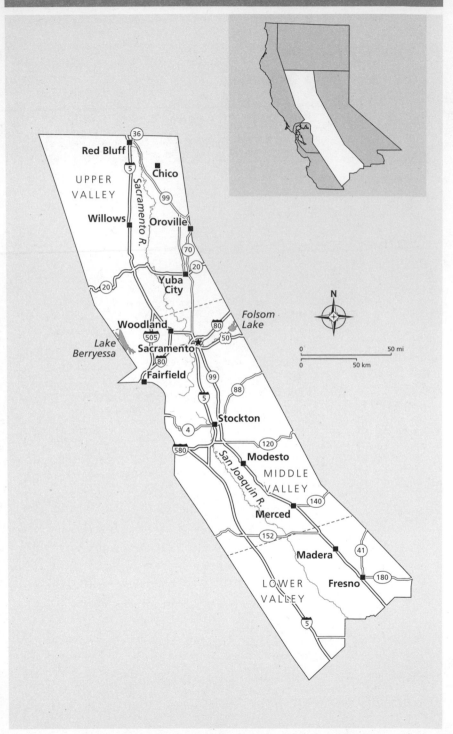

Red Bluff

Chico

UPPER
VALLEY

Willows

Oroville

Sacramento R.

Yuba
City

Woodland

Folsom
Lake

Lake
Berryessa

Sacramento

Fairfield

Stockton

Modesto

MIDDLE
VALLEY

San Joaquin R.

Merced

Madera

Fresno

LOWER
VALLEY

N

0   50 mi
0   50 km

Interstate 5 or Highway 99, which passes through most of the major towns and points of interest.

Lower Valley

Fresno and the rest of the sun-pummeled San Joaquin Valley may be short on visitor attractions, but one place is definitely worth a stop. ***Forestiere Underground Gardens*** began innocently enough in 1906, when a Sicilian immigrant named Baldasare Forestiere dug a shady cellar to escape the scorching summer heat. When he died forty years later, scores of rooms, patios, and passageways lay beneath a ten-acre plot north of Fresno.

Using only hand tools and skills learned digging subways in the East, Forestiere tunneled into the hard soil with grand visions of his subterranean home. Today you can walk through the living room, two bedrooms, kitchen, and library and still see scars from his pickax and a unique ventilation system that ensures the flow of cool, fresh air. But his residence was only the beginning; later came cheese and wine rooms, a ballroom with a stage, an aquarium, a chapel, Roman-style stone walls and arches, gardens with fruit trees (one citrus bears seven varieties), and an 800-foot-long auto tunnel!

trivia

"Snowbirds": Dark-eyed juncos spend summers in the Sierra Nevada, winters in the valley.

Despite the design and engineering complexities involved, Forestiere worked without a blueprint, and architects marvel at the sophisticated results. They are truly a monument to the spirit of one man with a shovel, a wheelbarrow, and a dream.

The Armenian Factor

Handwoven rugs to delight the eye, strange words to challenge the tongue, and delicious foods to tempt the palate are parts of the valley's rich Armenian heritage. Since the 1880s many thousands of immigrants have settled around the town of Fresno, where the culture of Armenia has taken root.

In markets and bakeries you can find *lavash* (cracker bread), honeyed-nut baskets, *peda* (yeast bread), and *lahmejun,* an Armenian "pizza" topped with ground lamb. Antique Armenian wool carpets can be seen in specialty shops, and everyone's favorite writer is William Saroyan, Fresno-born son of Armenian immigrants.

Forestiere Underground Gardens, 5021 West Shaw Avenue, is open in summer Thursday through Sunday, and weekends only September through November, April and May. Admission is charged, call (559) 271-0734 for hours and information on the group-only tours, or go to www.undergroundgardens .info.

Middle Valley

Sitting smack in the middle of the Central Valley, *Sacramento* has been called the "quintessential California city." It boasts sunshine, palm trees, high-tech companies, and produce stands, and is surrounded by freeways and suburbs. But the state capital has its own distinct identity as well. Two major rivers, the Sacramento and American, traverse it, and most major auto routes pass through or near downtown.

To celebrate California's Sesquicentennial (150 years since the gold rush and statehood), more than one hundred buildings were renovated. Among them were the first theater built in California, an 1876 railway station, and an historic waterfront with warehouses and paddle wheelers depicting an approximation of nineteenth-century riverside scene.

Sacramento's most pleasing feature is the quarter of a million trees in parks and along streets lined with Victorian homes. Mostly Dutch elms, they arch overhead and create cool green tunnels. There are a dozen top sights, including a remarkably well-restored capitol building, a superb railroad museum in Old Sacramento, and Sutter's Fort. But these places teem with visitors (especially busloads of schoolkids), and avoiding them means seeking out some of the lesser-known attractions.

In a city with 150 grand Victorian homes, the *Historic Governor's Mansion* may just be the grandest of the bunch. After all, it served as the

AUTHOR'S TOP TEN IN THE CENTRAL VALLEY

Forestiere Underground Gardens	Delta River Road
Historic Governor's Mansion	Western Railway Museum
California State Capitol	Hays Antique Truck Museum
B. F. Hastings Building, Old Sacramento	Oroville Chinese Temple
Jedediah Smith Memorial Trail	Bidwell Mansion State Historic Park

Walking the Walk

Old Sacramento offers living history actor-guided walking tours of its historic district. Tours leave from Sacramento History Museum at 101 "I" Street and proceed past a score of interesting sites. Among them may be the Lady Adams Building, the oldest in town and now home of a large costume museum and novelty shop; the Delta King floating hotel; a reconstruction of the Eagle Theatre, the first built in California; and an old schoolhouse that hosts an annual gingerbread house contest. Another stop on the walking tour, the Schroth Building, once housed the Eureka Swimming Baths, where the water was changed after every ten baths. Bathers competed for the coveted spots 1, 11, 21, and so on.

In the early days Sacramento was flooded many times by rising river waters, and at one spot near the banks of the American River you can see the original level of city streets. In 1862 the entire town was raised 12 feet with dirt dredged from the river and hauled over in wagons. For further information about the walking tours, go to www.oldsacramentolivinghistory.com.

official residence for thirteen leaders of the Golden State and their families, from George Cooper Pardee to Ronald Reagan. But after just three months, Nancy Reagan spurned its soaring gables and cramped closets in favor of a ranch-style home. Among the illustrious tenants was Earl Warren, who called the place home for a decade as governor before his appointment to the U.S. Supreme Court. (Today Arnold Schwarzenegger stays at the Hyatt Hotel when he's in town.)

The mansion now sits in a quiet neighborhood amid impeccably tended gardens, replete with tree-size camellias. Built in 1877 for a wealthy hardware tycoon, the home features the finest craftsmanship of its day, especially in the hardware department, with handcrafted bronze hinges and doorknobs. The state bought it in 1903 for the paltry sum of $32,500 unfurnished, then poured in vast sums, making it fit for a king, or at least a California governor.

Strolling through the sixteen rooms on an hour-long guided tour, you will see an Italian marble fireplace and French mirrors, handworked silver and gold-trimmed chinaware, thick Persian rugs and marble statues, and an 100-foot-long mahogany banister that was a dream for children of the household— no matter what the governor said.

The mansion was the site of four weddings and one assassination attempt—an anarchist group called the Wobblies (Industrial Workers of the World) dynamited the kitchen in 1917 and inflicted minor damage. In the bathroom off the master bedroom, Pat Brown's daughter Kathleen, who later ran for governor herself, painted the toenails of the claw-foot tub bright red.

TOP ANNUAL EVENTS IN THE CENTRAL VALLEY

Gold Nugget Days, Paradise (mid-April)

Bidwell Bar Day Celebration, Oroville (early May)

Silver Dollar Fair, Chico (Memorial Day weekend)

Sacramento Jazz Jubilee (Memorial Day weekend)

Crawdad Festival, Isleton (mid-June)

Folsom Championship Rodeo (July 4)

California State Fair, Sacramento (late August)

Gold Rush Days, Sacramento (Labor Day weekend)

Lodi Grape Festival, Lodi (mid-September)

Our Lady of Miracles Celebration, Gustine (mid-September)

Chico World Music Festival (late September)

Even when memories of society balls and political infighting have faded, that playful stroke will endure.

The Historic Governor's Mansion, a State Historic Park at Sixteenth and 1526 H Streets, is open daily with tours on the hour from 10:00 a.m. to 4:00 p.m. Admission charged. For information call (916) 323-3047.

The *California State Capitol,* modeled after the national counterpart in Washington, D.C., is of Roman-Corinthian design, with white columns and a 210-foot dome and cupola. Completed in 1874 and restored to its original splendor (1975–1981) at a cost of $70 million, the interior has magnificent tiled mosaic floors, murals, a soaring rotunda, massive staircases, crystal chandeliers, and stately legislative chambers. Seven historic museum rooms are open daily to the public (9:00 a.m. to 4:00 p.m.), with tours offered. Call (916) 324-0333 or see http://capitolmuseum.ca.gov. Outside, the grounds of Capitol Park cover forty acres (12 city blocks) and are planted with hundreds of trees and shrubs from around the world.

Sacramento's Old City Cemetery is rich in early history: mossy gravestones and elaborate tombs crammed into twenty-eight acres of greenery, including the Historic Rose Garden. Thousands of early settlers lie entombed here, among them John Sutter Jr. and railroad baron Mark Hopkins, whose sarcophagus was made with 350 tons of red granite. There are special monuments to the Civil War dead and volunteer fire department (featuring a 1,900-pound bell). The cemetery, at 1000 Broadway Street, is open daily from 7:30 a.m. to dusk, with longer hours in summer. Check www.oldcitycemetery.com for more details.

Capital Collections

Besides the dazzling California State Railroad Museum, the largest of its kind in North America, Sacramento boasts a mind-boggling array of museums for every taste. Among the best:

- California Military Museum contains more than 30,000 documents and memorabilia from the state's exciting history. Open daily except Monday; 1119 Second Street, Old Sacramento; (916) 442-2883; www.militarymuseum.org. Admission charged.

- California Museum explores the state's landscape, migrations, road to statehood, entrepreneurial spirit, and women's contributions. The museum's centerpiece is Constitution Wall, which spans six floors and towers over a courtyard. 1020 O Street; (916) 653-7524; www.californiamuseum.org. Call for winter–summer schedules. Admission charged. The California State Archives may also be used for genealogical research.

- California State Capitol Museum features tours, films, museum rooms, and changing exhibits on the state's government and history. Open daily from 9:00 a.m. to 5:00 p.m.; Tenth and L Streets; (916) 324-0333; http://capitolmuseum.ca.gov. Free admission.

- California State Indian Museum will move sometime soon to West Sacramento and become the California Indian Heritage Center. Until the move, displays of the rich and diverse cultures of California's Native American peoples may be seen at 2618 K Street. Open daily from 10:00 a.m. to 5:00 p.m.; (916) 324-0971. Admission charged.

- California State Railroad Museum is the largest and most innovative of its kind in the country, with twenty-one restored locomotives. Open daily from 10:00 a.m. to 5:00 p.m.; Second and "I" Streets, Old Sacramento; (916) 445-6645; www.csrmf.org. Admission charged.

- Crocker Art Museum, with expanded facilities scheduled to open in 2010, features two centuries of California art, old master drawings, Asian art, and rotating exhibitions. Open daily except Monday from 10:00 a.m. to 5:00 p.m.; 216 O Street; (916) 808-1184; www.crockerartmuseum.org. Admission charged.

- Leland Stanford Museum tours of the Victorian-era governor's house are a peek at how the Stanford University namesake and his wife lived in the 1860s and 1870s. Daily tours offered from 10:00 a.m. to 5:00 p.m.; 800 N Street; (916) 324-0575; www.stanfordmansion.org. Admission charged.

- Towe Auto Museum displays vintage cars and explains the history of the automobile in America. Open daily from 10:00 a.m. to 6:00 p.m.; 2200 Front Street; (916) 442-6802; http://toweautomuseum.org. Admission charged.

- Wells Fargo History Museum includes a restored Concord stagecoach, a gold scale, a telegraph, and other exhibits related to the bank's pioneering role in California history. Open weekdays from 9:00 a.m. to 5:00 p.m.; 400 Capitol Mall; (916) 440-4161; www.wellsfargohistory.com.

trivia

The Folsom Prison Museum at the famous penitentiary east of Sacramento contains artifacts and records dating from the 1800s.

Old Sacramento, with its trove of shopping and sightseeing treasures, is the city's most popular attraction. But most visitors overlook one low-profile site: the *B. F. Hastings Building.* Many old-town structures are reconstructions, but this is the genuine article. It first housed Wells Fargo offices, then became the western terminus for the legendary Pony Express service from St. Joseph, Missouri, 1,966 miles away. Today it houses the Old Sacramento Wells Fargo History Museum.

Riders had answered this want ad: "Skinny, wiry fellows not over 18. Must be expert riders, willing to risk death daily. Orphans preferred." One hundred joined up—among them fourteen-year-old Buffalo Bill Cody—for $25 a week and bragging rights. They transported half-ounce letters for $5 apiece in just ten days. But the service lasted only eighteen months, a victim of new technology called the telegraph.

Once again, the Hastings Building was in the thick of the action. The first coast-to-coast telegraph message was sent from here to Washington; in it members of the California Supreme Court assured President Lincoln that the state would remain loyal to the Union. Today you can sit down and click out a message to someone on the other side of the room, if you can manage to master the code. Ask to go upstairs, where the Supreme Court chambers appear just as they did when the first justices presided. The floor also contains a sitting room for "their honors" and the offices of Theodore Judah, the brilliant engineer who designed much of the transcontinental

trivia

The world's largest almond processing plant is Blue Diamond® Growers of Sacramento. Almonds are California's largest food export.

railroad. The B. F. Hastings Building is at Second and J Streets; call the Wells Fargo History Museum at (916) 440-4263 for more information. It is open for free daily from 10:00 a.m. to 5:00 p.m.

Sacramento's climate lends itself to outdoor activities throughout most of the year. It's the kind of place to rent a raft or kayak for a day, take in a AAA baseball game of the River Cats at Raley Stadium, or simply hop on a river taxi from Old Sacramento to the Garden Highway and enjoy an outdoor meal on a balmy summer evening. Old Sacramento marks the start of Jedediah Smith Memorial Trail for bicyclists and bird-watchers, jogging or walking pedestrians, and even dogs (on a leash). Leaving downtown, the paved pathway follows the American River Parkway and rambles 32 tree-lined miles out to Folsom Lake.

For information about the state capital and surrounding area, contact the Sacramento Convention & Visitors Bureau at (800) 292-2334; 1608 "I" Street, Sacramento, CA 95814; www.discovergold.org.

Movie director Sam Goldwyn once claimed the California Delta looked "more like the Mississippi than the real thing" and used it for filming *Huckleberry Finn*. Indeed, this dreamy farming and recreational area southwest of Sacramento, cut by two major rivers and several smaller streams, is quite unlike the rest of the state. More than

trivia

California's first dude ranch, Wonder Valley Ranch Resort, is located in Sanger, east of Fresno in the Sierra foothills.

a thousand miles of sleepy sloughs and quiet channels meander past rich farmland and small towns with landings for steamboats that will never come again. Some seventy bridges and five tiny ferries cross this intricate system of interlocking waterways, and you can drive through the heart of the Delta on the scenic *River Road*, starting just a few miles from the state capital.

During the gold rush the Sacramento and other rivers traversing the Delta served as a full-blown shipping highway, bringing picks, shovels, beans, and countless other necessities inland from San Francisco. Later, many dejected miners tried their hand at farming and discovered California's "green gold" in asparagus, pears, grapes, alfalfa, corn, and other crops. The only problem was that spring often brought floods that washed shacks and chicken coops downriver, a situation unsolved until Chinese immigrants arrived to put up miles of levees.

Scows and schooners serviced the river towns, and paddle wheelers arrived to cheering throngs just like in the movies. But by the 1930s river traffic had declined dramatically, and

trivia

Sherwood "Shakey" Johnson opened a pizza business in Sacramento, said to be the world's first pizza parlor, and definitely the first Shakey's Pizza outlet.

Delta towns became charming backwater anachronisms.

Today, the Delta has blossomed into an outstanding recreational paradise, where fishing and water sports abound. Houseboats set a pokey pace, and you can dally along for days without seeing the same channel twice, or tie up along a levee to fish Huck Finn–style (a practice called "gunk holing"). Yet, despite its popularity, the Delta rarely seems crowded.

Houseboats: Dawdling on the Delta

Huck Finn had the right idea: floating downriver and throwing a fishing line overboard; lying back in the warm sun and then jumping into the water to cool off. This lazy life-style can still be had on a houseboat with modern amenities—like wet bars and flush toilets—that Huck would never have imagined. Today you can truly rough it in luxury.

The California Delta has a thousand miles of navigable waterways and hundreds of islands, so there's lots of territory to explore. Several companies out of Stockton and Sacramento rent these 20- to 50-foot floating barges at modest rates (especially September through May). They say "no experience necessary," so even novices can handle the slow-moving boats after a couple of practice runs. Marinas are available for fuel, bait, beer, and groceries along the way.

The Delta is so big there's bound to be a surprise around every bend, whether a speedboat with water-skiers, a drawbridge, or an oceangoing vessel bound for one of the inland ports. (Beware of the wake!) The most popular area is called the Meadows, with shady trees and wild blackberry bushes crowding the banks and a sandy beach revealed at low tide. You can find a cozy anchoring spot on a secluded slough and stay as long as you wish; swimming, trapping crawdads, picking berries, casting a fishing line, or doing nothing at all, Huck Finn–style.

Contact the California Delta Chambers & Visitor's Bureau information line at (916) 777-4041 or check www.californiadelta.org.

The River Road snakes from bank to bank along the Sacramento River for about 35 miles between Freeport and Rio Vista, passing time-warp towns and old steamboat landings. The road sits atop the actual levee, and you can look right down on the river and irrigated fields. (You pick it up by taking I-5 about 7 miles south from downtown Sacramento to Highway 160 at Freeport.)

The first stop is *Courtland,* sitting in a sea of pear orchards and sumptuous mansions fringed with palm trees. Once a year, on the last Sunday in July, this somnolent settlement comes alive during the Pear Fair, with a parade and carnival, special pear foods and drinks like fritters and smoothies, and an award for the largest fruit. As you drive through, look for the ramshackle Wo Chong Co. "General Merchandise" Store and the defunct Bank of Courtland, standing proud as a Greek temple. One mile out of town, Highway 160 crosses the first bridge and continues toward Isleton. Be sure to stay on the River Road (County Road E13); *Locke* lies 6 miles straight ahead.

Locke (population eighty-one, elevation 13 feet) (www.locketown.com) is a place so picturesque it seems like a movie set. It's the only town in the country built entirely by and for Chinese, back in 1915, and most of the residents can trace their ancestry to the first settlers, if they weren't actually there themselves! A handful of wizened old men sit in doorways reading Chinese newspapers or creak along Locke's cramped streets, going nowhere in particular. One by one these old-timers are dying off, and no one (at least no one Chinese) is coming to take their place.

What you see is a ghost town in the making, a place of delightfully lopsided, wood-frame buildings with cockeyed balconies and doorways, rickety staircases, and sidewalks that croak when you step on the planks. Things weren't always so; in fact, Locke was once a mecca for gambling and other illicit vices. It had a hotel (still barely standing), an "opera house" for traveling troupes, and three brothels.

The spirit of those long-gone days resurfaces at the ***Dai Loy Museum*** on Main Street, housed in a former gambling den that prospered from 1916 until a sheriff padlocked the doors in 1950. Games are laid out as if in progress: dominoes for *dow ngow* (battling bulls), tin cups and buttons for fan-tan—and the table legs and crossbraces are worn smooth from years of nervous feet. The museum is open weekends noon to 4:00 p.m. Admission charged.

Other points of interest include the Joe Shoong Chinese School and Al's Place, an area wide hangout with a rowdy bar and a larger-than-life reputation for steak dinners. (A better dining choice is Locke Garden Chinese Restaurant.)

Sadly, Locke has become a tourist pit stop with cutesy gift shops, so if you find yourself jostled by a passing tour group, head down the road a mile to ***Walnut Grove*** (www.walnutgrove.com). Straddling the river, it's larger than

Savoring Crayfish

The Sacramento Valley is known worldwide for its tomatoes, rice, and other agricultural products, but in Sweden it's famous for its crayfish, known by some as crawfish or crawdads. In Europe consumers pay as much as $10 a pound for live California crayfish. It seems that signal crayfish found in the Sacramento River closely resemble the Swedish species wiped out during the 1960s, and most of those shipped to Sweden are eaten during a monthlong festival in August. Compared with Louisiana, the state's industry is small, but it's the California crustaceans that Europeans prefer. (About 90 percent of the local harvest is shipped abroad.)

Crayfish are caught in wire-mesh traps, marked by buoys, which are submerged in the river. These ingenious devices have one-way entrances so that the creatures can't escape once they've taken the bait, which can be anything from sardines to dog food. Crawdads look a lot like lobsters but are much smaller (about ten to a pound) and live in freshwater. They are usually boiled and picked out of the shell but are a challenge to eat.

trivia

The transcontinental railroad started in Sacramento. The famous Big Four—Leland Stanford, Charles Crocker, Collis P. Huntington, and Mark Hopkins—along with railroad designer/engineer Theodore Judah, met above a hardware store in downtown Sacramento in 1860.

Locke but quieter, with an old quarter likewise going to seed and small businesses that probably seemed dated in 1950.

Founded in 1851, it once had both a Chinatown and a Japantown, an impressive theater, and the neoclassical Bank of Alex Brown, an early resident. But unlike Locke, today there's a new bank and a respectable number of residents.

Cross the river again here and rejoin Highway 160 on Grand Island. At the tiny village of **Ryde,** the elegant Ryde Hotel has been impeccably restored to reflect the Delta's golden era. In the past it had a speakeasy and was owned by actor Lon Chaney Jr. You can still see a peephole in the door from Prohibition days. For reservations call (916) 776-1318 and view www.rydehotel.com.

Bloodless Bullfights

The Central Valley is home to many residents of Portuguese ancestry, and several small towns there host traditional festivals called *festas,* which combine religious rites, merrymaking, food and wine parties, and an old-fashioned carnival.

One of the largest *festas* is Our Lady of Miracles Celebration in Gustine in mid-September. It draws crowds up to 25,000 for three days of processions, folk dancing, solemn prayers such as the Blessing of the Cows, and old Portuguese *pezinho* music, which consists of emotional singing accompanied by a violin. Ethnic food includes fried sardines, octopus stew, and candied almonds.

The most unusual event at a Portuguese festival is the bullfight, held in a bullring called a *Praca de Touros.* About twenty bloodless bullfights are held annually in central California, almost always at the end of a *festa.* Bullfighting has been illegal in the United States since 1957, but an exception is made for the bloodless Portuguese style, which is the same as seen in Portugal itself. The animals are not killed or even hurt (at least in theory) because bullfighters use Velcro-tipped spears instead of traditional barbed lances to fend off the charges of the 1,000-pound fighting bulls. Their horns are also capped to prevent injury to the horses used in the spectacle, which is often the most horrific part of a Spanish or Mexican bullfight. Yet these are still very serious affairs, not just entertainment, and bullfighters include both local lads and professionals coming all the way from Portugal. For more information about the Gustine *festa,* call (209) 854-3712.

A handful of sumptuous old homes dot the California Delta, among them the *Grand Island Mansion* near Ryde. Standing stately amid rows of palm trees, this four-story, fifty-eight-room Italian villa was built for a fruit magnate in 1917. Once upon a time, wealthy and famous guests here must have danced on parquet floors and gazed into the gilt mirrors. Today it's open for Sunday brunch; check www.grandislandmansion.com or call (916) 775-1705 for reservations.

The final stop on your delta tour should be *Isleton,* with its wonderfully obsolete Main Street lined with the decrepit remnants of a once-thriving Chinatown, among them Hop Fat and Co. Formerly the Asparagus Capital of the West, Isleton still throws a humdinger of a crawdad festival every June, which draws crawdad connoisseurs from miles around. More than 20,000 pounds of crustaceans are devoured.

Head west on Highway 12, crossing the Sacramento River one last time to reach the town of Rio Vista. Here is a place guaranteed to leave you shaking your head, either in admiration or disgust. *Foster's Bighorn* (707-374-2511; www.fostersbighorn.com) on Main Street (between Front and Second) houses one of the world's largest private collections of animal trophies, all shot by famed big-game hunter Bill Foster (now deceased).

Looking out over the long, narrow bar and adjacent dining room are stuffed heads from around the world: Alaska to South Africa to Australia. Bears, lions, gazelles, apes, moose, wolves, rhinos, tigers, and many more (more than 300 creatures) reside here. There are even the stuffed, lifeless heads of a giraffe (long neck and all) and an African bull elephant, which may be the largest mounted mammal trophy in existence. Wall space not occupied by the trophies displays photos of the great white hunter himself.

Sixty years before BART (Bay Area Rapid Transit), the Sacramento Northern Railway ran between San Francisco and Chico via the state capital at speeds up to 70 miles per hour. Cars from this long-gone line, together with dozens of other relics from the golden days of interurban train travel, crowd a railway yard at Rio Vista Junction. The *Western Railway Museum* sits about 10 miles west of Rio Vista off Highway 12, easily reached from the Delta.

During the 1950s, in an era when interurban trains were being phased out, members of the Bay Area Electric Railroad Association obtained their first car, and a permanent home at Rio Vista Junction, former flag stop on the Sacramento Northern, was selected in 1960. About one hundred pieces now occupy the twenty-five-acre site, including trolleys, streetcars, steam locomotives, and cable cars, the largest variety of operating engines and cars in the West. Among the notable examples are a New York City "El" train car, a Gay Nineties San Francisco streetcar, a wooden electric interurban car that hauled eggs and poultry as well as passengers, and a tram from Melbourne, Australia, vintage 1930.

Volunteer greeters are spiffily dressed in the dark blue, gold-trimmed uniforms of conductors. All are electric train buffs. They will usher you onto one of the two train rides you can take. Streetcars leave every twenty minutes on rides around the museum grounds, and interurbans—bigger than streetcars—leave on the hour on leisurely 10-mile trips to Gum Grove station and back. As you hop aboard, bells clang, the air compressor thumps, and the motors growl.

trivia

The murals found in the State Library in Sacramento, painted by Maynard Dixon, are considered among the finest of their type. They depict the epic history of California in two parallel story lines, the Spanish-Mexican settlement and the American migration, which converge at one spot on the wall. Look for them after 2009–2010 restoration.

A dozen different cars are kept in operating condition and interchanged for the tours. You might be aboard a Peninsular Railway car built in 1903 and used until 1932. The second ride might be on a 51,000-pound streetcar called "the iron monster," which ran along San Francisco's Market Street at a top speed of 25 miles per hour. All but two of these giants were scrapped in the late 1950s. Sit on comfortable wooden benches that flip around and face the opposite direction when you come to the end of the line.

The 1.5-mile route passes more rolling stock, and two huge barns shelter more cars at various stages of restoration.

The Western Railway Museum, at 5848 Highway 12, is open from 10:30 a.m. to 5:00 p.m. on weekends year-round and Wednesday through Sunday from June through August. Admission, including unlimited rides, is charged. For information call (707) 374-2978 or go to www.wrm.org.

trivia

Knight's Ferry Covered Bridge east of Oakdale, built in 1864, is the longest west of the Mississippi.

The **Woodland Opera House,** at the corner of Second Street and Dead Cat Alley, sits haughtily as a reigning star in the town of Woodland, northwest of Sacramento. (From Highway 12 drive north on Highway 113 through Davis.)

From 1896 to 1913 the Victorian-style opera house was the pride of Yolo County, and smart ladies and their gents came from as far away as the capital to see and be seen in the glow of gaslights. During those years only two actual operas were staged (the term *opera house* was loosely defined at the time),

Burger Fever

California's great Central Valley is known for its prodigious output of food products. Seasoned travelers also acknowledge its reputation for serving up some of the best hamburgers in the state, if not the entire nation. Here are a select few places to chow down the all-American classic:

- Dave's Giant Hamburger makes classic cheeseburgers and chiliburgers and milkshakes you eat with a spoon, not a straw. Due to the size of the burgers no fries are served except by special order. 1055 North Texas Street, Fairfield; (707) 425-1818.

- Squeeze Inn claims that people drive for miles for a "squeezeburger with cheese." The diner's small size, only eleven stools and some picnic tables out back, belies its reputation. 7916 Fruitridge Avenue, Sacramento; (916) 386-8599.

- A&W Drive-In Restaurant inspired the film *American Graffiti,* made by Modesto native George Lucas. Here carhops on roller skates serve burgers and root beer floats. 1404 G Street, Modesto; (209) 522-7700.

but audiences were entertained with a steady stream of melodramas, minstrel shows, variety and magic acts, comedies, band concerts, and recitals. Among the many illustrious personages to appear were "Gentleman Jim" Corbett and John L. Sullivan, who starred in plays followed by sparring matches; John Philip Sousa and his rousing orchestra; and future Hollywood stars Sydney Greenstreet and Walter Huston.

Then hard times hit, and the opera house closed for nearly six decades. Regular tours explore the old theater from top to bottom: the double entrance doors, the stage and balcony, dressing rooms, and the gaslight control panel where oxygen and gas were mixed. Much of the original building has survived, including the brick walls, cast-iron posts, wooden pewlike balcony seats, and trap doors from the dressing rooms to the stage above.

After the historical tour, attend a live performance in the 532-seat theater. For information about tours and current productions, call (530) 666-9617 or go to www.wohtheatre.org.

Valley folk may have their cultural institutions, but for a real look at what life here is all about, visit the **Hays Antique Truck Museum** in Woodland.

trivia

Highway 99 running north–south down the heart of the Central Valley was the road taken by the Joads and other Okies in Steinbeck's *The Grapes of Wrath.*

This outstanding collection of mechanical workhorses stretches from 1903 to the 1950s and includes more than one hundred trucks representing dozens of makes. Most are fully restored and on display inside two giant sheds.

The majority come from the 1910s and 1920s, when brass lamps, wooden spokes, open cabs, and solid rubber tires were the norm. There are gasoline, diesel, and electric models made by forgotten companies like Yellow Knight and Ruggles, as well as the more familiar Mack, GMC, and Fageol. The museum also boasts the only extant Breeding Steam Truck and a section of the Old Plank Road that ran across the desert from Yuma, Arizona, to California.

trivia

The Hilmar Cheese Company in Hilmar is the world's largest single-site cheese production plant.

Mr. A. W. Hays bought his first vehicle, a Chevy, back in 1929 and just kept on collecting. Among the many noteworthy examples are a three-ton beast used by the army in World War I, a forest green gasoline delivery truck, an old fire engine with wooden running boards, an antique paddy wagon with wooden bars, and a 1930 Dodge half-ton pickup painted pistachio green. The Hays Antique Truck Museum forms part of the Heidrick Ag History Center, 130,000 square feet of interactive exhibits highlighting agricultural equipment from the valley's bygone days. The center, at 1962 Hays Lane, is open daily; admission charged. For information call (530) 666-9700 or go to www.aghistory.org.

Upper Valley

If you are headed north, a pleasant alternative to I-5 is **Highway 45,** which runs along or near the Sacramento River past towns and scenery reminiscent of the Delta's River Road.

Whichever road you take north, you will undoubtedly spot the most unfamiliar familiar place in the Central Valley: **Sutter Buttes.** Rising a measly 2,000 feet, this pint-sized cluster of peaks is known as the world's smallest mountain range. Yet because the surrounding terrain is so flat, Sutter Buttes thrust abruptly from the landscape like a stage set. Indeed, the buttes form the only significant rise in the entire valley.

Owing their existence to volcanic activity in some distant era, Sutter Buttes' twenty separate peaks form a rough circle about 10 miles in diameter, huddling together like a wagon train under attack. Native Americans called the place *ono lai tol* (the middle mountain), and it figures in their creation myths. Hot, dry summers and the dark volcanic soil and porous rocks mean semidesert conditions for the indigenous fauna and flora. Golden eagles nest on the craggy volcanic peaks, coyote and deer roam free, and cattle and sheep graze on the grass-covered lower slopes.

One reason the Sutter Buttes remain relatively unknown is that they lie partially within private land. Sutter Buttes is California's newest state park, although there is no public access yet—but you can visit with a little advance planning. All-day hikes with a guide (spring and fall only) range from gentle creekside rambles to strenuous climbs up to the buttes' highest peaks. Other excursions concentrate on the local plant and animal life. For information call the Middle Mountain Foundation at (530) 671-6116.

The town of *Oroville,* about 70 miles northeast of Sacramento in Butte County, is a gateway to the Feather River Country of the northern Sierra Nevada. Bidwell Bar upstream was the site of California's second major gold strike (the spot now lies at the bottom

trivia

Every January millions of geese and other birds flock to Sacramento National Wildlife Refuge at Willows.

of Lake Oroville), and among the eager prospectors to arrive were a large number of Chinese. When their settlement burned to the ground in 1856, the Asian gold seekers moved downriver and built a tent town.

This temporary settlement soon grew to become the largest Chinatown in California, and in 1863 the emperor T'ung Chich even helped residents build a place of worship, *Liet Sheng Kong,* the Temple of Assorted Deities for the three Chinese religions—Taoism, Confucianism, and Buddhism.

Today, the *Oroville Chinese Temple* sits in a quiet corner of town next to a river levee. Outside stands a two-ton bronze incense-burning urn presented by the royal family on their visit to California more than a century ago. Entrance to the original temple involves crossing a raised step and moving sharply to the right past the main door, obstacles designed to prevent "evil spirits" from entering. (Spirits supposedly travel only in a straight line.)

Inside are mirrors to further frighten the unwanted intruders with their own ugliness. There is a guided tour of the main room, where the carved figures on the large teakwood altar correspond to the three religions. All around lie the trappings of oriental mysticism: incense, candles, lanterns, fortune sticks, temple money for burning, and gongs for letting the gods know when an offering (in the form of smoke) is on the way.

Over the years buildings spread out from the main temple, and visitors are permitted to wander the grounds. The Council Room was reserved for business and social services, such as banking, settling feuds, and the reading and writing of correspondence by learned men for the often illiterate workers.

The Moon Temple upstairs became the place reserved for Buddhist worship. Enter through a circular brick doorway symbolizing the circle of life or eternity. Inside are bamboo lantern holders, a pewter altar set, and a parasol presented by the empress of China.

Across a tranquil courtyard lies Tapestry Hall, where the tradition and beauty of Chinese culture are highlighted with ancient pillar rugs, tapestries with embroidered dragons and lions' heads, shadow puppets, bronze mirrors, and other objects, mostly from Canton province.

trivia

The towns of Red Bluff and Redding both host three-day rodeos each spring.

The Oroville Chinese Temple, 1500 Broderick Street, is open daily from noon to 4:00 p.m. (but closed December 15 to February 1); admission is $2. Call (530) 538-2496 or check www.cityoforoville.org/chinesetemple.html for more information.

Oroville is now a quiet river town, but in times past it saw its share of gold-fever craziness. Around the turn of the twentieth century, one dredging company even offered to move the entire town lock, stock, and barrel in order to hunt for gold below. Citizens said no.

The source of all the wealth, the Feather River, was dammed in 1967 with the highest (770 feet) earth-fill dam in the country, creating *Lake Oroville* about 5 miles east of town. With its 167 miles of shoreline, the lake forms the centerpiece of a large state recreation area. From the visitor center a 47-foot tower overlooks the dam and reservoir and across a landscape of chaparral, oak, and pine. The center (530-538-2219) is open daily from 9:00 a.m. to 5:00 p.m.

Highway 70 follows the Feather River up into the Sierra, and 12 miles north of Oroville is a turnoff to the village of *Cherokee.* With only a dozen or so permanent residents, this former boomtown boasts an interesting collection of historic buildings.

Housed in a former boardinghouse, the Cherokee Museum displays a re-created miner's cabin, petrified mammoth bones, mineral specimens, and local Indian artifacts, as well as a hand-carved diorama of the town in 1880 (open weekends only from 11:00 a.m. to 3:00 p.m.). The village pays its respects to famous visitor Rutherford B. Hayes with Hayes Hall, a ramshackle, barnlike building crammed with memorabilia from his one-day 1880 sojourn. President Hayes Day is observed every September 24 with special exhibits and a jug or two passed around. Other sights include Pioneer Cemetery and the ruins of the old assay office.

Blast-furnace heat is part of summer life in the valley, and it causes most visitors to run for shelter. If you find yourself in the vicinity, make a beeline to the town of *Chico,* nicknamed the "city of trees" and probably the valley's shadiest spot (shady as in cool). Chico presents a pleasant version of small-town America, with a homey downtown and a bandstand on a grassy, elm-shaded square.

It also boasts one of the nation's largest urban parks, which sets the town apart from most other valley hotspots. *Bidwell Park* starts near downtown and winds along both sides of Chico Creek for 10 miles into the foothills, 3,618 acres of the best land in town. In the lower area the creek tumbles into Syca-more Pool, an old-fashioned swimming hole. *Chico Creek Nature Center* is devoted to exploring the many sides of Bidwell Park. The center sponsors nature walks and features an interpre-tive museum and nature lab. Call (530) 891-4671 or check www.bidwellpark .org for information on hours for the center's new facility.

> ## trivia
>
> Chico is home to the National Yo-Yo Museum, a collection of vintage Silver Bullets, Terminators, and other brands, as well as the world's largest wooden yo-yo. Every October the museum hosts the National Yo-Yo Contest.

The upper stretches of Bidwell Park are virtual wilderness reached by rigor-ous hikes up a steep canyon. Take a dip at one of three old-fashioned swimming holes. So arcadian is the park that early Hollywood filmmakers used it for parts of *The Great Waltz, The Adven-tures of Robin Hood,* and *Gone with the Wind.*

This green oasis sprang from the gift of Mrs. Annie Bidwell. The Bidwells were movers and shakers. John worked as a clerk for the famous Mr. Sutter in Sacramento, served in the Mexican-American War, then made his own gold strike on July 4, 1848. He later served on California's constitutional committee, was elected state senator and congressman, twice ran for governor, and owned one of the valley's largest farms.

In 1849 John Bidwell purchased 26,000 acres and proceeded to "plant" a town: He laid out Chico and gave away plots to anyone who would build. A nature lover and gifted amateur horticulturist, he introduced hundreds of variet-ies of trees and plants to the barren landscape and is chiefly responsible for the leafy canopy the town enjoys today. In 1865 General Bidwell decided to build the finest house in the state, and three years later it became a wedding gift for his bride, Annie, the pretty, dark-haired daughter of a Washington politician.

Join an entertaining tour of *Bidwell Mansion State Historic Park,* next to the campus of the state university at Chico (renowned as a fun-loving school). There is a large rose garden with several rare varieties in which Annie took great pride. Surrounded by a neat lawn and towering ornamental trees, the three-story home was designed in the style of an Italian palazzo, and its brick walls are covered with pink plaster.

Inside are twenty-six graciously furnished rooms that saw illustrious guests such as suffragist Susan B. Anthony, General William T. Sherman, naturalist John Muir, and President Rutherford B. Hayes. Mrs. Bidwell was an ardent suffragette and conservationist, and she joined her husband in an almost fanatical support of the temperance movement. In 1892, John Bidwell was nominated for president on the National Prohibition Party ticket.

trivia

The towns of Gridley and Corning are, respectively, the kiwi fruit and olive capitals of the United States. Corning packages more than half the olives sold in the United States.

The mansion claimed the first indoor plumbing in California, including one of the original fixtures from England, manufactured by Thomas B. Crapper. Also on display here are Annie Bidwell's petite almost doll-size shoes and undergarments garters, and a bootjack with a protective panel so that no one could catch a glimpse of her ankles (considered provocative at the time) as she donned her shoes.

Bidwell Mansion, at 525 The Esplanade, is open Wednesday through Sunday, with guided tours on the hour; admission charged. For information call (530) 895-6144.

Many people cool off by floating down the Sacramento on *inner tubes,* and Scotty's Landing is a popular local hangout on the river (12609 River Road; 530-893-2020). It's an informal restaurant and bar with a patio and beach volleyball court. Another way to stay cool is to visit Sierra Nevada Brewery, at 1075 East Twentieth Street, where guided tours and tastings of its famous pale ale and other varieties are conducted. For schedules and reservations call (530) 896-2198 or check www.sierranevada .com.

trivia

Tour the famous Jelly Belly jelly-bean factory in Fairfield mid-week when the candy-making machines are in action. More than one hundred other kinds of candy are also made here.

Chico is one gateway to Lassen Volcanic National Park, and Highway 32 takes you up through dense forests of conifers that provide welcome shade on the way to cooler altitudes high above the valley. (See the Shasta Cascade chapter for details on the park.)

Places to Stay in the Central Valley

LOWER VALLEY

Best Western Village Inn
3110 North Blackstone Avenue
Fresno
(559) 226-2110

Comfort Inn
5455 West Shaw Avenue
Fresno
(559) 275-2374

**Travelodge
Merced–Yosemite**
1260 Yosemite Parkway
Merced
(209) 722-6224

MIDDLE VALLEY

Amber House Bed & Breakfast
1315 Twenty-second Street
Sacramento
(800) 755-6526

Best Western Cordelia Inn
4373 Central Place
Fairfield
(707) 864-2029

Best Western Sutter House
1100 H Street
Sacramento
(916) 441-1314

Delta King Hotel
1000 Front Street
Sacramento
(916) 444-5464

Holiday Inn Express Convention Center Sacramento
728 Sixteenth Street
Sacramento
(916) 444-4436

Inn off Capitol Park
1530 N Street
Sacramento
(916) 447-8100

Valley Oaks Inn
600 North East Street
Woodland
(530) 666-5511

Vizcaya Mansion
2019 Twenty-first Street
Sacramento
(916) 455-5243

UPPER VALLEY

Best Value Inn and Suites
580 Oro Dam Boulevard
Oroville
(530) 533-7070

Holiday Inn Express
894 West Onstott Road
Yuba City
(530) 674-1650

Johnson's Country Inn
3935 Morehead Avenue
Chico
(530) 345-7829

Music Express Inn
1145 El Monte Avenue
Chico
(530) 891-9833

Safari Inn
2352 Esplanade
Chico
(530) 343-3201

The Villa Court Inn
1527 Feather River Boulevard
Oroville
(530) 533-3930

WORTH SEEING/DOING IN THE CENTRAL VALLEY

Anheuser–Busch Brewery Tour, Fairfield

Castle Air Museum, Atwater

Knights Ferry (historic mining town)

Old Sacramento Historic District

Sacramento Zoo

Sutter's Fort State Historic Park, Sacramento

Vacaville Premium Outlets (factory stores), Vacaville

HELPFUL WEB SITES FOR THE CENTRAL VALLEY

California Delta Chambers & Visitor's Bureau: www.californiadelta.org

California State Capitol Museum: http://capitolmuseum.ca.gov

California State Parks: www.parks.ca.gov

Chico Chamber of Commerce: www.chicochamber.com

Fresno Convention & Visitor's Bureau: www.fresnocvb.org

Merced Conference & Visitor's Bureau: www.yosemite-gateway.org

Modesto Convention & Visitors Bureau: www.visitmodesto.com

Old Sacramento: www.oldsacramento.com

Oroville Area Chamber of Commerce: www.orovillechamber.net

Sacramento Convention & Visitors Bureau: www.discovergold.org

Sacramento Parks: www.cityofsacramento.org/parksandrecreation/parks

Places to Eat in the Central Valley

LOWER VALLEY

The Branding Iron (American)
640 West Sixteenth Street
Merced
(209) 722-1822

Giulia's Italian Trattoria
3050 West Shaw Avenue
Fresno
(559) 276-3573

Grand Marie's Chicken Pie Shop (American)
861 East Olive Avenue
Fresno
(559) 237-5042

Santa Fe Basque Restaurant (Basque/Continental)
3110 North Maroa Avenue
Fresno
(559) 226-7499

Sir James (American)
1111 Motel Drive
Merced
(209) 723-5551

Vineyard Restaurant (Californian)
605 South "I" Street
Madera
(559) 674-0923

MIDDLE VALLEY

Cafe Bernardo (American)
234 D Street
Davis
(530) 750-5101

Centro Cocina Mexicana (Mexican)
2730 J Street
Sacramento
(916) 442-2552

Delta King Pilothouse Restaurant (American)
1000 Front Street
Sacramento
(916) 441-4440

Fat City Bar & Café (American)
1001 Front Street
Old Sacramento
(916) 446-6768

Il Fornaio (Italian)
400 Capitol Mall
Sacramento
(916) 446-4100

La Bonne Soupe Cafe (French)
920 Eighth Street
Sacramento
(916) 492-9506

**Natoma Bar & Grill
(Californian)**
702 Gold Lake Drive
Folsom
(916) 351-1500

**Paesano's Pizzeria
(Italian),**
1806 Capitol Avenue
Sacramento
(916) 447-8646

**Rio City Cafe
(Californian)**
1110 Front Street
Sacramento
(916) 442-8226

Tower Cafe (Continental)
1518 Broadway
Sacramento
(916) 441-0222

UPPER VALLEY

**Gooney Bird Bar
and Grill (American)**
3312 Esplanade
Chico
(530) 892-9534

**Nash's Restaurant
(American)**
1717 Esplanade
Chico
(530) 896-1147

Red Tavern (American)
1250 Esplanade
Chico
(530) 894-3463

**The Refuge Restaurant &
Lounge (American)**
1501 Butte House Road
Yuba City
(530) 673-7620

**Sierra Nevada Taproom
& Restaurant (American),**
1075 East Twentieth Street
Chico
(530) 345-2739

**Sultan's Bistro
(Greek/Middle Eastern)**
300 Broadway Street
Chico
(530) 345-7455

**Tong Fong Low
(Chinese)**
2051 Robinson Street
Oroville
(530) 533-1488

**Western Pacific Brewing
& Dining (American)**
2191 High Street
Oroville
(530) 534-9101

THE SIERRA NEVADA

At 430 miles long by 80 miles wide, the Sierra Nevada range is a formidable natural barrier. The mountains rise gradually from the valley floor to more than 14,000 feet, then plunge sharply to the high desert country of eastern California, a thin strip sharing more in common with Nevada and the Great Basin than the Golden State. Over millennia, glacial sculpting left a landscape of jagged peaks and hundreds of lakes, such as stunning blue Tahoe, crown jewel of the Sierra. Glaciers also carved out alpine valleys, including world-famous Yosemite, a national park so beautiful that it's in danger of being loved to death.

In 1827 mountain man Jedediah Smith became the first white person to cross the range, but just fourteen years later a wagon train loaded with settlers lumbered over the challenging terrain on its way to the promised land. Thousands more would join them. Then came the gold rush, when no barrier could hold back the floodwaters of immigration.

More than a century later, the Sierra Nevada is traversed by several major roads, and crossing it by car is a snap except during winter storms. The mountains offer countless outdoor activities. Although lying at an average of less than 2,000 feet,

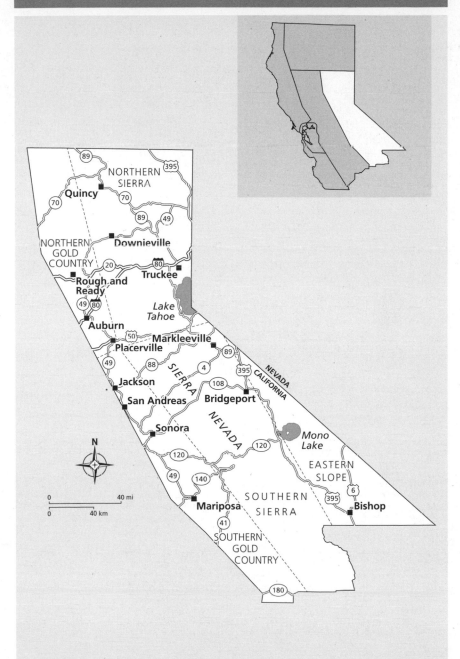

NORTHERN
SIERRA

Quincy

70 70

89 49

NORTHERN
GOLD
COUNTRY

Downieville

20 80

Rough and
Ready

Truckee

49 80

Lake
Tahoe

Auburn

50

Markleeville

Placerville

49

89

88

SIERRA

4

395

108

NEVADA
CALIFORNIA

Jackson

San Andreas

Bridgeport

NEVADA

Sonora

120

Mono
Lake

120

120

EASTERN
SLOPE

49 140

395

6

Mariposa

SOUTHERN
SIERRA

Bishop

41

SOUTHERN
GOLD
COUNTRY

180

N

0   40 mi
0   40 km

California's famous gold country unquestionably belongs to the Sierra Nevada. The mountains were the source of wealth. Gold had washed down streams over many thousands of years, and prospectors first on the spot found dust, flakes, pebbles, and even fist-size nuggets, so much gold that at first it was harvested rather than mined.

Early on, miners could stick their shovels into a river bottom and come up with more gold than gravel. One man unearthed a three-ounce nugget while digging a hole for a tent stake. Such stories lured gold seekers from around the world, and they flocked to a 300-mile strip along the western slope of the Sierra, where the climate was mild and the diggin's good. Some 500 mining towns, usually a scattering of tents or wooden huts, sprang up during the first decade after 1848. More than half of those have vanished; and many that remain are little more than colorful names on a map.

The spine of gold country is Highway 49, named for the forty-niners of the wild-and-woolly year of 1849. It runs for 318 miles from Oakhurst in the south to Vinton near the Nevada border, passing through grassy hills dotted with oak and pine and scores of former gold rush towns. Often the road narrows to become the Main Street of these settlements, which means window-rattling traffic and pollution. The most heavily traveled stretch is the 100 miles or so between Sonora and Nevada City, which happens to parallel the richest part of a gold-laden vein of quartz called the Mother Lode. Discovering the real flavor of gold country means getting off this main track and scratching beneath the surface.

Southern Gold Country

Near the southern end of Highway 49, the town of **_Mariposa_** ("butterfly" in Spanish) sits in a pleasant, wooded valley surrounded by cattle and timber

AUTHOR'S TOP TEN IN THE SIERRA NEVADA

Coulterville	Bodie State Historic Park
Calaveras Big Trees State Park	Mono Lake
Volcano	Downieville
Vikingsholm	Sardine Lake
Markleeville	Feather River Canyon

country. Although Mariposa features a fairly standard collection of historic and newer buildings, there are a couple of outstanding attractions here: the Mariposa Museum and History Center and the California State Mining and Mineral Museum.

First, stop at the old *courthouse,* scene of all official business within Mariposa County, which has no incorporated cities. Inside, maps show how Mariposa was at one time much larger, occupying one-fifth of the state when the original counties were laid out in 1850. The sprawling domain was later carved up to create six new counties and parts of five more. The courthouse, a sure sign that law and order had arrived to stay, has been in continuous use since 1854, making it the oldest in California. Located at 5088 Bullion Street at Ninth, it is open weekdays from 8:00 a.m. to 5:00 p.m.

Enter the *Mariposa Museum and History Center* and step into the wild and colorful era of the California Gold Rush. The recreated Gagliardo General Store's shelves are lined with patent medicines, chewing tobacco, and hard-rock candy. An 1850s street scene features the original press and print shop of the *Mariposa Gazette,* a classroom from Bull Creek School, a tailor's shop, an assay office, a drugstore, and Rattlesnake Ike's Saloon, purveyor of rotgut whiskey. An early stagecoach on display, the "Cannon Ball," made the run to Yosemite Valley. Peer into a typical gold miner's one-room cabin containing all his worldly possessions.

One of these crusty characters was Horace Snow, whose letters to his friend Charlie describe life in the mines. Bandit Joaquin Murrieta, who supposedly turned to crime after his wife was murdered and who, it was said, specialized in robbing Chinese immigrants, is another exhibit that earned the museum accolades from the Smithsonian Institution.

trivia

Gold is the state mineral, and serpentine is the state rock.

Outside, there's more: a stamp mill used for crushing gold-bearing quartz (each stamp weighs thousands of pounds); an authentic Indian village with bark houses and a sweat lodge; and a collection of mining equipment, including a mule-powered *arrastra* and steam pumps. The center, located at Twelfth and 5119 Jessie Streets, is open daily year-round (except January) from 10:00 a.m. to 4:00 p.m. Admission charged. For information call (209) 966-2924.

The outstanding *California State Mining and Mineral Museum* spent more than a century in San Francisco before being moved here. Since 1988 the 20,000-piece collection has had a permanent home at the county fairgrounds.

On display is a head-spinning sampling of the stuff that all the fuss was about—ore, nuggets, and little vials of flakes locked inside a massive safe—plus a wide array of rocks and minerals from around the world: rare Dalfi diamonds, colossal quartz crystals, malachite, broccoli-green azurite, rhodochrosite from Argentina that looks like a scrumptious cream dessert, and oddities such as a petrified egg and a replica of a 242-ounce nugget found in 1932.

Within the museum is a three-dimensional model of a mine's tunnels and shafts and a fully mechanized miniature stamp mill. A simulated mine tunnel leads you past muckers in flannel shirts and hard hats, a drifter machine for drilling horizontal holes, and other mining paraphernalia. The exhibit is open year-round; for information on hours and admission call (209) 742-7625.

A fascinating side trip from Mariposa goes to one of the most unspoiled gold rush settlements, **Hornitos,** where you will see a ghost town in the making. In former times a rollicking community of 15,000, Hornitos (whose name in Spanish means "little ovens") now has about fifty residents, occasionally seen drifting through the heat-hazed streets on their way to a Mexican-style plaza.

When the World Rushed In

The California Gold Rush was the largest mass migration in American history. More than 20,000 forty-niners came in 1849 alone, traveling overland on a harsh, eight-month journey. Thousands more took the longer, more expensive sea voyage around Cape Horn or used a shortcut across Central America. By 1852 there were several hundred thousand immigrants in California from dozens of countries, including about 25,000 Chinese.

The gold rush attracted a ready-made cast of characters for storytellers such as Mark Twain and Bret Harte. In a long line of desperadoes and scalawags, gentlemanly Black Bart (alias Charles E. Bolton) was the most infamous. He ambushed twenty-eight Wells Fargo stages, taking only the strongboxes and leaving his atrocious poetry behind.

Among the saucy ladies of the gold rush was dancer-actress Lola Montez, who once threatened to horsewhip a newspaperman who criticized her performance. This ex-mistress of mad King Ludwig I of Bavaria hit Grass Valley in 1853 and took the place by storm, keeping a bear on a chain in her front yard, among other stunts. Little redhead Lotta Crabtree, who lived up the street from Lola, learned how to entertain miners at raucous mining-town taverns. After finding fame and fortune in California, Lotta moved to New York and became one of American theater's first millionaires.

TOP ANNUAL EVENTS IN THE SIERRA NEVADA

Gold Discovery Day, Coloma (January 24)

Dandelion Days, Jackson (mid-March)

Mariposa Storytelling Festival (mid-March)

Calaveras County Fair & Jumping Frog Jubilee, Angels Camp (mid-May)

Mule Days Celebration, Bishop (Memorial Day weekend)

Columbia Diggins, Columbia State Historic Park, Columbia (late May)

California Bluegrass Association Father's Day Festival, Grass Valley (mid-June)

Tuolumne Lumber Jubilee, Tuolumne City (mid-June)

Mono Basin Bird Chautauqua, Lee Vining (mid-June)

Secession Day Celebration, Rough and Ready (late June)

Gold Rush Days, Downieville (late June)

Feather River Railroad Days, Portola (mid-August)

Chaw'se Big Time, Indian Grinding Rock State Park, Pine Grove (late September)

Coloma Gold Rush Live, Marshall Gold Discovery State Historic Park, Coloma (mid-October)

Victorian Christmas, Nevada City (December)

There the post office and other buildings survive in varying states of decay: Golden Stag Hall, Plaza Bar, and Roy's Cafe. One crumbling brick building nearby was where D. Ghirardelli, later of San Francisco chocolate fame, got his start running a general store.

Hornitos was born when Mexican miners were forcibly evicted from Quartzburg. Ironically, a big strike was made near the new town, and it became one of the richest and toughest of them all. Famous bad man Joaquin Murrieta, the "Robin Hood of the Mother Lode," used this as his hideout, specifically Rose Martinez's Fandango Hall and Saloon, where according to legend there was a secret escape tunnel.

Stroll up to *St. Catherine's Church* (1862), a curious specimen combining wood walls and stone buttresses. The town's boot hill is here, a mournful cemetery filled with crumbling tombstones and withered flowers. (Some say the name "Hornitos" came from the oven-shaped tombs here.) Surrounded by cacti, the old jail down the hill has 2-foot-thick granite walls and an iron door that would have made even Murrieta shudder.

Reach Hornitos via Mount Bullion, 6 miles north of Mariposa on Highway 49. Hornitos lies 13 miles away at 908 feet elevation, one of the lowest-altitude mining towns. To return, retrace this route or cut an 11-mile diagonal to Bear Valley.

From Hornitos, the town of **Coulterville** lies 16 miles away. Getting there means driving one of the least developed stretches of Highway 49, through countryside almost unchanged since the days of the forty-niners. From rocky, scrub-covered hills, you make a tortuous descent into the Merced River Canyon, so steep and hot in summer that miners dubbed it Hell's Hollow.

After plunging to the bottom, you arrive at Lake McClure, then start another series of hairpin turns back up the other side, finally reaching Coulterville. This bucolic settlement is one of the less developed gold rush towns, its historic buildings still weathered and time beaten, not yet prettied-up by developers, but surviving nonetheless.

Coulterville got its start in 1850, when Pennsylvania merchant George Coulter opened a supply business for miners. When the environs proved rich, the town grew to 10,000, including many Chinese immigrants, and life took on typically off-balance aspects. A slice of bread, for instance, cost a dollar ($2 if buttered). Coulterville burned to the ground three times before sturdier structures went up, and more than forty of them survive.

It's a town of covered boardwalks along **Main Street,** where twenty-five bars formerly stood. The renowned Hotel Jeffrey (209-878-3471; www.hotel jefferygold.com), which claimed Ralph Waldo Emerson and Teddy Roosevelt as guests, started as a Mexican cantina and fandango hall in the 1850s and has 30-inch-thick rock-and-adobe walls. Nearby are the local hanging tree, where Leon Ruiz was strung up for killing two Chinese miners, and the "Whistling Billy" locomotive, an eight-ton engine shipped around the Horn and hauled here by mule train. Among other historical relics are an old trading post, the Gazzala Station saloon and dance hall; Bruschi Brothers warehouse; and a pint-size stone jail—small but effective. You can have lunch at Coulter Cafe and General Store, formerly a rooming house for prospectors.

The adobe Sun Sun Wo Store (and part-time opium den), on the outskirts of town, is a remarkably well-preserved reminder of Coulterville's Chinese heritage. Right next door sits Candy's Place, which for years did a thriving trade in assorted vices—until its owner ran off with a prominent citizen, never to return (it's now a private residence).

Coulterville retains much of its frontier spirit and atmosphere and the big annual event is a Coyote Howl, held every May.

Uncovering the most picturesque mining towns generally means getting off Highway 49, which bears the brunt of tourist traffic. Farther north in Tuolumne County, **Jamestown** is one such place: Main Street is graced by a little park with a white gazebo and a row of brightly painted buildings with overhanging balconies. Most have been transformed into shops, hotels, and restaurants, so the place is hardly a throwback to the gold rush. Yet there's a certain aura of nostalgia hanging over the town. You can browse through piles of bric-a-brac at Emporium Antiques (1897), with its elegant arched facade; enjoy a fine meal across the street at the historic 1859 National Hotel; and then try your luck at prospecting. Look for a stuffed mannequin of a miner hanging from a gallows outside Gold Prospecting Adventures on Main Street. They promise to teach tinhorns how to use a sluice box and find the "pay streak" in a local stream. Of course, you get to keep any gold you find! Call (209) 984-4653 for information, or see www.goldprospecting.com.

After the first local strike in 1848, "Jimtown" mushroomed overnight in typical fashion and then served as gateway to the Mother Lode. The area really boomed with the arrival of the Sierra Railway that ran between Oakdale and Jamestown, and later to Angels Camp. This story is re-created just outside town at *Railtown 1897 State Historic Park,* which is the outdoor sister of Sacramento's famed railroad museum. In the old depot and fully working roundhouse and turntable, watch old train engines being restored and maintained, then stroll through a blacksmith shop and movie sets. (The park has been featured in more than 200 films and TV shows.) On weekends an old train chuffs around the property on a 6-mile tour. The park is open daily from 9:30 a.m. to 4:30 p.m. with shorter winter hours; fees are charged for tours and train rides (209-984-3953; www.csrmf.org/railtown).

From Jamestown, *Highway 108* is one way to get to the east side of the Sierra, U.S. Highway 395 at Bridgeport, although it's closed during winter and early spring. Scenic places to stop along the way are Pinecrest Lake (near Dodge Ridge Ski Resort), Donnell Vista Point, and the Columns of the Giants—striking rock formations, similar to the more famous Devils Postpile farther south, found just a half mile from the road. The stark, columnar cliffs were formed eons ago from basalt lava flows.

Kennedy Meadows Pack Station (www.kennedymeadows.com) near the Sierra summit offers summer guided trail rides and overnight trips by mule into the surrounding wilderness areas and the northern back country of Yosemite National Park, an area visited by few. From Kennedy Meadows the narrow, winding road climbs through spectacular scenery to Sonora Pass at 9,624 feet before making a rapid descent down the eastern slope.

If you stay on Highway 49 instead of taking this sidetrip, you will remain in the heart of gold country. *Moaning Cavern,* 4 miles east of Angels Camp at Vallecito, takes its name from the strange sound said to emanate from the entrance. Indians believed the caves to be sacred, and 144 winding steps lead you down to a graveyard of prehistoric bones, the remains of about one hundred unfortunate souls who either fell or were thrown from above. In the 1850s miners looking for gold lowered themselves into the cavern by rope, and today you can make the same descent on a challenging rappel tour, dropping 165 feet into the main chamber, which is large enough to hold the Statue of Liberty. For information call (209) 736-2708 or go to www.caverntours.com.

A century ago well-to-do travelers made *Calaveras Big Trees* a must on their grand tour of California. These inspiring giant sequoia redwoods along Highway 4 still receive a quarter of a million visitors annually. Most come in summer and flock to the popular 1.5-mile-long North Grove Trail, with imposing specimens such as the Old Bachelor, with its massive, gnarled limbs, and a trio of elegant redwood monarchs called the Three Graces.

trivia

Geologists estimate that 70 percent of California's gold has yet to be discovered.

The grove became well known in 1852, and before long the hucksters had moved in. Entrepreneurs erected scaffolding and stripped the foot-thick bark off one tree in numbered sections, then shipped it to England for reassembly at an exhibition. (With this protective shield gone, the tree died; it's now just a fire-blackened hulk.) Another group held a contest to see how fast it could fell the largest tree. You can climb to the top of the 24-foot-wide stump they left as a legacy; it was used as a dance floor and for church services, among other things. The trunk itself served as a bowling alley. So much for John Muir's "monarchs of the forest."

If you arrive during the busy season, you can escape the crowds by visiting the less accessible *South Grove,* about 10 miles from park headquarters on the other side of the Stanislaus River. This is the largest stand of sequoias north of Kings River some 150 miles away, and contains the Louis Agassiz Tree, the park's largest single specimen, 250 feet high and 25 feet across. South Grove Trail winds along Big Trees Creek, passing about a thousand redwoods, many of them alive when the New Testament was being written half a world away. The path is remote and primitive, crowded with sugar pines (known for their 2-foot-long cones), azaleas, and dogwood.

For information on Calaveras Big Trees State Park, call (209) 795-3840 or (209) 795-2334. The North Grove Visitor Center is open weekends only in winter and daily in summer. Call for hours.

Highway 4, the Ebbetts Pass National Scenic Byway, runs from Angels Camp into the high Sierra, joining Highway 89 about 5 miles south of Markleeville. East of Calaveras, the road climbs along a ridge above the Stanislaus River Canyon, flanked by granite outcrops and dense forests that are best seen from Liberty and Hells Kitchen vista points. The road continues to **Bear Valley** (209-753-2301; www.bearvalley.com), a year-round recreation area where you can ski at Mount Reba in winter or see classical music concerts in summer. Next comes Lake Alpine (www.lakealpine.com) at 7,350 feet, with superb mountain scenery and fishing. To the south is the 160,000-acre Carson-Iceberg Wilderness, which offers numerous soul-stirring hikes through pristine meadows and untouched lakes (www.fs.fed.us/r5/stanislaus/visitor/carson.shtml). From here the road climbs to Ebbetts Pass at 8,730 feet. (Note: Highway 4 past Bear Valley is closed from first snow until May.)

Amador County, with its seat at historic Jackson on Highway 49, lies in the heart of the gold country. But **Highway 88** is another less traveled west-east route into the Sierra Nevada in the direction of Lake Tahoe.

Long before the frenzied cries of "Gold!" rang through these hills, Native Americans were living a simple, peaceful existence. When gold fever hit, the Miwoks were driven out of their traditional homes. Even so, each year they returned for ceremonies and celebrations, games, and the gathering of acorns. One of these Miwok settlements is preserved at **Chaw'se Indian Grinding Rock State Historic Park,** about a mile off Highway 88. It's a haven of tranquil meadows, and a forest of manzanita, ponderosa pine, and the black oak trees that provided acorns, the staple food of the Miwok diet.

> ## trivia
>
> California's golden trout is found only in the icy streams of the High Sierra and is native to no other state.

The main historic attraction consists of 1,185 holes ground into a granite outcropping with stone pestles and used for pulverizing acorns and other seeds. The resulting "flour" was made into a beverage, bread, or mush, and a typical family consumed about 2,000 pounds of the stuff each year. Close inspection of the pockmarked rocks reveals the individual holes, or mortar cups, that were used until they became too deep.

It's easy to imagine the simple yet idyllic life before white people arrived to turn the Miwoks' world upside down. A well-marked path takes you to the largest roundhouse (reconstructed) in California, with an entry door facing the rising sun. Inside, you can sometimes smell traces of smoke from recent ceremonies. It's easy to imagine the native dancers attired in ceremonial garb and chanting nearby.

The best time to convert these fantasies to reality is during Big Time, the fourth weekend in September, when there are songs, dances, arts and crafts, and Indian football to supplement acorn gathering. At this rambunctious spectacle, players are allowed to pick up and run with opponents who are carrying the ball, but only if they are female.

Chaw'se Indian Grinding Rock State Historic Park, located on Pine Grove–Volcano Road, is open daily from sunrise to sunset. For information call (209) 296-7488.

Three miles off Highway 88, **Volcano** is a gold-country classic, a tiny one-time mining town amid the pines that continues to bask in the memory of its days of glory. Volcano is about as sleepy as they come, with a few historic buildings and shops that open sporadically, depending on the weather and other variables.

Volcano had California's first circulating library, first theater group and debating society, first law school and astronomical observatory. Volcano also had its requisite number of hotels, saloons, brothels, and bakeries, as well as a "court of quick justice."

Lying at the base of encircling hills, the town got its strange name from early miners who thought the site resembled the caldera of a volcano. The town grew to 10,000 residents, who scrapped and scraped for the gold stuff, and the valley once bragged of a 2.5-mile-long sluice box. The Chinese arrived late and literally cleaned up. By meticulously scouring all the old sluices and machinery with fine-haired brushes and scraping tools, they collected fortunes in gold dust.

The wonderful **St. George Hotel** (209-296-4458; www.stgeorgehotel .com), has been in continual use since 1862, not counting the three times it burned to the ground. The three-story, white-and-red-brick building is a gem of gold rush architecture, with suspiciously sloping balconies, pillars choked with climbing trumpet vine, and floors that creak even when you tiptoe.

trivia

The grizzly bear, which appears on the state flag and great seal, is now extinct in California.

The rooms range from elegant to sparse—iron-frame beds, old bureaus, wall hooks for your clothes—and bear names like "Poker Flat" and "Red Dog." The restaurant has been "serving food and grog since 1862." The **Whiskey Flat Saloon** in the hotel remains Volcano's social center, its ceiling covered with dollar bills and business cards, and the walls dripping with odd pieces from just about everywhere, like the "rattlesnake" (actually a python skin) used to trick visiting tinhorns.

In town, the old assay office in a tin-roofed lean-to that really leans is the visitor center. The Volcano Theatre Company performs inside in the Cobblestone Theatre, and outside in the Amphitheatre. The old country store has served customers since 1852. In a ramshackle shed around the corner sits a

Civil War–era cannon called Old Abe, which helped the Volcano Blues put down a threatened Confederate uprising. Other historic buildings include the Bavarian Brewery (1856) and the restored Union Hotel (1880), open for business, though some locals claim it's haunted.

Each spring four acres near Volcano burst forth in floral gold, as well as white, pink, and a rainbow of other colors. At **Daffodil Hill** more than 300,000 flowers (some 300 varieties) stand up and shout for a few weeks in March and April. (The exact blooming cycle varies from year to year.) In 1887, the McLaughlin family began planting bulbs at the rate of about a thousand per year. Their descendants have carried on and they fling open their private ranch during blooming season only. Daffodil Hill, located 3 miles northeast of Volcano, is open daily for the short season at no charge (209-296-7048).

Ten miles north in **Fiddletown,** a giant fiddle hangs above the community club, right next to the volunteer firehouse and a cafe. If this drowsy village seems a bit on the scruffy side, it's probably because ruffians of one description or another have been drifting in and out for 150 years.

According to local legend, Fiddletown was named after the original settlers from Missouri who spent their leisure hours playing music and dancing. A snobbish local judge, embarrassed at having to tell people he was from a place called Fiddletown, actually changed the name to Oleta for some years, before local pride resurfaced to claim its heritage. The annual Fiddlers' Jam contest is in September.

Fiddletown's most important historical site reflecting the sizeable Chinese community that once lived here is the **Chew Kee Store** (Dr. Yee's Herbal Shop), restored and filled with shelves of potions and elixirs. Located on Main Street across from the old Chinese Gambling House, the historic store is open Saturday from April through October from noon to 4:00 p.m.

Northward (east of Plymouth) lies the arcadian **Shenandoah Valley,** an area of rolling hills and vineyards, where you can get a whiff of traditional winemaking. Today there are about thirty wineries in Amador County. Among the pioneers was D'Agostini Vineyards, the state's fourth oldest, founded by a Swiss immigrant in 1856. It has since been renamed Sobon Estate, and you can wander through a cellar of huge oak barrels and try some zinfandel, a local specialty. Open for tasting daily from 9:30 a.m. to 5:00 p.m. at 14430 Shenandoah Road.

Shenandoah Vineyards resides in noble stone buildings at the top of a gentle rise and offers an art galley, in addition to wine tasting. Open daily from 10:00 a.m. to 5:00 p.m. at 12300 Steiner Road.

For both wineries call (209) 245-4455 or consult www.sobonwine.com for more information.

Southern Sierra

Returning to Highway 88 you climb steadily into the mountains through El Dorado National Forest, more than a half-million acres of get-away-from-it-all wilderness. (Take the Bear River turnoff.) The ascent to **Kit Carson Pass** (8,573 feet) skirts sparkling lakes and sawtooth peaks. Carson and John C. Frémont were the first to map a trail through these mountains, and it became a main avenue to the goldfields. Today it's the site of highly regarded Kirkwood Ski Resort (www.kirkwood.com). Just beyond the pass you can take Highway 89 north toward bustling Lake Tahoe.

Mark Twain wrote: "Three months of camp life on it would restore an Egyptian mummy to his pristine vigor and give him an appetite like an alligator." **Lake Tahoe** is a blue-green alpine jewel that encapsulates the best of the Sierra Nevada. Unfortunately, the lake's beauty and first-class recreational facilities bring legions of visitors summer and winter alike. Emerald Bay, toward the southwestern tip, is the most famous scenic spot, a must for anyone with a camera. Most people miss a top-notch sight just a 1-mile hike away—a sprawling, thirty-eight-room mansion modeled on a Scandinavian castle.

Vikingsholm was the dream come true of millionaire heiress Lora Knight, who built her summer residence here in a style popular at the turn of the century—the eleventh century, that is. Swedish architect Lennart Palme and Mrs. Knight traveled extensively in Scandinavia, studying castles and homes for the final design, which was based on a medieval Norse fortress.

The trail to Vikingsholm starts near Eagle Falls. On the way down, spot the little teahouse Mrs. Knight had built across a narrow strait on Fannette Island. At the trail's end you finally see the mansion. The setting is superb, and because no trees were cut down during construction and only natural materials were used, the home blends harmoniously with the woods.

Vikingsholm was built in just five months, with two hundred workers living on-site. Timber was barged across the lake, stone quarried nearby, and all metal pieces forged right on the job.

Enter the mansion, built around a circular courtyard, through a heavy wooden door and pass into a living room of antique furniture and carved beams, then on to the dining room. During its heyday the castle had a staff of sixteen maids, chauffeurs, and cooks, and today summer park rangers set out

At the Rim of the World

The Tahoe Rim Trail (TRT), open since 2001, is a 165-mile path that traverses the ridgeline of Lake Tahoe's crown of peaks. Its track and inspiring scenery is available for casual day hikers as well as backpackers, bikers, and horse riders from mid-June through October.

The TRT winds its way through valleys, along ridges, and up the granite peaks of the Carson Range, joining the rugged Pacific Crest Trail at some points. The flora changes according to season, from spring wildflowers to fall foliage. Among the many scenic highlights are Freel Saddle at 10,000 feet and Lake Aloha's islands of granite boulders. The best views can be found at Christopher's Loop, South Camp Peak, Twin Peaks, and Rose Knob Peak. Though much of the terrain is challenging, there's an easy 1.2-mile interpretive trail at Tahoe Meadows (8,740 feet) that's even wheelchair accessible. For more information contact the Tahoe Rim Trail Association at (775) 298-0012 or visit www.tahoerimtrail.org.

Mrs. Knight's elegant china. Upstairs, heavy Scandinavian rugs cover the floor of the bedroom where Mrs. Knight slept in a replica of a queen's bed found on a 1,200-year-old Viking ship.

Vikingsholm is open in summer only. For information visit www.vikings holm.com.

Rather than fighting the crowds at Lake Tahoe, you could turn south into Hope Valley on Highway 89 and drive about 20 miles along a highly scenic route of pine forest and granite outcrops. *Markleeville* is a picturesque hamlet and the seat of Alpine County—the state's smallest county, with fewer than 1,000 full-time residents spread over 727 square miles. The county boasts only one traffic light, a flashing yellow signal, which makes Markleeville (population under 200) a veritable urban center.

Tucked between mountain folds at about 5,500 feet, the town was named after founder Jacob Marklee, an ornery fellow who built a toll bridge across a local creek in 1861. Apparently this led to a heated argument in which Marklee was killed (the other man got off by pleading self-defense). This story is recounted at a small historical museum (open sporadically) devoted to silver mining.

The Markleeville General Store has been serving customers the basics since 1865. Across the road (on Highway 89 at Montgomery Street) sits the Creekside Lodge (866-802-7335) from the same period; it has a good restaurant heated

trivia

Portola's Western Pacific Railroad Museum along the Feather River Scenic Byway boasts a 115-plus car and locomotive vintage-train collection (www.wplives.org).

by an old Franklin stove. Next door is the Cutthroat Saloon, a rowdy bar whose walls sport a collection of mounted deer heads.

Visitors come to Markleeville for trout fishing, rafting, and hiking in summer, and for cross-country skiing and fireside relaxing in winter. Four miles from town ***Grover Hot Springs State Park*** sits in the shadow of 10,000-foot Hawkins Peak. It offers two outdoor pools, one fed by 104-degree water from six natural mineral springs and the other for cooling off. Relax after a long day of hiking or skiing local trails; at night you're sure to have that appetite Mark Twain wrote about!

Grover Hot Springs State Park is open year-round; call (530) 694-2248 for further information.

The Eastern Slope

From Markleeville, Highway 89 continues south and east to Monitor Pass (8,314 feet), then quickly descends the Sierra Nevada's east side to ***U.S. Highway 395*** in California's high-desert beginning of the Great Basin that stretches across three states all the way to the Rockies. Here tourists are few and the sights spectacular.

A drive along US 395 during winter or spring is the best way to see the jagged peaks and glaciers of the range in all their majesty. It's a region of extraordinary contrasts, with perennial snowfields at 13,000 feet overlooking sagebrush-dotted desert. For geologists the eastern Sierra provides a textbook example of fault-block mountains, created when a huge chunk of the earth's crust was detached and uplifted.

Take a side trip to ***Bodie,*** which some people claim was the "baddest" mining town of them all. Lying high (8,375 feet) in the windy, sage-strewn hills southeast of Bridgeport, 13 miles off US 395, it can certainly lay claim to being the West's most authentic ghost town.

trivia

The state's motto, Eureka!, is a Greek word meaning "I have found it." It refers to the discovery of gold in 1848.

The state parks service, while not doing restoration, keeps about 150 original pine buildings in a condition of "arrested decay," a kind of suspended animation so realistic it looks as if townsfolk just up and left one day. Naturally there's lots of dust, and things have begun to decay, but all the furniture is original, and the bedbugs in the sagging mattresses may still bite. You can peek into the old saloon and see a roulette wheel, poker chips, and decks of cards, and bottles of rotgut whisky. There's also a Methodist church with wooden pews and a pipe organ, proving that at least some folks here were not scoundrels. Unfortunately, the church held its last service in 1932, and later its interior was vandalized—even the Ten Commandments painted on oilcloth were stolen.

Bodie got its name from an early prospector, William S. Body, who froze to death in a storm. (Bodie winters include snow up to 20 feet deep, 100 mph winds, and temperatures down to forty below zero.) After gold was discovered, a camp went up nearby, and legend has it that a sign painter simply misspelled the name. Gold seekers and assorted parasites swarmed in, a ragtag collection of men who unearthed fortunes by day and squandered them by night.

Bodie was wild and wicked, with rotten whisky and mean men, opium dens, and ladies of easy virtue. Fistfights, stabbings, and robberies were commonplace, and during one violent period there was a killing a day. Even the weather was nasty, with bitterly cold winters and scorching summers. The town claimed sixty-five saloons and a flourishing red-light district along Maiden Lane and Virgin Alley. There's a story that one small child, upon learning that his family planned to move there, knelt down and prayed, "Good-bye, God, we're going to Bodie!"

A Mustang Sally

Incredibly, many thousands of horses still live free on unfenced lands in the West. It's possible to see some of these wild mustangs in their natural habitat along California's Eastern Slope, where the snow-dusted Sierra Nevada looks like a giant stage setting. Outfitters based in Bishop offer horseback treks through Inyo National Forest near the Nevada state line, where thousands of the animals live in remote canyons and on the open range. Both experienced riders and novices are welcome to join the small groups, which are led by seasoned wranglers along old stagecoach roads and high-desert country pocked with chaparral and sagebrush.

The small and wiry mustangs are descendants of the original barbs brought here by Spanish conquistadors and later mixed with other breeds. They run in groups of up to fifty animals, defiant in their freedom and very wary of people. But the tour groups usually get close enough for photos and to see and hear the wild horses cavorting as nature intended—truly a magnificent sight.

Mustang-viewing trips are offered by Rock Creek Pack Station in spring and early summer; call (760) 872-8331 or 935-4493 or go to www.rockcreekpackstation.com for details. Frontier Pack Train offers similar trips (888-437-6853; www.frontierpacktrain.net). In addition, about sixteen outfitters offering various kinds of horse and mule trips belong to the Eastern High Sierra Packers Association. For information check www.395.com/generalinfo/bcstock.cfm; call (760) 873-8405; or write to them c/o the Bishop Chamber of Commerce, at 690 North Main Street, Bishop, CA 93514.

The town's heyday ended about 1890, and it slowly declined, although mining went on until 1941. A small percentage of the original buildings remain, slouching and leaning like aging derelicts. But there's a lot to see: a well-stocked general store, the old hotel, a jail and iron bank vault, and a fine museum with an antique funeral carriage. The old schoolhouse retains its original desks and blackboard. Walk the dusty streets and plank sidewalks and be thankful you won't be leaving town in a pine box.

Bodie State Historic Park is open daily from 9:00 a.m. to 4:00 p.m. (and from 8:00 a.m. until 7:00 p.m. in summer), but the road is closed in winter due to harsh weather. Admission is charged. For information call (760) 647-6445.

A few miles south of Bodie lies iridescent blue *Mono Lake,* shimmering like a mirage as you approach, with the White Mountains looming in the background. Here the only sounds are the cries of birds and the crunch of the salt-encrusted mud as you walk a shoreline ringed with spire like mineral formations. This eerie landscape seems to belong to another time or another planet. Mark Twain called Mono Lake "the loneliest spot on earth."

Born more than half a million years ago, Mono Lake is a remnant of a once-vast body of water, one of a handful of lakes remaining in the Great Basin after the last ice age. Until recently scientists feared that time was running out for Mono Lake. In 1941 the thirsty city of Los Angeles (which had already sucked dry Owens Lake to the south) began diverting water from streams that emptied here. The lake's water level dropped about 45 feet, transforming islands into peninsulas, and the water became more saline as salt and other minerals were concentrated. Mono became two and a half times saltier than the Pacific Ocean, and the high alkalinity made it impossible for fish to survive. The lake seemed to be dying.

Then in 1994 the State Water Board resolved the long controversy by allowing the diverted streams to again flow into the lake. In the summer of 2006, the lake reached its highest point since 1972.

Life continues at the once-dying lake. In winter, blooming algae turn the lake pea-soup green, providing a feast for brine flies and brine shrimp in summer, when they reproduce in the billions. These creatures, in turn, provide food for astonishing numbers of seasonal birds: two million eared grebes, snowy plovers, California gulls, and about ninety other species that gorge on the abundant food. Visitors who decide to take a swim will find themselves floating on the highly saline water, which is slippery to the touch. The high

trivia

The ancient bristlecone pines of Inyo National Forest are the oldest living trees on earth, dating back to at least 2,000 years before the birth of Christ.

alkaline content makes it very cleansing, and old-timers claim that a soak in the lake will cure almost anything. Mark Twain remarked that the dirtiest clothes could be cleaned spotless by Mono Lake water.

The unusual mineral formations along the shoreline, called *tufa,* are created when calcium from freshwater, welling up from underground springs, combines with carbonates in the lake. The brittle calcite builds up around the mouths of the springs, forming towers up to 30 feet tall and other strange and spectacular shapes. About 85 percent of the California gull population comes each year to lay eggs on the tufa islands, which are safe shelters from coyotes and other predators. The best place to see tufa formations is the lake's designated South Tufa Area.

Another top sight is nearby **Mono Craters,** the youngest mountains on the continent. Some were formed as recently as 500 years ago. Rising more than 2,000 feet, the twenty-one craters are set in a valley of soft lava pumice atop a huge magma chamber. But be forewarned: Geologists say that future eruptions here are certain. For a close look take Highway 120 to Panum Crater, where a trail leads to the rim of a still-active volcano.

The Mono Basin Scenic Visitor Center, housed in a spectacular building, is located just north of the town of Lee Vining (the eastern gateway to Yosemite National Park). It features imaginative exhibits on the area, art and photography exhibits, an award-winning film, and free tours of the South Tufa area. Call (760) 647-6331. For more information, contact the Mono Lake Committee at (760) 647-6595, go to www.monolake.org, or stop by the information center and bookstore at the corner of Highway 395 and Third Street.

Northern Gold Country

Back on the western slope of the Sierra Nevada, Gold Country becomes mobbed along the stretch of Highway 49 from Jackson north to Nevada City (in California). That's hardly true about the sleepy burg of **Rough and Ready,** 4 miles west of Grass Valley, except maybe on Secession Day each June (the last Sunday), when local patriots and lots of visitors commemorate the town's brief independence back in 1850.

Founded by a miner who had fought under General Zachary "Old Rough and Ready" Taylor during the Mexican War, the town boasted rich diggings nearby. So when the government declared a tax on mining claims, residents officially seceded from the Union for three months, elected their own president, and drafted a constitution. But come July 4 they got sentimental and recanted without bloodshed. There are a couple of sights from those wild days, such as the original blacksmith's shop.

Since 1959 most visitors have come to make a union of a different sort at the ***Wayside Wedding Chapel,*** a one-room country church with stained glass and six white pews—ideal for a romantic wedding or renewal of vows. Unlike the quickies at nearby Reno, weddings here need to be planned, but everything can be arranged for a price, from the minister (all faiths) to witnesses. For further information call (530) 273-6678.

Gold prospectors were a wild-and-woolly breed, hell-bent on extracting the shiny stuff whatever the cost. When they became more desperate, as placer deposits dwindled in the 1860s, they employed hydraulic mining, a practice

The Tragedy of the Donner Party

Even before the gold rush, California beckoned. In April 1846 two Illinois brothers, George and Jacob Donner, gathered their families and possessions and headed west in six covered wagons. They joined others at Independence, Missouri, where George was elected wagon master of a group of eighty-nine men, women, and children.

Delayed along the trail, the exhausted and demoralized Donner party reached the eastern approach to the Sierra Nevada by late October. After a week of hesitation, they decided to press on over the pass toward Sutter's Fort (Sacramento). But winter came early that year, and one of the worst storms in history pummeled the hapless pioneers. Snowbound, they hunkered down around a lake that would come to bear their name. And food quickly ran out.

In December one group tried to escape and was hit by a Christmas storm. Half of that group died huddled under their blankets. Famished and despairing, the survivors resorted to cannibalism. When rescuers finally arrived in late February, they were shocked to find the evidence; but when another big storm hit, they too partook of all that was available at a place later named Starved Camp.

In winter Donner Summit is still brutally cold and the snowfall can be enormous, up to 400 inches. The lake is beautiful and seldom crowded, as motorists whiz by on Interstate 80 between the Central Valley and Reno. A monument erected at Donner Memorial State Park near Truckee marks the snow depth of that horrific winter of 1846–1847 at about 22 feet.

The Emigrant Trail Museum here has a map of the 2,000-mile California Trail and numerous railroad and ski exhibits. The real draw is the Donner story. There's a list of those who survived—forty-seven of the original eighty-nine—and those who perished: their names, ages, and identification (eleven people from the rescue groups were also eaten). Near the museum a short trail leads to cabin sites where some of the Donners dined and died.

The museum at Donner Memorial State Park is open daily from 9:00 a.m. to 4:00 p.m. For camping and picnic sites, reservations are necessary in summer; call (530) 582-7892 for more information.

that was particularly disastrous for the environment. The process is clearly seen at ***Malakoff Diggins State Historic Park,*** located 29 miles northeast of Nevada City on a remote and little-visited site.

Here the miners literally blasted gold from the hillsides with high-pressure water hoses shooting liquid at more than two million gallons an hour. The water then flowed through a series of sluices to extract the ore, and this process turned mountains into molehills and sent thousands of tons of mud downstream, so much that the runoff created havoc with valley farmers and even caused major floods like the one at Marysville in 1875. Hydraulic mining was finally banned after eighteen years of devastation.

Enter the park through a huge man-made ravine with fluted cliffs and contorted rocks that are strangely beautiful in their starkness, reminiscent of the Dakota badlands or deserts of Utah. Up to 50,000 tons of earth were washed away each day, leaving a pit more than a mile long and 600 feet deep. A 6.5 mile trail walk around its rim and floor shows what a few gold-maddened men with water cannons accomplished.

The diggings are a short walk from the old mining town of ***North Bloomfield,*** with about thirty dilapidated buildings and a dozen reclusive residents. A fistful of historic exhibits includes an old livery stable, a church, and a general store (with miners' clothing, oil lamps, and so forth) as well as a small museum that chronicles the destruction wrought over nearly two decades. Curious displays include 12-foot-long skis and a portable undertaker's table.

To reach the park take Highway 49 north from Nevada City for 12 miles, turn east on Tyler-Foote Road, and proceed 17 miles along a winding mountain road. For information about schedules and fees, call (530) 265-2740.

Of all the old gold rush towns, ***Downieville*** is the one that should not be missed. It was originally called the Forks because of its site at the confluence of two rivers, but Major William Downie bribed enough residents into renaming the settlement in his honor. Rich placer deposits were discovered nearby, producing the kind of stories that set people's blood racing. One woman found $500 worth of gold while sweeping the earthen floor of her kitchen.

Typical boomtown growth hit, and by 1851 about 5,000 gold seekers had arrived. But Downieville had nowhere to grow; it's hemmed in by steep hillsides, and old homes cling to the slopes above town like terrified mountaineers. Although the present population hovers at only about 400, the town is the seat of Sierra County.

A trip to Downieville is twice as nice because the road getting there, ***Highway 49*** out of Nevada City, is among the state's most scenic, especially the stretch beyond Camptonville along the Yuba River. The landscape gradually becomes higher, cooler, and less crowded passing through a narrow

Riding the Rails

You can ride through Donner Pass and the massive Sierra Nevada in a style pioneers would have happily enjoyed aboard Amtrak's Super Liner, the *California Zephyr.* This double-deck train runs year-round between Chicago and Oakland along a route considered one of America's most beautiful, and many people from the Bay Area travel the stunning stretch to Reno for a bit of weekend action. (It's said that the eastbound trains are always more festive than the westbound.)

Pulling out of Emeryville (near Oakland) in the morning, the *Zephyr* skirts San Pablo Bay and the Carquinez Strait, then heads into the valley with a stop at Sacramento. The splendid scenery begins after Roseville as the tracks start to climb toward Colfax in the high Gold Country, taking on what railroaders call "the Hill." The Sierra is soon revealed in all its glory, and from glass-encased observation cars travelers see awe-inspiring real estate, such as the American River Canyon, not visible from the road.

When the train finally reaches Truckee and Donner Summit, it's around lunchtime. In addition to the dining car, a lounge car serving snacks doubles as the train's social center. Many people bring their own food and drink. The trip over the Sierra Nevada to Reno takes about six hours, and the service is top-notch, including an onboard sightseeing guide.

Though the amenities may be modern, the route is hardly new—trains have traveled these rails for more than a century. Amtrak's *California Zephyr* follows the route of the first transcontinental railroad built by the Central Pacific. This incredibly rugged stretch was finished in just five years as 10,000 men, mostly Chinese laborers, raced east from Sacramento and up 7,000 feet into the Sierra, then down the other side to Nevada and on to Utah, where they met workers from the Union Pacific coming from the opposite direction.

For further information on this thrilling trip, contact Amtrak at (800) 872-7245 or check www.amtrak.com.

canyon and rock-strewn river basin. At last the picture-perfect town of tin-roofed houses, cradled in a canyon where the Yuba and Downie Rivers meet, leaps out just ahead.

Downieville is a place of narrow streets lined with weathered wood-frame buildings and covered sidewalks, where you can ponder the scene in the shade of an overhang or dine on a terrace fronting a rushing stream. The salmon-colored Craycroft Building was formerly a courthouse, saloon, and dance hall, and the Mackerman Building is home to the *Mountain Messenger,* the first newspaper (1853) in these parts and still going strong as California's oldest weekly. It has 3-foot-thick walls and fireproof iron doors for the inevitable fires that ravaged all mining towns. At St. Charles Place bar next door, a sign outside reads: CHECK ALL GUNS AND LONG KNIVES.

Downieville can claim the only authentic gallows left in California, conveniently built next to the old courthouse, which was destroyed years ago. This grim wooden landmark is protected by a group called Friends of the Gallows. A Main Street plaque recalls a rare event, even in this wild country—the execution of a woman. The unfortunate Juanita, who stabbed Jack Cannon to death after a quarrel, swung from a Downieville bridge in 1851, a few years before the gallows were built.

The **Sierra County Museum** on Main Street, with gold nuggets and the usual collection of mining artifacts, sits in an attractive brick building that once housed a Chinese gambling den. At Lions Memorial Park near the fork of the two rivers, mining history lives on as discarded hardware, including a steam boiler and a rusting iron car filled with hefty chunks of quartz.

A good deal of gold prospecting still takes place in this area. A pleasant drive awaits on the 12-mile stretch from Downieville to **Sierra City,** a pretty hamlet at 4,000 feet with just 200 residents. Miners arrived about 1850 and started building in a narrow canyon overlooked by the Sierra Buttes. The

trivia

Used just once, in 1885, Downieville Gallows is preserved as a state historic monument.

settlement was leveled three times by avalanches sweeping down the canyon, but the diggings were so rich that miners refused to abandon their little pieces of ground.

Just east of town is the **Kentucky Mine Museum** at a former mining site drilled into solid granite. The tour here gives a good idea of the entire process of hard-rock mining, including "jaw crushers" that broke chunks into smaller rocks and a stamp mill that ground them into powder. Later, mercury was used to extract the precious gold flakes for further refining. Call (530) 862-1310 for admission and tour schedules.

Northern Sierra

Highway 49, "the Golden Chain," continues to Yuba Pass in the high Sierra. An alternate route 5 miles east of Sierra City, **Gold Lake Road,** leads to a spectacular alpine region with several beautiful lakes. Among them is exceptionally picturesque **Sardine Lake,** whose waters mirror the ragged spires of the Sierra Buttes, lording over the landscape at 8,587 feet. When there's snow on the peaks, you may just think you're in the Swiss Alps. The 2-mile hike to Upper Sardine Lake, along a wide trail accessible to four-wheel-drive vehicles, offers a good workout and spectacular scenery; bring water and a picnic lunch. Another nearby spot in nearly pristine condition is Packer Lake, which has a lodge and a few rustic cabins for families and trout fishermen. About a mile away is the trailhead for a great hike to the top of Sierra Buttes. One very worthwhile detour from Gold Lake Road takes you to beautiful Frazier Falls. Here an easy trail leads to several lookout points, including a bird's-eye view from just a few feet above where the water from Frazier Creek plummets over a cliff.

From here, it's a short hop to Plumas County and **Feather River Country,** the final piece in the Sierra Nevada puzzle. This region is not easy to define, especially as there's no single Feather River until the various branches link up at Oroville on the fringes of the Central Valley. The area is roughly bordered by Highways 49 and 70 and includes portions of five counties (primarily Plumas) and two national forests. Elevations range from 1,000 feet in the west to the summit of Mount Ingalls (8,377 feet). This northernmost part of the Sierra Nevada is much less crowded than the Lake Tahoe region, but it offers great scenery and plenty of outdoor activities on more than 1,000 miles of rivers and one hundred lakes.

Heading north from Gold Country, you reach the former lumber town of **Graeagle** (www.graeagle.com), now a neatly planned little community of red

Getting High in the Sierra

Standing dizzy and fear-frozen on a meshed grate, desperately clutching the metal railing, I look straight down a 1,000-foot vertical drop and wonder. Am I mad? I actually busted a gut to get here. But as the nausea and nervousness subside, I feel a certain euphoria at having reached this beautiful place all by myself.

The two-hour climb to the top of Sierra Buttes is one of the best hikes anywhere. This walk-of-a-lifetime starts at the Packer Saddle Trailhead near the Packer Lake Lodge (a good place for coffee before and a brew after). The trail climbs about 1,700 feet over 2.5 miles, but there are numerous switchbacks to make things easier. The first half or so rises gradually, and there's time for a rest at a mountain terrace; then the real climb begins. Finally the trail emerges above the forest at the craggy spires, and you soon see the soaring forest-service lookout station—the final challenge. Crowning the 8,587-foot summit of Sierra Buttes, it is an engineering wonder to behold, reached by climbing a series of metal stairs jutting out miraculously over the abyss. It's downright scary to reach this lofty pinnacle, but you'll never regret it for a minute. The views of Gold Lakes Basin and far beyond are truly inspiring.

For information about this and other hikes in Tahoe National Forest, contact the North Yuba River Ranger District, 15924 Highway 49, Camptonville, CA 95922; (530) 288-3231; www.fs.fed.us/r5/tahoe.

mill-workers cottages transformed into shops with a lake, golf courses, with a wooden Indian named Chief Graeagle to welcome visitors. A few miles west, in the Mohawk Valley, is the Eureka Mining complex, centerpiece of **Plumas-Eureka State Park.** The park headquarters and visitor center occupy the former bunkhouse of a once-thriving gold mine, right down the road from scenic Johnsville.

During 1851 miners exploring near Jamison Creek came across an exposed ledge of quartz and gold some 400 feet long and 20 feet wide, sitting 4 feet above the granite base. Many claims were filed over the next few years. A tent city grew into freewheeling Jamison City, and tramways were built to bring ore down to the central mill near Johnsville. (One of these was said to have served as the world's first ski lift, used by the fun-starved miners.) Mining went on until 1943, resulting in 63 miles of shafts and tunnels.

From just outside the visitor center, the **Mining Trail** leads past a smattering of mining equipment—"chill wheels" used to crush quartz, a waterwheel to power the stamp mill, an air compressor, and other remnants from the days when hundreds of men toiled here. The old Mohawk Mill has been partially reconstructed with new timbers. At one point the mill had sixty stamps, each weighing 600 to 950 pounds, which crushed small pieces of ore into sand. With each stamp dropping up to eighty times a minute, the slamming could be heard for many miles around.

The museum has a fully operational model of a stamp mill (ask to see it turned on) and various displays on mining and skiing history. The first organized ski races in America were held at nearby Onion Valley in 1861, and there's a pair of oak skis used by Snowshoe Thompson, the famous Sierra character who for two years ferried up to eighty pounds of mail on his back between Placerville, California, and Genoa, Nevada, a distance of 90 miles! The museum is open daily from 8:00 a.m. to 4:30 p.m. in summer and variable hours the rest of the year. Call (530) 836-2380 for information.

If heading north from here, turn off into the spectacular **Feather River Canyon** (along Highway 70) or continue on Highway 89 to Lake Almanor

trivia

A ten-ton water-powered wheel, supposedly the world's largest, is found at the Northstar Mine Powerhouse & Pelton Wheel Museum in Grass Valley.

at the far northern edge of the Sierra Nevada range. Created by damming the North Fork, Almanor is a large, virtually undeveloped lake framed by pines, with majestic Lassen Peak looming to the north. The lake offers excellent fishing (trout, bass, king salmon) and warm summer water temperatures for swimming and other sports.

Designated a National Scenic Byway, Highway 70 takes you along the steep, rock-strewn Feather River Canyon of the North Fork, a route that traverses three tunnels and nine bridges. Railroad tracks run parallel to the road, and en route you will probably spot a train or two passing through the canyon. There is camping in Plumas National Forest and a few small resorts at towns such as Portola and Quincy.

The Feather Falls Scenic Area shelters granite domes and sheer ravines northeast of Lake Oroville. The main attraction of the 15,000-acre preserve is the waterfall, which Native Americans attributed to an angry and noisy monster living in a chasm. A 4.5-mile-long trail to the falls winds in and out of canyons, along streams, through a forest of firs and ferns, and finally along a steep ridge to a dramatic overlook. Hikers watch the Fall River cascading from a high cliff onto scattered boulders in a box canyon below. At 640 feet, Feather Falls ranks as California's highest waterfall outside Yosemite Valley.

Another attraction is South Branch Falls, a series of seven beautiful cascades on the Feather River that range from 30 to 150 feet in height. The best time to visit the Feather Falls Scenic Area is spring, when the snowmelt has swollen the river and wildflowers are flaunting their colors. The heart of the preserve is located about 30 miles from Oroville via Highway 162, but it can also be reached from La Porte on the east side. For more information and a map with detailed directions, call (530) 534-6500 or check http://www.fs.fed.us/r5/plumas.

Places to Stay in the Sierra Nevada

SOUTHERN GOLD COUNTRY AND SIERRA

Creekside Lodge
14820 Highway 89
Markleeville
(530) 694-2511

Eureka Street Inn
55 Eureka Street
Sutter Creek
(209) 267-5500

The Foxes Inn
77 Main Street
Sutter Creek
(800) 987-3344

Hotel Jeffrey
5001 Main Street
Coulterville
(209) 878-3471

Hotel Leger
8304 Main Street
Mokelumne Hill
(209) 286-1401

Kit Carson Lodge
Highway 88 at Silverlake
Kit Carson
(209) 258-8500

Meadow Creek Ranch
2669 Triangle Road
Mariposa
(209) 966-3843

Miners Inn
5181 Highway 49 North
Mariposa
(209) 742-7777

National Hotel
18183 Main Street
Jamestown
(209) 984-3446

Sorensen's Resort
14255 Highway 88
Hope Valley
(800) 423-9949

St. George Hotel
16104 Main Street
Volcano
(209) 296-4458

Sutter Creek Inn
Highway 49, Main Street
Sutter Creek
(209) 267-5606

EASTERN SLOPE

The Cain House
340 Main Street
Bridgeport
(760) 932-7040

Chalfant House B&B
213 Academy Avenue
Bishop
(760) 872-1790

Joseph House Inn
376 West Yaney Street
Bishop
(760) 872-3389

Lake View Lodge
51285 Highway 395
Lee Vining
(760) 647-6543

Tioga Lodge
54411 Route 395
Lee Vining
(760) 647-6423

NORTHERN GOLD COUNTRY AND SIERRA

Deer Creek Inn
116 Nevada Street
Nevada City
(530) 265-0363

Downieville River Inn & Resort
121 River Street
Downieville
(800) 696-3308

The Featherbed Inn
542 Jackson Street
Quincy
(530) 283-0102

Gray Eagle Lodge
5000 Gold Lake Road
Graeagle
(800) 635-8778

Herrington's Sierra Pines Resort
104 Main Street
Sierra City
(530) 862-1151

The Lure Resort
100 Lure Bridge Lane
Downieville
(530) 289-3465

Northern Queen Inn
400 Railroad Avenue
Nevada City
(530) 265-5824

Pullman House Inn
256 Commercial Street
Portola
(530) 832-0107

Riverside Inn
206 Commercial Street
Downieville
(530) 289-1000

Sardine Lake Resort
990 Sardine Lake Road
Sierra City
(530) 862-1196

Yuba River Inn
Highway 49 at
Wild Plum Road
Sierra City
(530) 862-1122

WORTH SEEING/DOING IN THE SIERRA NEVADA

Columbia State Historic Park

Devils Postpile National Monument, Mammoth Lakes

Empire Mine State Historic Park, Grass Valley

June Lake Loop

Lake Tahoe, North Shore

Marshall Gold Discovery State Historic Park, Coloma

Placerville's Hangtown

Yosemite National Park

HELPFUL WEB SITES ON THE SIERRA NEVADA

Alpine County Chamber of
Commerce: www.alpinecounty.com

Bishop Visitor Bureau:
www.bishopvisitor.com

California Campgrounds:
www.californiacampgrounds.org

California State Parks:
www.parks.ca.gov

Chester/Lake Almanor Chamber of
Commerce:
www.chester-lakealmanor.com

Gold Country Visitors' Association:
www.calgold.org

Inyo County: www
.theothersideofcalifornia.com

Lake Tahoe Visitors Authority: www
.bluelaketahoe.com

Mariposa County Tourism Bureau:
www.homeofyosemite.com

Mono County Tourism Commission:
www.monocounty.org

Mono Lake Committee:
www.monolake.org

Plumas County Visitors Bureau:
www.plumascounty.org

Sacramento Visitors Bureau:
www.discovergold.org

Tahoe Rim Trail Association:
www.tahoerimtrail.org

Tuolumne County Visitors Bureau:
www.thegreatunfenced.com

Yosemite Area Traveler Information:
www.yosemite.com

Yosemite National Park:
www.nps.gov/yose

Places to Eat in the Sierra Nevada

SOUTHERN GOLD COUNTRY AND SIERRA

Incahoots BBQ Pizza & Grill
9486 Main Street
Plymouth
(209) 245-5544

National Hotel Restaurant (American)
18183 Main Street
Jamestown
(209) 984-3446

Sutter Creek Palace Restaurant & Saloon (Continental)
76 Main Street
Sutter Creek
(209) 267-1300

Wolf Creek Restaurant (American)
14830 Highway 89
Markleeville
(530) 694-2150

EASTERN SLOPE

Latte Da Coffee Café
51 Highway 395
Lee Vining
(760) 647-6310

Tioga Toomey's Whoa Nellie Deli (American)
22 Vista Point Road
Highway 120
Lee Vining
(760) 647-1088

Whiskey Creek at Bishop (American)
524 North Main Street
Bishop
(760) 873-7174

NORTHERN GOLD COUNTRY AND THE SIERRA

Grizzly Grill (American)
250 Bonta Street
Blairsden
(530) 836-1300

Iron Door (American)
Main Street
Johnsville
(530) 836-2376

Longboard's Bar & Grill (American)
402 Poplar Valley Road
Graeagle
(530) 836-1111

Sardine Lake Lodge (Continental)
990 Sardine Lake Road
Sierra City
(530) 862-1190

Sweet Lorraine's (American)
384 Main Street
Quincy
(530) 283-5300

Trolley Junction (American)
400 Railroad Avenue
Nevada City
(530) 265-5259

SHASTA CASCADE

COME TO ANOTHER CALIFORNIA, the signs and bumper stickers proclaim. If this sounds like advertising hype, the message is not. This often forgotten corner of the state is truly a world apart.

Most Californians are only vaguely aware of the Shasta Cascade region, and if they visit, it's along fast, impersonal Interstate 5. Stretching from the eastern slopes of the Coast Range to Nevada and from the Oregon border to the southern fringes of the Cascades, it is sparsely populated and largely untouched.

This unspoiled chunk of the Golden State offers tremendous diversity: volcanoes (including the biggest plug dome on earth); many of California's largest lakes; the world's second-highest man-made waterfall; and a peculiar version of the Abominable Snowman, called Bigfoot. Spotted from time to time (usually during snowstorms), these hairy creatures are said to stand up to 12 feet tall and weigh 800 pounds. If visitors manage to steer clear of these beasts, they can find nearly unlimited outdoor opportunities in Shasta Cascade—whether angling for salmon and steelhead or snowshoeing beside bubbling lava pits.

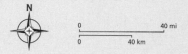

N

| 0 | | 40 mi |
| 0 | | 40 km |

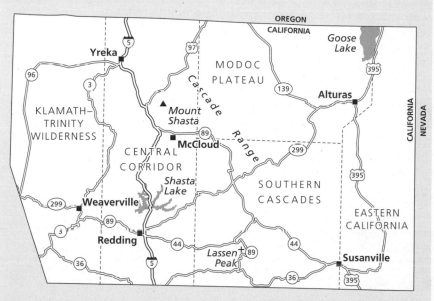

OREGON
CALIFORNIA

Goose
Lake

Yreka

96

3

5

97

MODOC
PLATEAU

139

395

Alturas

KLAMATH–
TRINITY
WILDERNESS

▲ Mount
Shasta

89

McCloud

Cascade Range

299

CENTRAL
CORRIDOR

Shasta
Lake

SOUTHERN
CASCADES

395

299

Weaverville

89

3

EASTERN
CALIFORNIA

Redding

5

44

Lassen
Peak

89

44

Susanville

36

36

395

CALIFORNIA
NEVADA

Getting there is easy: I-5 forms the north–south backbone, and Highway 299 is the main east–west route. The two cross at **Redding,** unofficial capital of Shasta Cascade, with about 85,000 residents. It's considered the hub of the region, and it can be used as a base for exploring.

Redding's **Turtle Bay Exploration Park,** located less than a mile from downtown, is an urban oasis spread over 300 acres along the Sacramento River. Its educational focus is on the interrelation between humans and nature. The excellent interactive museum, a marriage of building and site, is an homage to the river and the blue-collar origins of the town's economy. Across the river are the McConnell Arboretum and Gardens, 200 acres devoted to California, the Mediterranean, South Africa (where 80 percent of all flowering bulbs originate), and other botanical regions. The highly popular Sacramento River Trail begins here.

The **Sundial Bridge,** an architectural and engineering masterpiece designed by Spaniard Santiago Calatrava, connects the south and north sides of the park. The span is supported by 4,300 feet of steel cable suspended from a single white, 217-foot pylon that casts its shadow on hourly markings on the plaza below, creating a sundial. Across the bridge, a wide pedestrian walkway of nonskid glass is illuminated at night to create a striking visual effect.

Klamath–Trinity Wilderness

Trinity County is larger than the state of Delaware but has only about 14,000 residents. A full 97 percent of the land is forested and includes such primitive

AUTHOR'S TOP TEN IN THE SHASTA CASCADE

Weaverville	McCloud
Trinity Alps Wilderness	Lassen Volcanic National Park
Castle Crags State Park	Burney Falls
Dunsmuir	Lava Beds National Monument
Mount Shasta	Cedarville

terrain as the Shasta-Trinity National Forest, the second-largest slice of virgin land in California. Nearly one-third of the county's inhabitants live in **Weaverville,** one of the state's oldest towns, about 45 miles west of Redding on Highway 299.

In July 1848, Major Pierson B. Reading found gold on a sandbar in the Trinity River, which launched the familiar stampede. Three prospectors built the first cabin and they drew straws to decide the name of the new settlement: John Weaver won. Like so many other mining towns, Weaverville was soon big enough to support two theaters and attract Lotta Crabtree, a highly touted performer, in 1855. Later, nearby LaGrange Mine became one of the world's largest hydraulic gold-mining operations.

Its streets still lined with wood-framed houses, picket fences, and honey locust trees, Weaverville has changed little over the years, except for the relentless traffic thundering down Main Street. Stroll under covered walkways past several notable buildings, painted rust red with white trim. Among them is the Court House, with iron shutters and thick walls for fireproofing. Erected in 1856, it served as a hotel, saloon, and store before changing roles in 1865, after the original courthouse became infested with bedbugs.

Weaverville is known for its spiral staircases, hand forged by a blacksmith from Bavaria. They were designed to sidestep the problem of different ownership of upper and lower stories and to preserve valuable Main Street frontage that might otherwise go to building staircases. The **Weaverville Drug Store** (oldest in California) has been serving customers at the same location (219 Main Street) since 1852. On display are patent medicines, a "suppository machine," and bottles of whiskey used for "medicinal purposes." Spirits are also sold across the street at the **Diggins Tavern,** complete with swinging doors and customers dressed in buckskin.

Many Chinese immigrants came to the "land of the golden mountains," and a town within a town developed here, with its own shops, opera house, and gambling parlors. The Temple of the Forest Beneath the Clouds was constructed in 1853, burned down twenty years later, and was rebuilt in 1874.

The **Weaverville Joss House** (Joss being Chinese pidgin English, from the Portuguese word for God, *deos*) is one of the oldest surviving Chinese temples in America. It sits amid gardens and a stream crossed by an arched stone bridge and looks north toward the Trinity Alps.

The temple was designed exactly as in China except that wood was used instead of stone and tile, and the facade was painted white and blue to resemble masonry. Intricate carvings of fish and dragons on the roof were meant to ward off evil spirits, especially needed, it was believed, because funeral processions for whites passed right in front of the temple.

TOP ANNUAL EVENTS IN THE SHASTA CASCADE

Kool April Nights Car Show, Redding
(mid-April)

Sacramento River Festival, Dunsmuir
(late April)

Redding Rodeo Week, Redding
(mid-May)

Old Lewiston Peddlers Faire
(early June)

July 4th Celebration, Weaverville
(July 4)

**Paul Bunyan Mountain and Blues
Festival,** Westwood (early July)

Scott Valley Bluegrass Festival, Etna
(mid-July)

Intermountain Fair, McArthur
(Labor Day weekend)

Balloonfest, Alturas (mid-September)

Rails to Trails Festival, Susanville
(early October)

Just beyond the main entrance are two tall wooden doors designed as spirit screens to keep out evil spirits. Inside, a state ranger reels off a brief history of the place, pointing out pictures of immortals painted on glass, a lion-dance headdress, an abacus, opium pipes, and other curiosities. Worshipers prayed before the three altars, but they were forbidden to ask specifically for riches. "Joss money" was burned in offering to the gods, and to gain their attention a drum and bell sounded during the ceremony.

All around the room are grinning and frowning deities and signs written by immigrants in Chinese. Among them is this simple request: "I want to make my fortune and go home again." Estimates are that about one-third of the immigrants did return; the rest stayed on, hoping to realize their golden dreams someday. The Taoist temple is active with worshippers praying and burning joss sticks. Lion dancers perform on Chinese New Year and July 4. Call (530) 623-5284 for information.

There were less peaceful sides to Chinese life. The *J. J. Jackson Memorial Museum* exhibits tridentlike spears and other weapons used in the infamous Weaverville Tong War of 1854. Two rival Chinese factions found themselves in a feud and began battle preparations. They placed orders for weapons (spears, shields, swords, tin hats) with local blacksmiths and drilled for a month, while townspeople wagered on the upcoming encounter. Finally, in a spot east of town called Five Cent Gulch, a two-minute melee took place before throngs of cheering spectators. When the dust cleared, seven Chinese were dead and twenty wounded.

The museum also houses a good collection of mining and Indian artifacts, antique firearms, an aspirator used to remove body fluids, and authentic jail cells, complete with graffiti, moved over from the courthouse. Call (530) 623-5211 or check www.trinitymuseum.org for more information.

Weaverville is home to one of two ranger stations for the ***Trinity Alps Wilderness.*** These mountains thrust upward in sharp, snowcapped ridges, with glacial canyons and alpine lakes sprinkled amid thick forests of fir and ponderosa pine. The landscape of granite peaks rising to 7,000 to 9,000 feet (Mount Thompson is the highest), resembles the Sierra Nevada but is much more compact. The timberline is lower here, too, and the area is wetter and greener because of its proximity to the coast.

trivia

Shasta Dam has the highest overflow spillway in the world and is three times higher than Niagara Falls.

The Trinity Alps are laced with hundreds of miles of trails throughout a 500,000-acre wilderness area. These are perfect trails for solitary adventures, unless you encounter a wolverine, pine marten, mountain lion, or black bear. Trinity National Forest claims a large concentration of California's bears in California, about one per square mile.

One popular trek goes to the exceptionally beautiful Caribou Lakes Basin, with four lakes cradled in a spectacular granite setting. Another leaves from Hobo Gulch, northwest of Weaverville, and takes in lakes, waterfalls, and an abandoned gold mine. Many trailheads into the wilderness start near the west shore of sprawling Trinity (Clair Engle) Lake. Lewiston Lake is one of the prettiest of all the drive-to lakes in Northern California. It is ringed by Douglas fir, with the Trinity Alps providing a backdrop.

For more information on the area, contact Shasta-Trinity National Forest, P.O. Box 1190, 360 Main Street, Weaverville, CA 96093; (530) 623-2121; www.fs.fed.us/r5/shastatrinity.

Heading west from Weaverville, this stretch of Highway 299 has been dubbed the ***Trinity River Scenic Byway.*** The churning river cuts through some impressive mountain scenery dotted with campgrounds and cottages and is very popular with fishermen and river rafters. Along the way are a few points of interest: the one-time La Grange hydraulic mining operation, Simon Legree's Bar (at Ironside), and China Slide, where some Chinese prospectors were buried under 200 feet of mud in 1890. But for the best views, you need to pull over and peer right down into the narrow river canyon.

trivia

Shasta Lake is called the Houseboat Capital of the World, with more than 400 commercial residence vessels for rent.

trivia

The famous Alcan Highway (U.S. Highway 97) to Fairbanks, Alaska, starts not in Canada or even Washington but in the town of Weed near Mount Shasta.

The town of **Willow Creek** (in Humboldt County), sitting amid a vast forest of Douglas fir trees, is known as the gateway to Bigfoot Country, with a 25-foot wooden sculpture greeting visitors parking at the Willow Creek–China Flat Museum (open summer; 530-629-2653; http://bigfootcountry.net/home). From here Highway 96 pushes north along the little-traveled **Bigfoot Scenic Byway,** following the North Fork of the Trinity and Klamath Rivers, both renowned for trophy-size fish and white-water rafting. The route passes right through the Hoopa reservation, whose main settlement offers the artifact-rich **Hoopa Tribal Museum** (www.hoopa-nsn.gov/departments/museum.htm) and the bustling Lucky Bear Casino. The village of Weitchpec, perched beside a bridge overlooking the Klamath, lies in the heart of Bigfoot country, rugged mountains that have yielded lots of speculation and a few grainy photos and plaster casts of oversized footprints.

At the old logging town of **Happy Camp** (82 miles from Willow Creek), there's another Bigfoot sculpture outside the post office and the Karuk People's

Bigfoot: Legend or Fact?

Native Americans talk about "Sasquatch," and Tibetans have their Yeti, an "Abominable Snowman." Here in northwestern California, powerful creatures of similar stature rule the wild Siskiyou and Klamath Mountains between Willow Creek and Happy Camp. According to a scattering of unconfirmed reports, the "Bigfoot" creatures stand about 8 feet tall and weigh 500 pounds or more, with a light covering of body hair that easily distinguishes them from the furry brown bears common in the area. Those who claim to have spotted a Bigfoot, usually peeking through the trees or around rocks near a campsite, describe their high-pitched voices and wide, flaring nostrils.

Some folks believe that humanoids similar to Bigfoot roamed much of the earth before the end of the last ice age, about 12,000 years ago, and that a handful survived in isolation.

Historical references to California's Bigfoot trace back to the 1880s, and over the years numerous reports surfaced from miners, loggers, and campers, more than forty separate incidents in all. Plaster casts were made of footprints and even a few photos and a home movie taken of one creature running away, whose authenticity have been vigorously challenged. In fact, most scholars and authorities think the whole legend is utter nonsense. But those who claim to have seen a Bigfoot in the flesh swear they are real.

Will the North Rise Again?

They say the folks around Yreka have an ornery streak that surfaces from time to time. Back in 1941 this little blue-collar town north of Mount Shasta led a brief movement to secede from California and create (along with part of southern Oregon) a new state named Jefferson. Even today a spirit of self-determination lingers in this distinct region of loggers, prospectors, and other rugged individualists.

At the time locals were having trouble getting their copper to market (due to the war in Europe, the price of transportation had rocketed), and in November of 1941 disgruntled miners met at Yreka. Here they formed an alliance with miners from southern Oregon suffering from similar problems, and what began as a protest against bad roads quickly snowballed into the so-called Jefferson Rebellion. Grizzled men armed with hunting rifles set up roadblocks and handed out proclamations of independence from California to bewildered motorists.

Siskiyou, Trinity, and Del Norte Counties joined forces with Curry County in Oregon, and they elected a governor and provisional government. They even chose a state seal: a double cross on a gold pan to "symbolize" how both California and Oregon had treated them. Secession had succeeded, and reporters from around the country arrived to see what state officials in Sacramento would do next.

But fate stepped in—just three days after the new governor's inauguration, the Japanese bombed Pearl Harbor, and the Jefferson snowball quickly melted as the nation's attention turned elsewhere. Some people claim the movement pushed the government to improve the roads, and sure enough Interstate 5 makes a puzzling jog west to skirt the town of Yreka, which boasts three highway exits.

T-shirts and bumper stickers sold here proclaim "Jefferson, a state of mind" and similar sentiments showing that the dream lives on. Said one local sage, "You can't tell what folks up here will do when they get a notion."

Center tribal museum, with some fine woven Native American basketwork (64236 Second Avenue; 530-493-1600; http://karuk.us/peoples%20center/peoples%20center.php). This is the heart of the would-be State of Jefferson (see "Will the North Rise Again?" sidebar).

Here Highway 96 turns east and follows the Klamath River through forested hills alive with songbirds and wildflowers, passing an evocative old cemetery (1869) filled with mossy tombstones at Fort Goff. Farther on, the route enters an entirely different landscape, treeless and volcanic, near I-5. A scenic shortcut through the Shasta River valley (Highway 263) heads south to Yreka, the Siskiyou County seat.

People drive I-5 if they are in a hurry. A slower but much more scenic alternate for north–south travel is *Highway 3* between Weaverville and Yreka, the old California–Oregon wagon road. The southern portion runs parallel to

Trinity (Clair Engle) Lake and the Trinity Alps, although you have to leave the main road to get a good look at the lake.

Trinity Lake was created in 1961 behind a 538-foot earth-fill dam, and at full capacity it's 20 miles long with 145 miles of shoreline sheltering many secluded coves. A part of the Whiskeytown-Shasta-Trinity National Recreational Area, the lake is known for its trout, salmon, and bass fishing, and most facilities are located on the west side in the shadow of the Trinity Alps. Completely equipped houseboats are available for rental, and, unlike busy Shasta Lake, you may find yourself alone with the fish.

Highway 3, dubbed the ***Trinity Heritage Scenic Byway,*** continues north past pine-draped slopes and craggy cliffs but seldom another car. Finally, at Scott Summit (5,401 feet) the road straightens out and descends into idyllic *Scott Valley,* a little patch of rural paradise first settled by beaver trappers. Among the small towns here is Callahan, at the headwaters of the Scott River (John Scott was an early gold miner). This former stage stop and trading center is slowly succumbing to time; its famous Emporium, once called "the biggest little store in the world," is now padlocked shut.

The town of *Etna* (12 miles north) is quiet—you have to leave the main road to find it—but merits a quick drive around. Originally called Rough and Ready, the town supplied local miners. Today you can visit Etna's historic cemetery and the Native Daughters of the Golden West Museum, above the library at 520 Main Street. Etna Hardware (420 Main Street) has been around for more than 120 years. The Etna Brewing Company, at 131 Callahan Street, produces a variety of "all natural" beers, including root beer, and offers tours and tastings. For details call (530) 467-5277.

trivia

The Shasta Cascade region is about the size of Ohio and boasts seven national forests and eight national or state parks.

Fort Jones was established in 1852 to protect the area from attacks by the bellicose Rogue River Indians. Ulysses S. Grant was ordered here and declared AWOL when he failed to take command (he later showed up with a good excuse). Now it's a quiet town with stores such as Fort Jones Frontier Hardware, selling "sporting goods and tourist supplies." The Indian Rain Rock and burial rock are among the displays at the Fort Jones Museum at 11913 Main Street; call (530) 468-5568 for more information.

From here another beautiful stretch leads to Forest Mountain Summit, at 4,097 feet, for a panoramic view of Scott Valley. Highway 3 ends at *Yreka* (at the junction with I-5). Few people know about this town's very respectable collection of Victorian homes, about seventy-five of them, including many listed in the National Register of Historic Places.

They are found chiefly on Miner Street, the old commercial hub, and nearby residential streets such as James Place. Other stops of interest are the Native American Heritage Park, with a full-size replica of a traditional sweat lodge, and a gold display at the Siskiyou County Courthouse, at 311 Fourth Street. Among the eye-catching pieces, carefully watched by two sheriffs, are a crucifix made from a single nugget, a solid gold watch, and one nugget called "the shoe," roughly the size of a child's foot. Yreka is also home to the 1-hour *Blue Goose* excursion steam train, which runs in summer to the town of Montague. Call (800) 973-5277 and check www.yrekawesternrr.com for schedule.

Central Corridor

If traveling north from Redding and Shasta Lake along I-5, don't miss **Castle Crags State Park,** about 6 miles south of Dunsmuir at Castella. Called *Castillo del Diablo* (Devil's Castle) by Spaniards, the glacier-scoured granite peaks rising from the forest are truly spectacular. Unrelated geologically to its more famous neighbor, Mount Shasta, Castle Crags was formed millions of years ago when hot granitic material below the surface was forced upward like a rising air balloon. Much later the forces of erosion—ice, water, and wind—sculpted and polished the gray white rock into stark shapes thrusting up 4,000 feet from the valley of the Upper Sacramento River.

At a scenic overlook called Vista Point, reached via a 1-mile corkscrew road, the landscape spreads out like a textbook on geology of the last 300 million years. The river and I-5 run along a fault zone between the Cascade and Klamath mountain ranges, to the east and west respectively. Castle Crags belongs to the Klamaths, formed when the sea floor crumpled and thrust upward with the collision of two tectonic plates. Just across the valley sits Girard Ridge, the western edge of the Cascades, and, beyond that, snow-shrouded Mount Shasta.

Ambitious hikers can take the 2.7-mile Crags/Indian Springs Trail from Vista Point, which is a bit strenuous as it rises 2,250 feet to the base of Castle Dome, thrusting skyward like a clenched fist. Serious rock climbers say Castle Crags is far less crowded than Mount Shasta in summer and provides equally great challenges, such as a nearly vertical outcrop of Castle Dome nicknamed the Cosmic Wall.

Quicksilver rather than gold was mined here, and the area is still a favorite of rock hounds and amateur archaeologists, who have found an abundance of Native American rock art (all of which is off-limits). In 1855 a violent encounter

Visiting Shasta Abbey

Standing in the snow outside an iron gate, I'm greeted cordially by a man dressed in a fur cap to cover his shaved head and a brown robe made of coarse cloth. I've requested a visit to Shasta Abbey, a Buddhist monastery tucked beneath Black Butte on the fringes of Mount Shasta City. The "reverend" and I begin our stroll around the spacious grounds.

Shasta Abbey was founded forty years ago by an English woman as its head abbess. The order of Buddhist contemplatives here practice the tradition known as Soto Zen. In this region of astounding spiritual diversity, where dozens of religious groups are based, Shasta Abbey is a fully recognized seminary for the Buddhist priesthood.

The American reverend accompanying me on this tour swears that the mountain's famed mystical powers have nothing to do with the abbey's location. He has spent the past two decades here and, like most of the three dozen monks in residence (including some females), has no intention of ever leaving. Indeed, they all seem content, smiling and bowing to each other as they pass in the corridor or perform chores.

The abbey has its own vegetable gardens and is largely self-contained, and we walk along covered walkways lined with firewood past solid stone buildings. We stop at an odd exhibit of old toys and discarded objects called Quon Yin's Garden, which is supposed to represent the universe's many spiritual realms. Next we look into a large hall reserved for morning services, adorned with lanterns and several Buddhas carved in gold. A typical day here begins at 5:30 a.m. with meditation and prayers, followed by a meal, and chores, more meditation, another meal, and so on until the evening service.

The abbey opens to outsiders for retreats and seminars teaching Buddhist precepts and meditation techniques. Shasta Abbey is located at 3724 Summit Drive, Mount Shasta; for further information call (530) 926-4208 or go to www.shastaabbey.org.

between Modoc Indians and white settlers took place nearby, the so-called Battle of the Crags. The Modocs fought from a towering stronghold using only bows and arrows and were soundly routed, but not before California poet Joaquin Miller was seriously injured by an arrowhead.

Castle Crags State Park is open daily year-round, sunrise to sunset. Vehicle admission charged. Campsites are available, but reservations are required in summer; call (530) 235-2684 for information.

For a really different experience, try the ***Railroad Park Resort*** in Dunsmuir within sight of Castle Crags. You can sleep in an antique caboose or deluxe box car, among many others, and each is furnished in period style with antiques and special touches like claw-foot tubs. A restaurant and lounge occupy other retired railroad cars, each embellished with hand tools, lamps, steam gauges, and other memorabilia. Call (530) 235-4440 or go to www.rrpark .com for reservations.

Dunsmuir was formerly an important stop on the regular Southern Pacific line between San Francisco and Portland, and the historic downtown retains a feel of those bygone times. It's a dyed-in-the-wool railroad town, and locals relive the past every June during Railroad Days. Wander down from Dunsmuir Avenue for a whiff of the old ways, then take in the Upper Sacramento River Exchange Center, a hands-on museum and information center for fishing, hiking, and ecology located at 5937 Dunsmuir Avenue (530-235-2012; www.riverexchange.org). Other nearby attractions are the botanical gardens in Dunsmuir City Park (530-235-4740; www.dunsmuirbotanicalgardens.org) and Hedge Creek Falls, located off Dunsmuir Avenue from the Highway 101 Dunsmuir/Siskiyou exit.

trivia

Glass Mountain is the largest obsidian glass flow in the West.

"Lonely as God and white as a winter's moon." was the way poet Joaquin Miller described **Mount Shasta,** and famous naturalist John Muir claimed his

Skiing Mount Shasta

Long in the shadow of Lake Tahoe ski resorts, Shasta Cascade offers some excellent downhill and cross-country skiing right on the slopes of the famous mountain. Opened after an avalanche demolished the old station, Mount Shasta Ski Park on the mountain's south side is a family-oriented resort with mostly intermediate skiing: Thirty-two trails spread over 425 acres with 1,400 feet of vertical drop. Views from on high are superb: across the Sacramento River Canyon to Lake Siskiyou, Castle Crags, and the Trinity Alps.

This idyllic winter area is located just 12 miles off I-5, about halfway between Mount Shasta City and McCloud, so it's very convenient from points north and south. In addition, many hotels offer stay-and-ski packages. Though elite skiers might eschew these slopes, the snow conditions are good from November through April, a 130-day season, and the station features a large night-ski facility and two terrain parks.

There's also on-site Nordic or cross-country skiing with miles of groomed trails through peaceful forest. For information on the ski park, go to www.skipark.com.

More cross-country skiing is available along Everitt Memorial Highway (the road to the old Ski Bowl) leading up the mountain's west side from downtown Mount Shasta. There are marked trails at Sand Flat and Red Fir Flat at about 6,000 feet and limited parking. For more information contact the Mount Shasta Ranger Station at (530) 926-4511.

"blood turned to wine" when he first saw it. Soaring to 14,162 feet, the snow-clad, dormant volcano dominates the landscape for hundreds of miles in all directions. Unlike higher peaks such as Mount Whitney, lost among a cluster of summits, Shasta stands alone, rising majestically about 10,000 feet from the surrounding terrain.

Shasta has a permanent cap of ice and snow, and runoff from its five glaciers feeds dozens of streams, most importantly the McCloud, Shasta, and Sacramento Rivers. Although no eruptions have occurred during the past two centuries, hot sulphur springs near the summit show that the volcano, like many other Cascade peaks, is far from extinct.

Shasta is probably an Indian word, but others claim it derives from the French *chaste* (pure) or even the Russian *tshastal* (white or pure). Local Indians believed that the Great Spirit created it by dropping ice and snow through an opening in the sky. He then converted the mountain into his tepee and built a fire in the center (the smoke that appears during volcanic activity). Out of respect to the Great Spirit, Native Americans would not step foot above the timberline.

Several metaphysical groups flourish in the nearby town of Mount Shasta. Some believe that inside the mountain are secret cities inhabited by Lemurians, descendants of an ancient race that fled the continent of Mu when it sank into the Pacific. The most famous of this race is Phylos, who supposedly appears in a flowing white robe and invites climbers into a golden temple to listen to soft music.

Other mountaineers claim that kindly dwarfs have shown them caves of gold, or that they have spotted strange lights and fogs and heard booming bells. The Yaktayvians of the Secret Commonwealth have bells tuned so precisely that they create giant landslides whenever outsiders come too close. Naturally, UFO sightings are common.

A 15-mile paved spur road winds up Shasta's southwest flank to just above the timberline at about 6,800 feet. From here a 2-mile uphill hike along Bunny Flat Trail leads to **Horse Camp,** site of a Sierra Club lodge and beginning of one of the West's great hiking adventures: the ascent of Mount Shasta. The 6,000-foot-plus climb over volcanic rubble, ice, and snow can be punishing, but it is accessible to anyone in good physical condition with basic climbing gear. (Mountaineering equipment is not required.)

Every summer several thousand climbers attempt the summit; about half succeed. But success takes planning, conditioning, and luck. The mountain makes its own weather and is often hit by violent, fast-moving storms. For an information packet on the climb, contact the USDA Forest Service at (530) 926-4511 and check www.fs.fed.us/r5/shastatrinity and www.climbingmtshasta.org.

Another first-rate hike is Black Butte Trail to the summit of a steep, nearly treeless cone of andesite west of Mount Shasta. This pile of dark volcanic slag was formed by four successive eruptions about 10,000 years ago. Northbound I-5 aims straight for it, only to veer away at the last minute. The steep, rocky trail is about 2.5 miles from the trailhead to the summit at 6,325 feet (vertical climb is 1,845 feet). It can get very hot in summer, so carry water; and beware of rattlesnakes napping on sunny rocks. At trail's end traverse a narrow ledge to the remains of an old lookout where it can get very windy—but the views are stunning.

The town of **_Mount Shasta_** boasts an eclectic blend of residents, from regular outdoor types to New Agers and followers of numerous spiritual traditions. Among many local shops with a metaphysical flavor and several art galleries, most are along Mount Shasta Boulevard.

Look in Mount Shasta City Park for the headwaters of the Sacramento River. From a lava tube deep within the mountain, icy clear water gushes forth into Cold Creek amid an arcadian scene of ferns and moss-covered rocks. On the east side of the mountain lies the postcard-perfect community of **_McCloud,_** queen of the old lumber towns. There is the setting, a magnificent backdrop of Mount Shasta pasted against the sky. The architecture is a charming collection of simple cabins and wood-framed houses laid out neatly, as if someone planned the whole thing. They did.

McCloud was a company town for mill workers, who paid with scrip at the company store and lived in houses built with lumber they had milled.

Riding into the Sunset

For the perfect blend of mountain scenery, old-fashioned railway travel, and gourmet dining, hop aboard the Shasta Sunset Dinner Train. The elegant service runs most of the year round-trip between McCloud and Mount Shasta City (with an alternate route east to McIntosh Vista), taking diners for a three-hour sightseeing trip capped with a four-course feast. (The trains poke along at just 10 to 22 mph.)

The McCloud Railway Company uses both steam and diesel engines to pull its collection of four vintage railway cars, olive green with gold-leaf lettering outside and brass fittings and mahogany paneling inside. Dinner, served on white linen set with fine china and cutlery, includes a choice of entrees and desserts (try the Decadent Turtle Cheesecake). Each meal ends with a complimentary glass of port to sip while pulling into McCloud Station (and back to reality) at around 9:00 p.m.

For rates and schedules contact the Shasta Sunset Dinner Train at (800) 733-2141 or www.shastasunset.com.

trivia

McCloud Golf Club, built in 1927, is the oldest public golf course in Northern California.

(The first settlement dates from 1827, when Alexander McLeod led trappers to the area in search of beaver.) Learn more at the Heritage Junction Museum on Main Street.

The Mercantile Building, a log structure housing stores and a cafe, is also on the graceful Main Street. The McCloud Railway Company, which offers the Shasta Sunset Dinner Train excursions, is at 328 Main Street. The historic yellow and white McCloud Hotel (1916) at 408 Main Street (800-964-2823; www.mccloudhotel.com) has been restored and remodeled as a bed and breakfast inn. A stroll away is the Stoney Brook Inn (800-369-6118; www.stoneybrook inn.com), popular with New Agers for its soul-stirring views of the mystical mountain.

Another overnight option is the McCloud Guest House (530-964-3160, www.historicalmccloudguesthouse.com), which served as home of the lumber company's president and later welcomed visiting VIPs. Among them were Herbert Hoover, Jean Harlow, and various members of the Hearst family, who own a fair amount of property near McCloud. (William Randolph Hearst built a huge castle called Wyntoon on the McCloud River.) They came for the mountain and for spectacular McCloud Falls, as visitors do today.

Southern Cascades

Lassen Peak was the Mount Saint Helens of its day. On May 30, 1914, after centuries of slumber, the volcano blasted out rock and smoke at a foreboding rate. Over the next year, about 150 small eruptions kept locals on edge. Then, suddenly and ferociously, Lassen blew its top in a tremendous explosion that tossed twenty-ton boulders around like pebbles and spewed ash 30,000 feet in the air, covering the streets of Reno hundreds of miles away. Later, an 18-mile-long mud flow, triggered when scalding lava poured onto the ash-laden snowfields, killed vegetation for miles around.

Smaller eruptions continued over the next seven years, leaving the landscape littered with debris. All this makes **Lassen Volcanic National Park** a living laboratory for the study of volcanoes. With about 80,000 acres of wilderness, this park looks more like Montana or Wyoming than what you expect to find in California. Parts are dry and lava encrusted, looking like a battlefield or moonscape; other sections are heavily wooded with conifers or splashed with wildflowers. There are fifty cobalt blue lakes, six of them accessible by car, and countless hot springs, geysers, and boiling mud pots. In addition, 150 miles of trails (including 17 miles of the Pacific Crest Trail) weave through a landscape alternately luxuriant and devastated.

Standing at 10,457 feet, Lassen Peak is considered young by geological standards. It's also a mole hill compared to an ancient volcano called Tehama, which once covered the entire area before collapsing like a deflated balloon. At **Sulphur Works** thermal area, you can see a diagram of Tehama's 11,500-foot profile and spot your position some 4,700 feet below its former peak.

This was the location of Mount Tehama's central vent, and the volcano still whispers. Fumaroles hiss; hot springs bubble; mud pots boil, splatter, and sputter; and from deep below, immense cauldrons of red-hot magma belch evil-smelling fumes. Water seeping down into the earth is heated by this magma and rushes upward in the form of searing steam, reaching 195 degrees Fahrenheit (the boiling point of water at this altitude). A short walk from Lassen Park Road, Sulphur Works is the most accessible place to view volcanic activity, with easy trails on elevated walkways. Not far away, a trail leads to Bumpass Hell, the world's hottest hot springs at upward of 200 degrees Fahrenheit. The odd name comes from Kendall Bumpass, who discovered the spot in 1865 and lost a leg after plunging through the shallow crust into a sulphur pool.

trivia

Ahjumawi Lava Springs State Park near McArthur is accessible only by boat.

A 30-mile road wraps around the mountain, climbing to 8,500 feet, where a 2.5-mile trail zigzags to the summit. (It takes about two hours to climb the 2,000 feet.) From here a staggering view takes in the milewide caldera. Other sights reached via the park road are the Devastated Area, about 3 square miles of scorched terrain, and Manzanita Lake (near the northwestern entrance). The Cinder Cone nature trail (4 miles round-trip) winds past stark, black chunks of lava, vast cinder and ash fields, and heat-scorched trees, on the way up to a 700-foot cinder cone.

The park's biggest drawback is the closure of the main road due to snow from about October through mid-June. The rest of the year visitors can only enter at the fringes for a peek. (The best place to do so is the southwest entrance on Highway 89 stopping at the Kohm Yah-mah-nee Visitor Center.) Excellent cross-country skiing and snowshoe trails partially compensate for this inconvenience.

The park has information centers at the northwest Manzanita Lake entrance and at the Kohm Yah-mah-nee Visitor Center at the southwest entrance. For details contact Lassen Volcanic National Park, P.O. Box 100, Mineral, CA 96063; (530) 595-4448; www.nps.gov/lavo.

From Rail to Trail: The "Bizz"

Imagine walking alone through the forest along a gently sloping path or gliding silently on skis through fresh virgin snow. The only sounds you hear are wildlife and the rushing water of restless Susan River. That's the scene on the Bizz Johnson National Recreation Trail near Susanville, which follows the old Fernley–Lassen railway line for 25 miles along rugged Susan River Canyon. The rail-trail has become a local favorite with hikers, horseback riders, mountain bikers, and cross-country skiers. Fishermen and kayakers also use the cliff-flanked trail to access the river, but it is little known outside this area.

Named in honor of a former U.S. congressman, the wide and relatively easy trek starts at historic Susanville Depot (601 Richmond Road) and heads west to Mason Station near Westwood. The latter settlement became a lumber company town after the area was developed around 1890 by Minnesota loggers. The railway was built to haul out lumber but was abandoned during the 1950s. All the old rails and ties were torn up to make way for the trail, famous for colorful fall foliage. For further information and a trail map, contact the Susanville Bizz Johnson National Recreation Area at (530) 257-0456; www.blm.gov/ca/st/en/fo/eaglelake/bizztrail.html.

The town of **Susanville,** about 60 miles east on Highway 36, witnessed the Sagebrush War of 1862. This four-hour gun battle, followed by a beer-drinking session, determined that nearby Honey Lake Valley belonged to California, not Nevada. The town has a short list of attractions, including the William H. Pratt Museum (just off Main Street) with lots of lumbering artifacts. Adjacent is Roop's Fort, built in 1854 as a trading post and the first building in the county. Susanville is the eastern gateway to Lassen Volcanic National Park and to a full menu of attractions in the southern Cascades and northern Sierra Nevada, the Bizz Johnson Trail and Lake Almanor among them.

Eagle Lake is 16 miles north of Susanville. It's the state's second-largest natural lake, with more than 100 miles of shoreline, and sits in a basin fringed with sagebrush and juniper to the north, pine and fir to the south. The public recreation complex at the south end (including a marina, store, campground, and swimming beach) is positively Lilliputian by California standards—perfect for anyone trying to get away from it all.

Eagle Lake is a favorite with scientists. Its highly alkaline water supports an astonishing variety of animal life, including jumbo trout (up to 20 inches

trivia

California has three active volcanoes: Lassen Peak and Mount Shasta in the Cascade Range, and Mammoth Mountain in the Sierra Nevada.

long) that can survive nowhere else and seventy-five species of birds. Antelope, porcupines, and other animals come to drink at its shores.

The lake abounds with creatures that were thought to be extinct until they were rediscovered here. Among them are prehistoric snails and ice crickets. Ordinary garter snakes are weirdly colored here, and two types of rattlers have combined to create a species of snake found nowhere else.

American Indians called waterfalls "laughing waters," a good description of **Burney Falls.** Burney Creek splits just before reaching a spectacular 129-foot drop, and the two silver threads are joined by hundreds of secondary cascades that form a lacy curtain of water seeping from the mossy rock. On sunlit mornings, a rainbow appears in the mist below. Teddy Roosevelt supposedly called the falls the eighth wonder of the world.

McArthur-Burney Falls State Park lies halfway between Mount Shasta and Susanville, about 60 miles east of Redding. A 1-mile nature trail glides past the falls and through a landscape of sharp lava rock, ponderosa pines, and Douglas firs. From an observation platform near the parking lot, there's a slow descent into a gorge with new perspectives on the falls at each bend in the trail. Cool spray clings to the face. Even on the hottest days, the ambient temperature is about 65 degrees Fahrenheit while the water is a cool 42 to 48 degrees. Each day, between 100 and 200 million gallons of water rumble with a constant roar over the falls into a deep emerald pool filled with trout. Behind the shimmering sheet of water live hundreds of black swifts, nesting in lichen-covered cavities from March through October and easy to spot because of their erratic, batlike flight.

The trail continues alongside a slope covered with black basalt chunks, at one time part of a horizontal layer on which the creek flowed. The canyon is littered with basaltic debris left behind as the falls moved upstream, relentlessly eroding the sediment below.

Crossing the creek and weaving up the other side, the trail passes the spot where the water plummets over the edge. Burney Creek springs from a subterranean source, and in dry summer weather, it emerges from the porous lava about half a mile upstream of the falls. The exact size and origin of the underground reservoir that makes all this possible remain a mystery.

McArthur-Burney Falls State Park is open daily from sunrise to sunset for $4 per car admission. For further information call (530) 335-2777.

Modoc Plateau

The **Modoc Volcanic Scenic Byway** provides a rich mixture of geology, wildlife viewing, and history and is the most exciting way to reach Lava Beds National Monument and Tule Lake in the state's far north. Good but unpaved roads in sections permit driving the full 120-mile route from June through mid-October.

Leaving Highway 89 on Highway 15, thirty minutes east of McCloud, the drive comes to Medicine Lake Highlands, a broad shield volcano larger than Mount Shasta. Its collapsed crater formed a huge basin where water deposits created Medicine Lake, said by Native Americans and New Agers to be a powerful energy vortex.

Sights en route include cinder cones, lava tubes, and a huge pile of jet-black obsidian called Glass Mountain. The Modoc Plateau is a slab of rocky volcanic residue covering some 13,000 square miles, fields of lava flow from eons ago now covered with sagebrush. In "California's Empty Quarter," there are a handful of settlements, with mile after mile of nothing but a barn or a fence to mark the horizon. **Lava Beds National Monument** near the Oregon border is remote and looks deserted. Over a period of thousands of years, rivers of liquid rock from Medicine Lake Shield Volcano spread over the land. When cool, the rock formed a fantasyland of lava tubes, yawning chasms, ice caves, towering cinder cones, and vast fudgelike lava flows punctuated by an occasional tree or bush.

trivia

Siskiyou County boasts the largest mule and black-tailed deer herds in California.

The area also witnessed California's only major Indian conflict. During the Modoc War (1872–1873), a handful of braves held off the U.S. Army for six months. The Indians called this "the land of burnt-out fires" and thought no one would want it. They were wrong.

For an overview of both natural and Native American history, drive to the visitor center, 16 miles from Highway 139. The easiest landmark to explore is **Mushpot Cave,** right outside the center, with lights and interpretive signs explaining the geological story. This lava tube was created when rivers of liquid basalt hardened on the surface (which cooled faster) but continued flowing below, forming narrow, elongated tunnels.

This cave and others were formed about 30,000 years ago by flows from Mammoth Crater on the monument's southern boundary.

About 450 of these cylindrical tubes honeycomb 72-square-mile Lava Beds; the largest is some 75 feet in diameter and several miles long, and the smallest is too cramped to crawl through. Tubes lie near the surface, and about twenty of them are developed—that is, accessible with flashlight and "bump hat"—most of them along Cave Loop Road near the visitor center. Be prepared to crouch in places to pass low ceilings dripping with "lavacicles."

Merrill Ice Cave boasts a frozen river and a waterfall formed when rain collects inside and freezes. Because lava is such a good insulator, the ice remains year-round, even if it's 100 degrees outside. From December through March, rangers lead strenuous advance-reservation tours of Crystal Ice Cave. Big Painted Cave and Symbol Bridge have a number of Indian paintings on the walls, and Fossil Cave has yielded the bones of a mastodon and a camel, long extinct in these parts. Saturday tour advance reservation admission to Fern Cave with a ranger guide is possible from mid-May to October, to protect sensitive plants and animals inside.

Gillem Bluff, a high wall of lava rock splashed with green vegetation, rears up just west of Devils Homestead Lava Flow. Schonchin Butte, one of the larger cinder cones at 5,341 feet, provides an exceptional view over the entire monument, a barren world covered with scrawny grasses and clumps of sagebrush all the way to Medicine Lake Volcano and Mount Shasta. Astronauts trained here before heading to the moon.

Mankind's role in this rugged landscape has been nearly as violent as nature's. Not far from Gillem's Bluff was the main camp of the U.S. Army during its efforts to flush out the Modoc Indians from their stronghold. War broke out in 1872 when the government tried to force the Modocs onto a reservation shared with the Klamaths, their traditional enemies.

Finally, a charismatic leader named Kientpoos, or Captain Jack as he came to be known, led 160 men, women, and children into hiding. Sixty fighters holed up in *Captain Jacks Stronghold* held the army at bay for months, inflicting heavy casualties while suffering few themselves. The Modocs brilliantly used the narrow, trenchlike corridors between thick lava walls that were formed by

trivia

The Sacramento River, California's longest river entirely within the state, begins as a tiny spring at Mount Shasta and flows all the way to San Francisco Bay.

fissures in the crust. The harsh terrain proved ideal for defense, the Modocs sniping from behind rocks while the army advanced in a straight line, as in Civil War battles. One officer reported that he lost several men one day without ever seeing a single Indian.

Canby Cross marks the site of a bloody massacre. Goaded on by those who shunned compromise, Captain Jack pulled out a pistol during peace talks and murdered General Canby. An Indian agent named Meacham was partially scalped during the fracas but recovered to tell many a tale. Jack was hanged, and his people were rounded up and herded to Oklahoma. Fortunately, the Modocs survived as a living people.

Lava Beds National Monument is open continuously, and the visitor center stays open from 8:00 a.m. to 6:00 p.m in summer and 8:30 a.m. to 5:00 p.m. the rest of the year. Admission is $10 per car; for further information call (530) 667-8100. For Fern Cave and Crystal Cave Tours, call (530) 667-8113 three weeks in advance.

Not far from Captain Jack's Stronghold, the West Wildlife Lookout offers a good panorama of Tule Lake, which was eight times larger when the Modocs made their last stand. You can drive to the lake directly from Lava Beds on a dirt road, or return to Highway 139 and proceed to the monument's north entrance.

Northeast of the national monument's main unit, lying on a flat, dry plain that was formerly part of the lake bed, is the Petroglyph Section, where an abundance of prehistoric art has been found. *Petroglyph Point* is a sheer stone wall about 1,200 feet long and 100 feet high. According to archaeologists, a stratum of soft volcanic tuff from ground level up to 15 feet high was incised with hundreds of symbols, including serpents and other figures, concentric circles, and drawings resembling floor plans of large buildings that are not typical of local Indian art.

Tule Lake National Wildlife Refuge boasts one of the world's most impressive displays of bird life. Named for the bulrush that flourishes in marshy areas, Tule Lake shares the Klamath Basin (at about 4,000 feet) with the Lower Klamath Refuge further west. Both refuges hug the Oregon border. Every year, approximately two million ducks and one million geese from as far away as Siberia stop here to feed and rest, and when a large flock arrives or departs together, the sky is literally darkened by the sheer numbers.

trivia

Tulelake is the horseradish capital of the world, producing one-third of America's harvest.

The migration starts in early September with pintails and white-fronted geese, and by late October other waterfowl have joined them in the largest concentration on the continent. Endless flocks of ducks and geese stream by both day and night. Many birds land and take up temporary residence, feeding and chattering incessantly. Come November, thousands of hunters flock here as well.

Although the big show is seasonal, any time of the year is good for bird-watching. From December through February, hundreds of bald eagles from Alaska prey on the wintering waterfowl and local rodents while nesting in cliffs overlooking the lake. In spring many other species stop to rest and feed on the way to Canadian breeding grounds, and from May through August tens of thousands of ducks, geese, and marsh birds are born and raised here. Midsummer is a good time to see pelicans, egrets, herons, gulls, terns, and other marsh birds, which usually stay until October.

> ## trivia
>
> Nearly 19,000 Japanese-Americans were forced to live at the Tule Lake Segregation Center from 1942 to 1946. In 2008, the site was designated part of the World War II Valor in the Pacific National Monument.

The refuge is open daily during daylight hours. You can drive a self-guided 10-mile auto tour route, canoe 2 miles of marked channels from July through September, or hike to an overlook. For more information stop at the Klamath Basin National Wildlife Refuge Visitor Center at 4009 Hill Road, Tulelake, Monday through Friday from 8:00 a.m. to 4:30 p.m. and from 9:00 a.m. on weekends (530-667-2231; www.fws .gov/klamathbasinrefuges).

Between the village of Canby (at the junction with Highway 139) and Alturas, Highway 299 weaves across 20 miles of a rocky plateau known as the Devil's Garden. The town of *Alturas* is the best place for accommodations while visiting the Modoc Plateau. The surrounding countryside is a blend of dry scrubland and good farmland spotted with grazing cattle and sheep, irrigated fields, lava rock, and a smattering of pine forest. This kind of land was a magnet for Basque sheepherders and farmers. One of Alturas's more popular restaurants, the Brass Rail (395 Lakeview Highway; 530-233-2906), specializes in Basque cuisine.

The *Modoc County Historical Museum*'s fine local collection emphasizes the taming of this wild country. There are crude Indian arrowheads and tomahawks, stones and fossils, a rattlesnake skin and mounted animals, a Swiss bow gun, and branding irons. Firearms steal the show. Guns and bullets of all calibers are laid out for inspection, from a pint-size thirty-caliber "gartergun" to a homemade shotgun with four ten-gauge barrels that could bring down one hundred geese with a single blast. The museum, at 600 South Main Street, is open May through October from 10:00 a.m. to 4:00 p.m., Tuesday through Saturday. Call (530) 233-4434 for more information.

Eastern California

Alturas is the gateway to the **Warner Mountains,** which form a natural boundary between the Modoc Plateau and the arid Great Basin sweeping eastward across Nevada and Utah in a sea of desert sagebrush. This isolated range, a remote spur of the Cascades, offers few trails and fewer signposts, but it does provide rugged scenery and solitude, even in summer. If the Warners were near a city, they would probably be famous and crowded; instead, they are filled with wildflowers in spring and wildlife all year-round.

The highest and most scenic part is the **South Warner Wilderness,** sprawling over almost 70,000 acres of the Modoc National Forest (530-233-5811; www.fs.fed.us/r5/modoc). The 27-mile Summit Trail here skirts the three tallest peaks and looks out on Nevada and much of the Shasta Cascade region. It starts at the Patterson Ranger Station, 42 miles from Alturas, and ends at Pepperdine's Camp. Trout fishing is superb at Patterson Lake, and you can see mule deer in abundance. Several companies offering horseback trips into the South Warner Wilderness are based in Alturas.

The only paved road across the Warners is Highway 299 through 6,305-foot Cedar Pass, where there is a small ski area and campground, part of Modoc National Forest. From here, the road drops quickly through a wild canyon to the sleepy hamlet of **Cedarville** in the Surprise Valley, 23 miles from Alturas. Main Street here looks like an old snapshot, with a row of pillared and porticoed western-style structures such as the old brick Kressler and Bonner Building from more than a century ago. Today it's gone modern, with a bookstore, art gallery, pizzeria, and custom saddle shop. Main Street is lively with shops, restaurants, and a beauty parlor.

One nice spot a block away is a little park crossed by a creek, site of the **Kressler and Bonner Trading Post,** Cedarville's first building (1865), which supplied wagon trains bound for Oregon. The rough-hewn log structure with shingled roof is surrounded by a split-rail fence; to one side a historical marker states that the original settlement, called Deep Creek, was established by James Townsend, who was killed by Indians. In 1886 Kressler and Bonner purchased the post, and it served in that capacity for another decade.

From Cedarville Highway 299 head east toward Nevada, and a sign reading NO SERVICES NEXT 100 MILES speaks for itself. But to visit the most remote spot in the entire state, closer to Boise than San Francisco, drive north from

Cedarville along the **Surprise Valley Barrel Springs National Back Country Byway** (530-279-6101), a 93-mile loop passing ranch land and alkaline lakes where the spirit of the American West lives on. A century ago this valley was deemed "the Bloody Ground" for its history of mind-numbing violence, first between settlers and Indians and later feuds among farmers, sheepherders, and cattlemen.

About 25 miles to the north, a white church steeple poking through the trees marks the approach of **Fort Bidwell,** a former army post established in 1865 at the foot of the Warner Mountains. Nothing remains of the fort, but Main Street boasts a couple of lopsided historical buildings, and a redbrick schoolhouse stands forlornly on a hill. The Fort Bidwell General Store on Bridge Street (1876) was built of stone with heavy iron doors and windows, and terrified residents used to hide inside its fireproof walls during Indian raids when the troops were on patrol. The town's historic cemetery sits on a slope overlooking Surprise Valley, with dozens of weathered tombstones of cavalrymen and their families. They stand as testimonials to the harsh frontier life, where hostile attacks and disease, drought, and winter storms always threatened. Among the most poignant is the story of Sergeant Frank Lewis of the First U.S. Cavalry, "who died by his own hand at Camp Bidwell on January 2, 1877, aged 30," according to the plaque dedicated by his grieving fellow soldiers. Even today the grave is never without flowers, and some say the sergeant's ghost still appears late at night on the porch of the old general store, where he died tragically so long ago.

The real attraction here is being so far off the beaten path. Viewed from the cemetery, the ribbon of road heading east becomes a gravel track along the old Emigrant Trail. Like a mirage, it peters out in the desert somewhere near the Nevada state line in the middle of nowhere, as far as you can travel and still be in California.

Places to Stay in Shasta Cascade

REDDING AND WEAVERVILLE AREA

49er Gold Country Inn
718 Main Street
Weaverville
(530) 623-4937

Baymont Inn
148 Moonlit Oaks Avenue
Yreka
(530) 841-1300

Best Western Hilltop Inn
2300 Hilltop Drive
Redding
(530) 221-6100

Clearwater Lodge
24500 Pit One Powerhouse
Road
Fall River Mills
(530) 366-5005

Coffee Creek Ranch
HC2 Box 4940
Trinity Center
(530) 266-3343

Motel Etna
317 Collier Way
Etna
(530) 467-5330

Tiffany House
1510 Barbara Road
Redding
(530) 244-3225

Trinity Alps Resort
1750 Trinity Alps Road
Trinity Center
(530) 286-2205

Trinity Canyon Lodge
27025 Highway 299
Junction City
(530) 623-6318

CENTRAL CORRIDOR

Cave Springs Resort
4727 Dunsmuir Avenue
Dunsmuir
(530) 235-2721

Drakesbad Guest Ranch
Warner Valley Road
Chester (Lassen Volcanic
National Park)
(530) 529-1512

McCloud Hotel
408 Main Street
McCloud
(800) 964-2823

McCloud River Inn
325 Lawndale Court
McCloud
(800) 261-7831

Mount Shasta Ranch B&B
1008 Barr Road
Mount Shasta
(530) 926-3870

Mount Shasta Resort
1000 Siskiyou Lake
Boulevard
Mount Shasta
(800) 958-3363

Stoney Brook Inn
309 West Colombero Drive
McCloud
(800) 369-6118

Swiss Holiday Lodge
2400 South Mount Shasta
Boulevard
Mount Shasta
(530) 926-3446

SOUTHERN CASCADES

Best Western Trailside Inn
2785 Main Street
Susanville
(530) 257-4123

Burney Mountain Guest Ranch
22800 Hat Creek PH#2
Cassel
(530) 355-4087

High Country Inn
3015 Riverside Drive
Susanville
(530) 257-3450

WORTH SEEING/DOING IN SHASTA CASCADE

Lake Shasta Caverns, O'Brien

Lake Siskiyou, Mount Shasta

Shasta Lake

Shasta State Historic Park, Old Shasta

Sisson Museum, Mount Shasta

Whiskeytown Lake

HELPFUL WEB SITES IN SHASTA CASCADE

Alturas Chamber of Commerce/ Modoc County:
www.alturaschamber.org

Dunsmuir Chamber of Commerce:
www.dunsmuir.com

Klamath Basin National Wildlife Refuges:
www.fws.gov/klamathbasinrefuges/

Lassen County Chamber of Commerce: www.visitlassen.com

Mt. Shasta Chamber of Commerce and Visitors' Bureau:
www.mtshastachamber.com

National Park Service: www.nps.gov

Redding Convention and Visitors Bureau: www.visitredding.com

Shasta Cascade Wonderland Association: www.shastacascade.com

Shasta Mountain Guides:
www.shastaguides.com

Shasta-Trinity National Forest:
www.fs.fed.us/r5/shastatrinity/

Siskiyou County Visitors' Bureau:
www.visitsiskiyou.org

Trinity County Chamber of Commerce: www.trinitycounty.com

Volcanic Legacy Scenic Byway:
www.volcaniclegacybyway.org

Rippling Waters Resort
16241 Highway 89
Hat Creek
(530) 335-7400

Shasta Pines Motel
37386 Main Street
Burney
(530) 335-2201

MODOC PLATEAU AND EASTERN CALIFORNIA

Cockrell's Ranch & High Desert Lodging
Star Route 11-A
County RR 31
Cedarville
(888) 279-2209

Ellis Motel
2238 Highway 139
Tule Lake
(530) 667-5242

Fe's Bed and Breakfast
660 Main Street
Tule Lake
(877) 478-0184

JK Metzker House
520 Main Street
Cedarville
(530) 279-2650

JNR Hotel
581 Main Street
Cedarville
(530) 279-2423

Rim Rock Motel
22760 Highway 395
Alturas
(530) 233-5455

Places to Eat in Shasta Cascade

REDDING AND WEAVERVILLE AREA

Buz's Crab Seafood Restaurant (seafood)
2159 East Street
Redding
(530) 243-2120

Jack's Grill (American)
1743 California Street
Redding
(530) 241-9705

La Grange Cafe (Continental)
520 Main Street
Weaverville
(530) 623-5325

**Rivers Restaurant
(American)**
202 Hemsted Drive
Redding
(530) 223-5606

Trinideli (American)
201 Highway 3
Weaverville
(530) 623-5856

CENTRAL CORRIDOR

**Cafe Maddalena
(American)**
5801 Sacramento Avenue
Dunsmuir
(530) 235-2725

**Casa Ramos Restaurant
(Mexican)**
1136 South Mount Shasta
Boulevard
Mount Shasta
(530) 926-0250

**Cornerstone Bakery &
Cafe (Californian)**
5759 Dunsmuir Avenue
Dunsmuir
(530) 235-4677

**Grandma's House
(American)**
123 East Center Street
Yreka
(530) 842-5300

**Highland House
Restaurant (American)**
1000 Siskiyou Lake
Boulevard
Mount Shasta Resort
Mount Shasta
(530) 926-3030

Lilly's (American)
1013 South Mount Shasta
Boulevard
Mount Shasta
(530) 926-3372

**McCloud Hotel Dining
Room (American)**
408 Main Street
McCloud
(530) 964-2822

SOUTHERN CASCADES

**Alpine Drive In
(American)**
37148 Highway 299 East
Burney
(530) 335-2211

Art's Outpost (American)
37392 Main Street
Burney
(530) 335-2835

**Black Bear Diner
(American)**
2795 Main Street
Susanville
(530) 257-4447

**Chinese Kitchen
(Chinese)**
2455 Main Street
Susanville
(530) 257-6228

**Fall River Hotel
(Continental)**
24860 Main Street
Fall River Mills
(530) 336-5550

**MODOC PLATEAU AND
EASTERN CALIFORNIA**

**Captain Jack's
Stronghold Restaurant
(American)**
Highway 139
Tulelake
(530) 664-5566

**Country Hearth
(American)**
Main Street
Cedarville
(530) 279-2280

Index